MW01275713

Selling Ethically: The C.A.R.E. Methodology

A practical playbook with frameworks for growing revenue with integrity, closing deals without compromising your values, and building authentic relationships without selling your soul.

Chin Hing Chang

https://caremethodology.com/

Copyright © 2024 Chin Hing Chang
Edited and proofread using ChatGPT-4
All rights reserved.

C.A.R.E. Methodology is a trademark of ClassyNarwhal Canada.

Website: https://www.classynarwhal.com/
https://caremethodology.com/

ISBN: 9798332358678

ABOUT THE BOOK

Developed in conjunction with the consultative sales and challenger sales framework, the C.A.R.E. Methodology primarily seeks to alter your mindset and beliefs. This transformation enables you to confidently assist clients in a manner authentic to you while also being comfortable challenging them when it serves their best interests.

It's not so much about tactics, which can often be manipulative if not employed correctly, but rather about adopting a framework. This framework aims to minimize the uncertainty and discomfort surrounding sales, providing clear guidance to transition your prospects from being curious to closed.

This book also delves into strategy, process, and automation – not to diminish human interaction, but instead to alleviate workload, allowing more time for genuine human connection.

DISCLAIMER

This publication is designed to provide accurate and authoritative information regarding the subject matter covered. It is sold with the understanding that neither the author nor the publisher is engaged in rendering legal, investment, accounting, or other professional services. While the publisher and author have used their best efforts in preparing this book, they make no representations or warranties concerning the accuracy or completeness of the contents of this book and specifically disclaim any implied warranties of merchantability or fitness for a particular purpose. No warranty may be created or extended by sales representatives or written sales materials. The advice and strategies contained herein may not be suitable for your situation. You should consult with a professional when appropriate. Neither the publisher nor the author shall be liable for any loss of profit or any other commercial damages, including but not limited to special, incidental, consequential, personal, or other damages.

https://caremethodology.com/

CONTENTS

ACKNOWLEDGMENTS

This book took the better part of a year to complete, much of which wouldn't have been possible without the incredible support and mentorship from my network. Here are a handful of the most impactful individuals whom I'm grateful to have influenced the creation of this book:

Keith Ippel (Spring Activator): The exceptional mentorship and guidance I received during my tenure at Spring significantly shaped my view on utilizing business as a force for good and contributed to the formation of my current network of mentors, experts, and professionals.

Mike Winterfield (Active Impact Investments): Although brief, our engagement through the 2X Program was eye-opening and imparted some key lessons in sales that I still heavily use to this day.

Shannon Ward (Genus Capital): Your human and empathetic approach to selling has been a big inspiration. You've always had a wonderful way of explaining key concepts using relatable analogies.

Paul Brassard (Volition Advisors): Though we've never worked together directly, through the many opportunities I've had to collaborate with you and Volition Advisors, I've learned a ton both about business and about how to approach building relationships.

Tran Tri Dung (SwissEP): For the many opportunities to involve me in the Vietnamese startup ecosystem. I've learned as much as I've been able to support and wouldn't have been able to grow my network in the region without your advocacy. Observing how business is done in Asia always helps put things in perspective and keeps me mindful of the differences and similarities in business ethics.

Ziad Sahid (Tech Yukon): For continuing to involve me in supporting entrepreneurs in Yukon. Your continued patronage made it possible to complete this book in the past year. I've also learned a lot about slowing down and being tactful with communication through your wisdom in working with different funding agencies and politicians.

To the mentors I've never had:
Eric Ries (The Lean Startup): His books and writing have been a cornerstone to my understanding and development of various sales models and approaches.

Ramit Sethi (I Will Teach You To Be Rich): Always gives great actionable advice on all things business.

Reid Hoffman (Greylock): I've been a follower and big fan of the Masters of Scale podcast since it began and have listened to every single episode. Many of the insights gleaned from interviews with various founders have helped shape my perspective and approach to doing business.

Roy H. Williams, Ryan Chute, Jeff Sexton, Stephen Semple, and David Young (Wizard of Ads and The Empire Builders Podcast): Though most of their content is marketing-centric, a lot of it also applies to sales. Highly recommend their bi-weekly newsletters and the podcast series. Big thanks to Tammy Beese from WhatsUpYukon for exposing me to them!

PREFACE

This is not the very first sales-themed book; it's merely one of the many out there. So why should you care?! Why did I believe it was worth my time to contribute to the already crowded literature on this topic?

Sales is a well-established topic with many tested and proven processes, methodologies, and techniques. Many of these are developed on the tenets of behavioral psychology and will endure regardless of market trends, technological advancements, or economic circumstances.

However!

We're navigating a perpetually changing environment due to the continual advancement of technology, with each new generation adopting unique purchasing habits, utilizing diverse channels, and favoring distinct interaction preferences.

Today's consumers care more about transparency, authenticity, and aligning themselves with brands that speak to their values and represent their sense of identity. The modern consumer isn't solely buying a solution to their problems or a product; they're buying an experience, a relationship.

Today's employees (especially sales representatives) care more than ever about selling solutions that they believe in. They want to feel like they're more than a cog in the wheel, they want to know that what they're doing is meaningful and contributes to a greater impactful purpose. They seek companies that allow them to freely express themselves and be authentic.

And today's founders and executives alike are starting to recognize the importance of #doinggoodbusiness. Not only to make the world a better place, but also because doing good benefits the bottom line and leads to more profit.

Yesterday's lessons aren't designed for the businesses of today.

I find that too much of what's already out there focuses on tricks, techniques, and psychological manipulation. It's no wonder that salespeople have developed a bad reputation. Because of that, despite understanding the importance of sales, many founders still hesitate to prioritize sales-related activities and develop their sales skills.

I'm out to change that, especially so for social ventures (many who struggle to be financially sustainable) with great solutions that aim to make the world a better place. You can create meaningful impact *and* be highly profitable, and there's absolutely nothing wrong or unethical with doing both.

I'm Chin Hing Chang. born and raised in Malaysia but moved to Canada in 2005 as a 1st generation immigrant. I share who I am to help you understand the lens, ethos, experience, and values from which my lessons on the topic of sales come.

After graduating from the University of British Columbia (UBC) with a Bachelor of Science in Psychology, I started my career in sales because I believed, and still do, that sales is the most crucial skill both in business and personal life. Understanding sales = understanding persuasion. It helps you not only understand how to get customers and bring in profit but also sell your

> *Self*: in an interview (if you're looking for a job or to switch)
>
> *Vision and ideas*: in a pitch/presentation to your team, seniors, or even investors (if you're a founder).
>
> *Brand/product/reputation*: in your marketing campaigns.
>
> *Culture*: if you're recruiting and trying to attract, galvanize, and motivate the right people to support your endeavor.

As a vital life skill, sales also teaches us how to

- Be curious
- Communicate
- Negotiate
- Empathise and be an active listener

- Problem Solve, be adaptive, and think critically
- Manage our time and prioritize
- Improve our charisma
- Be more resilient
- And even be happier (Really?! More on this when we discuss (E)XPECTATIONS: page 87)

Everything is sales, sales is everything.

My formal sales training stems from the consultative sales framework learned during my time in the telecommunications industry. Consultative selling revolves around a needs and values-centered approach. It prioritizes understanding our prospects before pitching, enabling us to customize the optimal solution or recommendation for them. Having sold high ticket items (typically $300+) and also learned modern techniques and frameworks (SPIN, Challenger, NEAT, SNAP, etc.), I've incorporated them into lessons in this book as well.

Another interesting point to highlight: Although I have achieved top-performing status in some of my previous roles and can apply the techniques and frameworks to excel, I was by no means a natural-born salesman. While some individuals naturally possess charisma and persuasive abilities, if you don't, great sales skills can still be developed through consistent practice and rigorous testing! My expertise lies in teaching, training, coaching, and management—and it's through these avenues that I aim to empower you with the insights in this book.

Besides sales, I have been heavily involved in entrepreneurship support work since 2014. Specifically with social ventures (a.k.a. social enterprise/social impact business). If you're unfamiliar with the term, social ventures are companies that aren't only in it for the money, they are for-profit businesses that believe business can also be used as a force for good – for people, planet, and purpose. Since then, I've worked with over 500 such organizations across the globe, across every imaginable industry from food & beverage, education, fashion apparel, gaming, consultancies, to B2B software as a service (SaaS). This experience has taught me a lot about the importance of not only making money but doing so without selling your soul. About how to sell authentically without being manipulative.

Many of these companies I've worked with are early-stage businesses, a.k.a. Startups. While "startup" is often synonymous with software technology companies, every fledgling business is technically a startup. Since altering culture, addressing detrimental behaviors, and changing habits can be incredibly challenging without a significant overhaul – often costly and time-consuming – I'll draw from my experience working with startups to offer insights into establishing solid foundations and systems from the outset.

Side note: A lot of people perceive social ventures as unprofitable. That's not true, you *can* be highly profitable while doing good business (in fact, you *should* be highly profitable if you aren't already). Profit allows you to amplify your impact.

I don't mean to patronize, but a memorable quote from a speaker I once heard was

"You can't help the homeless by joining them".

Of course, there are many organizations that "greenwash" in an attempt to leverage #dogood as a marketing angle too. My advice to both social ventures and greenwashing companies alike: Remember, you still *need* to have a great solution. Consumers don't buy from you simply because you #dogood, they buy good solutions that solve their problems or satisfy their desires. Doing good is the icing on the cake, influencing their opinion only when all other factors between you and alternative vendors are equal. Greenwashing is patronizing when it's inauthentic. Also, recognize that offering good solutions is *necessary*, but alone isn't *sufficient.* "Build it and they will come" doesn't work, you still need to learn how to empathize with others and help them navigate their uncertainties to get out of their own way.

Finally, as an Asian immigrant in North America, my awareness of cultural differences in communication, persuasion, negotiation, and relationship building gives me a unique perspective on how to approach these topics.

Each of these experiences alone isn't unique and much of what I'll share aren't new grandiose ideas or methodologies that I've conceived. However, my unique combination of Sales + Startup + Social Ventures + working with businesses from diverse industries will give you lots of ideas and insights. I'll help you revisit your product/service offerings, how you present them, and how you interact with prospects and customers alike.

Lastly, I'm not here to teach you how to brainwash prospects to buy. Numerous techniques are intentionally manipulative, and many, if used without careful consideration, can unintentionally become manipulative. Instead, I believe good sales starts with understanding your personal misconceptions, shifting your mindset, and applying the right structures and processes so that it no longer becomes a fearful activity because you know what to expect and how to react.

Sales is not a bad word. If you're feeling pushy, or if people say you are, you're not doing it right.

HOW TO USE THIS BOOK

Is it really better to sell ethically?
The biggest concern I often hear is

> *"Traditional sales techniques work! Even if they are manipulative, they are still necessary for high sales performance and business success. Does ethical selling equate to poorer or slower conversion?"*

Yes, there's no debate; many manipulative techniques work and are actively used because they deliver results. But is it worth sacrificing long-term value for short-term gains? Souring the relationship, leaving them feeling icky, all for the sake of closing a sale today? In today's digital age, consumers are more informed than ever. Manipulative techniques are easily exposed and the reputational backlash that results will take years to repair. Exaggerating benefits or pushing for a close without addressing a prospect's concerns not only erodes trust but also often results in disappointment and regret over their purchase. In contrast, providing honest information, setting realistic expectations, and focusing on building long-term relationships reduces the likelihood of buyer's remorse and improves your organization's reputation and brand image.

A bridge built with sticks and stones will still help you achieve your objective of getting to the other side, but is it worth the risk and danger? Sure, it might get you there, but it will only last for a few days before it collapses. Sometimes it's worth slowing down in the right ways to build a more stable and enduring foundation to move forward with. If you're looking to build a venture-scale business that only cares about growth *at all costs*, this isn't for you. But if you want to do so in a way that's right by your customers, allows you to stay human, and leads to long-term business success, this book is all about that.

Attribute
Feel free to copy and use any of the concepts or examples, but please acknowledge and attribute the creators accordingly (some of which don't originate from me).

Be mindful of your context, goals, and values.
Because I work across different industries and have supported all sorts of products and services. Some concepts shared are generalized. Most will apply to every company, but the degree of importance or priority should be subjected to scrutiny and evaluated against your personal values, goals, market behaviors, and customer's purchasing patterns. I'll try my best to give many different examples so that you can see how various organizations have implemented them depending on their context.

I've also made an effort to incorporate as many real-life instances from genuinely ethical companies whenever feasible. Yet, it's worth noting that some examples may come from companies that are possibly greenwashing or lack authenticity in their ethical practices, or even outright non-ethical companies. Despite this, I've included them because they effectively illustrate certain concepts and showcase excellent execution. In those instances, I'll offer additional context to illustrate how to apply them ethically without resorting to manipulation.

Don't boil the ocean

Take what applies to you and don't overwhelm yourself by trying to do everything at once. Any improvement is better than nothing.

Just-in-time Learning

Growth is one of my personal values. If you are like me, you probably have the urge to constantly learn new things too. However! I preach "just-in-time" learning: Knowledge is best when it is relevant and can be immediately applied and practiced. This improves retention and more importantly, ensures that you're learning knowledge that gives you results and adds value immediately.

This digital playbook will be heavily hyperlinked for you to easily skip ahead to sections of interest or review a concept. It does not need to be read linearly. Feel free to jump around and explore areas you believe are most relevant or urgent for you and your organization.

Educate others

Lastly, depending on who you are and your role in your organization, I recognize that this book will give you some ideas to implement but you may lack the authority to do so. That's OK and totally normal. Be patient, educate those above you, challenge them to improve (both themselves and the organization), and show them how these ideas will help them in their role too.

♦♦♦

GLOSSARY

Here are some personal definitions to ensure we're on the same page:

Churn/ Churn rate	The rate at which customers/employees leave.
Customer (Cx)	Distinguishable from a prospect/lead, a customer is someone who has *already purchased* your solution.
Demo	Demonstration.
E-commerce	Buying/selling goods and/or services online.
Freemium	Free with basic features, paid upgrade to unlock premium features.
Funnel	Similar to a physical funnel, the customer's journey or your process is often depicted as a sales or marketing funnel. More individuals enter at the top (leads), but fewer proceed to the next stage, and even fewer make a final purchase.
Lead Magnet	An incentive provided in exchange for contact information from a prospect.
Pivot	Any change (both big or small) you decide to make with your business. E.g. pursuing a different target customer, adjusting your offerings, or even tweaking pricing.
Prospect/ Lead	Someone who is either interested, or you've identified as a potential buyer, but has yet to purchase.
Solution/ Offerings	Since some of you sell products, while others sell services, I'll use solutions/offerings interchangeably as replacement terms instead of saying "products and services" or "products or services".
Strategy/ Plan	High-level path to achieving your end goal. Includes everything you'll put into place (assets), how you'll structure the organization, campaigns you'll run, channels you'll use, activities you'll do, etc.
Process	Specific workflows, actions, or funnels. Processes are like a sequence of events or steps you take.

	Your strategy/plan is made up of multiple independent or interrelated processes.
Methods/ Methodology	Cultivated through training, they help improve efficiency/skills. Methodologies are your frameworks, they inform HOW you sell/your selling style: SPIN, Challenger Sales, etc. To understand how Strategy, Process, and Methodology are different yet related, here's an example: To clean 500 dishes, you could employ dishwashers or ship them to a commercial cleaning facility (strategy). They can be cleaned by hand (method): Rinse, Scrub with soap, Rinse, Dry on the rack (process), and/or by dishwasher (method): Load, Insert dishwashing liquid/tablet, Run (process).
Techniques	Specific ways to accomplish something. E.g. closing techniques or overcoming objections. Techniques are like different tools that help you get the job done.
Value(s)	The perceived benefit(s) of your solution. Not to be confused with the "price" of your offerings.
Values	If I'm using the plural term (and I'll try to be clear when I do), I'm usually referring to the underlying personal or organizational values that define our decision-making process (e.g. integrity, freedom, authenticity, etc.).

COMMON ACRONYMS:

ACDC	Awareness, Consideration, Decision, Close framework by HubSpot: For describing the stages of the customer journey.
Ad	Advertisement.
AI	Artificial Intelligence.

AKA/a.k.a.	Also known as.
BANT	Budget, Authority, Need, Timeline. A framework for qualifying prospects.
B2B	Business-to-Business. Businesses that sell directly to other businesses.
B2C	Business-to-Consumer. Businesses that sell directly to general consumers.
B2B2C	Business-to-Business-to-Consumer. Businesses that sell indirectly to consumers through another business. E.g. selling a product through a distributor or retailer.
B2G	Business-to-Government.
CRM	Customer Relationship Management. A tool (usually software these days) to help you keep track of and manage the relationships between all your prospects and customers.
CTA	Call to Action. The specific action you'd like your prospect to take and your invitation for them to do so. E.g. "Download the template" or "Book a consultation".
FAQ	Frequently Asked Questions.
HR	Human Resource. The division of business responsible for all things related to employees.
KPI	Key Performance Indicator. Metrics that track against an organization's and/or individual's performance goals.
ROI	Return on investment. What do prospects get in exchange for their time/money invested into your solution? Return should exceed Investment for them to feel it's worth their while.

SaaS	Software as a Service.
SDR	Sales Development Representative/Salesperson.
SEO	Search Engine Optimization.
SQL	Sales Qualified Lead
MQL	Marketing Qualified Lead
MOU	Memorandum of Understanding. A non-legally binding agreement that precedes a formal contract.
UBP	Usage-based Pricing
WoM	Word of Mouth.
CAC	Customer Acquisition Cost / Cost of Acquiring a Customer. How much it takes to market to a prospect and convert them into a customer.
LTV	Lifetime Value. How much you make from them over their lifetime as your customer.

INTRODUCTION

Before we begin, let's review some terms to ensure we're on the same page. Cooking is an excellent analogy to explain the differences:

Strategy: In cooking, strategy is the overall approach you take to create a meal. For example, to cook a healthy, vegetarian dinner. This guides decisions regarding the dishes you'll make, the ingredients you'll use, and the cooking techniques you'll employ. It's your "big picture" plan.

Tactics: Are the right combination of methods and techniques to create a specific dish. Tactics might involve deciding to braise a tough cut of meat to make it tender (technique), then adding herbs and spices to enhance the flavor (method). Tactics also include timing, sequencing, and the order in which you perform methods and techniques to achieve the desired outcome in a recipe.

Strategy is your overall plan, while tactics are the specific steps and decisions you take to put that plan into action.

Process: Is the structured framework and sequential series of steps involved in preparing a meal. Like in business, the process of cooking includes fundamental stages such as planning (choosing the recipe), preparation (gathering ingredients and tools), execution (cooking), and presentation (serving the meal). It's the roadmap that guides you from start to finish when creating a dish.

Methodology: The *collection* of rules, principles, and guidelines you follow when applying techniques and methods. It encompasses how you do things, such as the precise order of adding ingredients, cooking times, or seasoning choices. An example is following a specific cultural tradition in cooking, like Italian or Indian.

Method: A specific step or procedure within a process. A fundamental way of performing a particular task. For example, sautéing onions, grilling a steak, or boiling pasta are all methods. These methods are like individual building blocks used in various recipes. Each method focuses on a specific aspect, such as heating, cooking, or preparing ingredients.

Method is a specific step, while Methodology encompasses your broader philosophy and guiding principles that influence your cooking decisions across various recipes and culinary experiences.

Technique: A broader and more general concept. It encompasses a set of skills, practices, and methods you use to perform a wide range of tasks. Techniques are fundamental and often require precision and expertise. For instance, knife skills, which include chopping, dicing, and julienning, are techniques used in preparing ingredients for different dishes. Roasting, baking, and braising are techniques that involve specific cooking methods but can be applied to diverse recipes.

Here's a comparison for added clarity:

	Cooking	**Sales**
Strategy	Vegetarian Dinner	Targeting enterprise clients
Tactics	Vegetarian lasagna, and Caesar salad	Cold email, cold calling, and LinkedIn outreach.
Process	Instructions and steps for baking vegetarian lasagna (preheat oven, line baking tray, etc.)	Email conversion funnel (specific drip sequence and if-this-then-that actions)
Methodology	Italian style	Challenger sales approach
Method	A specific way of sauteing mushrooms	Tailoring insights, asserting commercial teaching, leading the sales conversation
Technique	Knife skills, baking technique.	Active listening, objection handling, and closing technique

Don't stress it if you're still confused; some people use these terms interchangeably, and it doesn't matter too heavily in practice. I'm sharing my definitions to help you logically orient yourself as we delve into each layer of the concepts mentioned above.

1: MINDSET & METHODOLOGY

Changing how we perceive ourselves as salespeople and how we sell.

I won't show you how to "hack" your business to grow 100X. Don't believe the hype from so-called gurus. There's no magic pill, no one-size-fits-all. I'm not your guru, but I will be your guide and help you find the authentic way that works best for you.

Selling is like cooking, you can use the same ingredients and processes but still create a variety of dishes depending on the specific methods you use. There are many out there, such as SPIN selling, Challenger selling, N.E.A.T. selling, etc., but it's important to recognize that no single methodology works best. Tailor your approach to align with your prospects, with what your reps are comfortable with, and with what works best for your processes and the offerings you're selling. If you're interested in a summary of the 12 most popular methodologies, check out: https://blog.hubspot.com/sales/6-popular-sales-methodologies-summarized.

BUT first! We need to address our mindset and perception of sales before we can even begin fine-tuning our methods. Selling should never be about convincing someone to buy something they don't need. To emphasize, I paraphrase the late Steve Jobs:

"You're not allowed to sell.
Enrich people's lives through education of our products"

Notice that Apple hires "Specialists", not "Sales" in their retail stores. Guy Kawasaki, an early employee brought on to market their Macintosh computer line popularized the term *evangelist* in marketing. The same applies to sales: exceptional salespeople possess a sincere passion and truly believe in the value of their offerings. When you authentically believe you have a great solution and it genuinely benefits your prospect, the interaction shouldn't feel transactional. Rather than seeing yourself as a salesperson, adopt the mindset of an evangelist. By attracting the right customers, guiding them through appropriate processes, and prioritizing their best interest, what might feel like uncomfortable sales transforms into authentic service, and profit will naturally follow suit.

Mindset 1: Intention

Focus on what they want,
not what you want (to close a sale/build rapport/etc.).

The initial significant change in mindset entails prioritizing the best interests of your prospects (helping them with their decision, educating them, enhancing their experience, and adding value) over your own (such as meeting sales quotas or maximizing revenue for your organization).

Profit is important, but don't let profit be the purpose. Instead, it is the natural result that ensues when you focus on adding value and assisting your prospects.

Tactics are acceptable if used with the sincere intent to:

- Make the prospect comfortable.
- Help you confront your prospect with hard truths that they've been avoiding and aren't serving them.
- Make your SDRs (Sales Development Representatives) or yourself more authentic and natural in your sales process.

Intention is everything. A little off tangent, but I'm reminded of a debate we had at Spring Activator, the social venture incubator/accelerator where I used to work.

Certain impact investors are overly selective in how they define a social venture. Even if a venture can't meet impact criteria today (e.g. through certification like B-Corp or others), it shouldn't mean that it should be immediately disqualified for investment consideration. The reverse is also true; some organizations leverage greenwashing as a marketing tactic. What's more important is to understand if they have honest intentions and are continually working towards improving their alignment on people, planet, and profit.

For instance, a small startup might not be able to afford eco-friendly packaging because they lack the scale to make it economical (not because they don't want to). If they're truly purpose-driven, they'll readily switch to more environmentally friendly solutions once they're able to. It's the trend and pattern of behaviors that matter. Are they actively looking to improve their impact, or are they simply trying to check a box to meet certain criteria?

You won't go wrong if you prioritize putting the prospect first in every sales interaction. View it as an exploration between two parties to create a vision for a better future with a clear path to getting there. Not every prospect who starts on this journey will reach the end, and that's OK! Don't force it.

Aim to leave your prospects better than when you found them, regardless of whether they buy from you or not.

Mindset 2: Be Authentic

You have to believe in the value of your own solution and be genuinely passionate about your mission or industry. If you don't, you're working for the wrong company. No amount of training can enhance the performance of an SDR who lacks enthusiasm. Beyond the obvious, you'll need to find a style that aligns with your *values.* You shouldn't have to force yourself to match your prospect's personality, cadence, or preferences.

Realize that "self" is not singular; it's plural. There is no such thing as one true authentic self. We have different archetypes or modes of being when we're with different people, and we might behave differently with our best friends than with our grandparents. Yet, we can confidently say that both of those are authentic versions of ourselves. We develop these different archetypes because it's valuable to select the right mode of being depending on the situation.

(Split, 2016 American film, by M. Night Shyamalan)

For instance, you might not swear or make fart jokes (that you d your friends) in front of your grandma (although some of you might, and that's a beautiful thing!). Similarly, it isn't always the most helpful to be overly friendly at work, lest your employees find it difficult to take you seriously. It's entirely normal to have a work or sales "mode" and different personalities or identities depending on who you're interacting with. That doesn't make you inauthentic or fake.

You'll need to discover for yourself what your personal style is, where you draw the line between these archetypes, and when to employ them. Authenticity means not feeling the need to be someone you're not, to avoid any sense of being forced. Your archetypes are your personal designs, and more importantly, they all reflect the same set of personal values and ethical ethos that make you who you are. Never apply sales tactics that you aren't comfortable with or that conflict with your ethos.

Mindset 3: Think Long-term

Manipulative tactics may boost results in the short term, but they're almost guaranteed to come back and haunt you with higher customer churn, negative reviews, or fewer referrals. Abandoning conversion-centric tactics to favor relationship building may result in small short-term sacrifices but almost always pays dividends in the long run. Not only directly through profit, but it will also improve employee engagement and culture in your organization.

Mindset 4: Be a Challenger

The Challenge Sales approach aligns with this principle. The idea of being a Challenger sounds aggressive, but it isn't about pushing prospects to buy something they don't need. Instead, it's about understanding what's best for your prospects, even when they may be unaware, hesitant to admit, or reluctant to confront certain aspects that are detrimental to them.

Challengers compassionately guide their prospects. This is achieved by adopting an empathetic approach. It involves informing prospects about their blind spots, overlooked opportunities, and how the offering you're promoting can enhance their situation.

Relationship Builders	Challengers
• Prioritize being accepted. • Avoid conflict or difficult conversations that might make the prospect uncomfortable, even if it's what they need to hear. • Focused on convenience.	• Strong understanding of the prospect's business, even more so than they know themselves. • Knowledge grounded in research and experience. • Willing to push the prospect out of their comfort zone if it's right by them. • Unafraid of healthy and respectful debate. • Focused on maximizing customer value.

Don't take the above as a suggestion that relationship builders aren't good salespeople. Instead, it's a recommendation to go a step further if you really care about your prospects. Being a true Challenger requires not only integrity but kindness. It doesn't imply a lack of concern for your clients' needs. On the contrary, it's precisely because you possess a deeper understanding than they do about their challenges, peers, marketplace, and industry that you can effectively assist them. This additional knowledge allows you to set yourself apart from competitors by introducing fresh insights that help your prospects reframe their perspectives. Coupled with investing attention into comprehending their individual needs and specific context, it empowers you to tailor your solution to suit them.

Challengers also need to excel at controlling and guiding conversations, not in a manipulative sense, but because prospects often lack awareness of what's best for themselves. It's not uncommon for prospects to become defensive when confronted with insights that challenge their long-standing preconceptions. Be emotionally resilient and understand that their defensiveness isn't directed at you personally.

KIND VS. NICE

While they may seem synonymous, kindness and niceness are completely different. Understanding what you're genuinely doing and how to truly be kind is the first step toward correctly adopting a Challenger approach.

"You can be nice and be passive. You can be nice and just not cause troubles, but to be kind, you need to solve those problems. You can be nice and be polite, but to be kind, you need to be honest. And to be honest, you need to have the strength and the courage to say what needs to be said at the right time."
– Daniel Lubetzky, Founder @ Kind Snacks

Being kind doesn't make you weak. It's more challenging and confrontational to be kind; hence, we often default to being nice. To genuinely be kind, we have to be willing to tell the hard truths, to explain why, even if it makes us and/or the person we're addressing uncomfortable. In sales, this might even mean willingly letting go of a prospect if you know that your solution isn't best suited for supporting them and others are better.

It is worse when you avoid necessary confrontations to be nice. People-pleasing is a form of assholery. When you try to be nice, you're being disingenuous and inauthentic.

"You're not giving them the dignity of their own experience and (assuming) they can't handle the truth. It's patronizing"
– Whitney Cummings in her interview with Tim Ferris

However, it's equally important not to use kindness as an excuse to be uncouth; you still need to be tactful and mindful of how you present your feedback if you genuinely care and want the receiver to accept it.

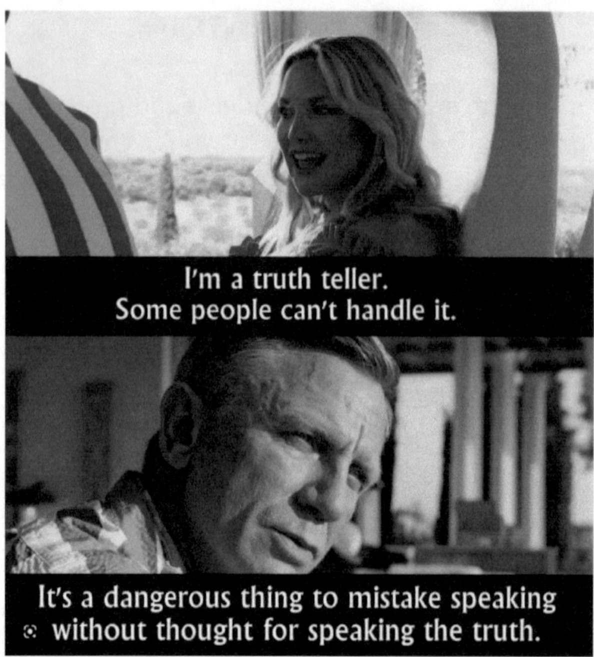

I'm a truth teller.
Some people can't handle it.
It's a dangerous thing to mistake speaking
without thought for speaking the truth.

(Quote from the movie – Glass Onion: A Knives Out Mystery)

Be intelligent and kind. Speak thoughtfully, making your insights comfortable for the other party to receive. You might even have to be discreet if a public situation deems it necessary. It's not only about giving constructive feedback and dropping facts – take it or leave it, it's their problem. If you truly care about helping others improve, be mindful of how you present such that they won't feel hurt, and in turn, become overly defensive or outright ignore your feedback or suggestions.

Before we proceed, take a moment to consider the ultimate irony: to excel as a salesperson, your approach should entail letting go of the notion of selling and, instead, prioritizing understanding your prospects. Be genuinely curious and ask plenty of questions without harboring any ulterior motives. Prospects can sense a hungry salesperson from a mile away!

C.A.R.E.

With kindness in our hearts, we're finally ready to sell with C.A.R.E.

CONNECT
ASSESS
RESPOND
ENGAGE

C.A.R.E. is a framework that helps guide our sales interactions. It involves gradualization (page 230) in the form of relationship-building and collaborative problem-solving. Not every prospect needs to go through the same series of steps, so don't rely on C.A.R.E. as you would on a crutch; instead, view it as a roadmap that helps you understand what to do next depending on where you are right now.

Adjust to your prospect. If they want to get straight to business, do so. On the other hand, if they don't want to be disturbed while they discuss something with a partner, refrain from disturbing them. Forcing the conversation will only create discomfort and make them defensive.

(C)ONNECT

Connection matters more than anything, including a great product. If someone doesn't like or trust you, they won't buy whatever you have to offer. In building connections, even though we like to think we aren't shallow, we are quick to judge others. First impressions matter. We form impressions in less than 7 seconds from as far as 10 feet away.

This can manifest in various ways, depending on how your prospects discover and initiate first contact with you. If it's an ad, it's your choice of imagery and the messaging in your headline. On your website, it's what they see at first glance above the fold before needing to scroll for more information. In an email, it's your email subject and first sentence.

Your goal isn't to impress or exert authority, it's actually pretty basic:

1. Be likable
2. Build trust

BE LIKEABLE

In traditional sales training, SDRs are taught to initiate interactions with *Non-Business Conversations (NBC)*, find *common ground* (interest, events, or experiences that you share), and use *positive body language* that will help you appear more relatable and build rapport with your prospects. These techniques alone aren't wrong, but without proper application and intention, they come across as inauthentic and may do more harm than good in relationship building. For example, positive body language techniques include:

- Nodding: Communicates active listening and validation. Indicates you are following the conversation and empathizing with their perspective. It signals agreement and understanding.
- Maintaining Eye Contact: Demonstrates confidence, sincerity, and attentiveness. It shows the customer you are engaged and interested in what they are saying.
- Smiling: Conveys warmth, friendliness, and approachability. Helps put the customer at ease.
- Leaning Forward: Signals interest and attentiveness, showing that you are focused on the customer and eager to assist them.

Yes, body language is important. But what's even more important is to be authentic about it. Instead of being overly conscious about your body language and trying to express the "right" signals, focus on empathizing, and the right body language should come naturally.

Don't try too hard to be likable, take the pressure off by focusing on making your prospect feel welcomed. This will come back to you in the form of increased likability. Your prospects feel welcomed when you:

Be human

There's an outdated saying that suggests you shouldn't bring your personal issues to work. Not only is it okay, but I believe it's better to do so. For instance, if you're having a particularly bad day, it's entirely acceptable to apologize for and explain your low energy rather than putting up a fake smile. Prospects can tell, will understand, and they appreciate your authenticity. I'm not suggesting turning the interaction into a consultation about your personal issues.

Be intentional, be present

It takes effort to build a relationship, be fully present, and actively listen rather than engage in idle conversation. Finding common ground isn't about identifying interesting points that they care about and pretending you share the same experiences or interests. Instead, it's about mindfully paying attention to real commonalities and shred interests. It doesn't only happen in conversation; it could be through observing something they're wearing today or learning that they have children through your background research.

There's nothing wrong with preparing for an interaction in advance. It doesn't make it artificial or scripted. Prospects appreciate the work you put into tailoring the interaction to them; it makes them feel special, just as you would if you went to a restaurant on your birthday, and they sang you a song and gave you free dessert because they took the time to get to know their frequent customers. Brainstorm conversation starters that more easily surface common ground you're excited to engage and relate with. For example, if you are a foodie, the simple question "What did you have for lunch?" could be a great opener that helps you build a strong foundation with your new prospects.

Empathize

It's sometimes a stretch to find common ground with someone who is the polar opposite of ourselves. Even in those cases, it's still possible to build a solid rapport with someone if we empathize. As human beings, we all share the same spectrum of emotions. Focus on connecting through emotions rather than experiences.

My friend Stevie shared his experience of sitting next to the vice president of Universal Studios Singapore on a flight. At the time, Stevie was a student and had no clear common ground with such a senior executive. Small talk led to the vice president venting his frustrations about his team. Despite Stevie's lack of workplace-related experience, he engaged not only by

- Sympathizing: expressing that he could imagine what it must be like,
- But also, by empathizing: sharing his struggles managing his team as a club president. But not in a one-upmanship manner

or for the sake of saying "Me too".

Sympathy is the ability to acknowledge and show concern for the feelings of others without necessarily sharing their emotional experience. It isn't inherently bad but can come across as patronizing. On the other hand, empathy creates a deeper level of connection when you try to understand and share those emotions.

Here's an example of both sympathetic and empathic responses to someone sharing the news that they have been diagnosed with cancer:

Sympathetic Response:

- Friend: *"Oh no, that's terrible news! I'm so sorry to hear that. If there's anything I can do to help, just let me know. I'll keep you in my thoughts."*
- The friend expresses sorrow and offers support, but the emotional connection is at a distance. The focus is on expressing concern and offering assistance without fully immersing in the emotional experience.

Empathic Response:

- Friend: *"I can't imagine how overwhelming and scary this must be for you. The fear, uncertainty, and the myriad of emotions you must be going through. I want you to know that I'm here with you every step of the way. If you want to talk about it or just sit in silence, I'm here to support you."*
- The friend not only acknowledges the situation but also attempts to understand and share the emotional experience. The response goes beyond expressing concern to actively putting themselves in the other person's shoes, fostering a deeper emotional connection.

There is still genuine concern and support with a sympathetic response. It's not a bad thing to do and we often find ourselves unconsciously sympathizing with others. However, if you want to connect at a deeper level, learn to empathize by sharing in the emotional journey.

Share in the suffering, against a common enemy

Sharing and going through a painful experience together tends to bring people together. I'm not advocating for creating a masochistic experience; instead, consider how you might frame the problems you solve from the perspective of emotions and behaviors.

- Emotions: What pain points compelled you to create your solution? If you've experienced the problem firsthand, discuss your experience and how it has made you feel. Empathize.
- Behaviors: What are the behaviors or circumstances that led to these emotions?

For instance, if you provide a recycling sorting service for multi-residential buildings, why is there a need for it?

> *"It makes my blood boil (angry) when I see neighbors putting plastic into the compost bins or contaminating the paper bins with mixed containers and vice versa. I'm frustrated that people can't follow simple instructions to properly sort their waste and saddened because this creates more waste as recyclables need to be discarded. It renders the additional effort of others to recycle wasted and can even lead to damaging the equipment"*

Painful emotions: anger, frustration, sadness

Behaviors/Circumstances: laziness, not following instructions, or perhaps the recycling process itself is more complicated than necessary.

These behaviors or circumstances are the common enemies responsible for your suffering. Identifying and calling them out helps your prospects understand you're on their team.

It's not:	Them (prospect)	vs.	You
it's:	Us (you + prospect)	vs.	Them (the problem).

Be sincere

Don't give shallow compliments to try and flatter your prospects. If you're not used to expressing positive sentiments, it does take some effort and practice to notice and genuinely appreciate the things you sincerely admire. Start practicing mindful praise with your friends and family; it'll greatly improve the quality of your relationships too.

BUILD TRUST

Likability is also an element of trust. Some of the other elements include credibility, confidence, and social proof. Here are a few ways to build trust; you don't have to deploy all of them, and you'll do well if you don't go overboard. Remember, focus more on their needs, and less on your desires. The goal isn't to make a sale, it's to make them feel welcomed and comfortable in your presence.

Credentials
What certifications, licenses, or awards have you earned? It could even be your job title itself or your specialized role in your organization. Highlight these to demonstrate that you're a qualified expert in the field.

Experience
How long have you been in this industry? At this job? How many clients have you worked with? Have you worked with someone who's faced a similar situation as them?

(Y Combinator's website)

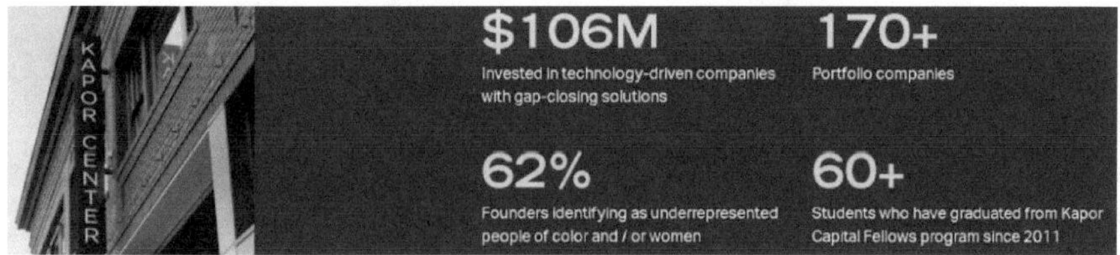

(Kapor Capital's website)

Knowledge
Never brag and avoid dropping jargon. You don't want to accidentally make them feel dumb or ignorant. Instead, approach this by highlighting common misconceptions, matching their level of understanding, and teaching them about potential blind spots.

Passion
Prospects expect you to passionately advocate for your product or the company you're working for. After all, that's what you're paid to do. Go a level deeper by sharing your honest passion for this type of solution or your infatuation with the industry at large. If it's lacking, perhaps it's time to consider a career or company change.

Play on their team
They won't trust you if they feel like it's you/your company vs. them. Yet, it befuddles me that many sales teams adopt this mindset. Position yourself with them, even if they don't end up becoming a customer. If you've personally navigated the same situation they have, share your experience as a fellow consumer trying to help another.

Be confident
If you know your stuff and understand what's best for your prospects, be confident in your recommendations and don't hesitate to lead the conversation. It's not about putting on a false sense of bravado or confidently bullshitting your way through questions when you don't know the answer. If you genuinely don't know something, it's better to admit it and get back to them with a proper answer after you've done your research.

Confidence isn't about asserting dominance by being commanding. It's about earning respect by demonstrating a calm competence that comes with experience and knowledge.

Dress the part
You don't always have to wear a suit and tie; in some cases, it's better not to. Be yourself by dressing in what makes you comfortable and confident, but also be realistic and dress the part to align with expectations. You would be worried if your doctor came in to see you in flip-flops, a hoodie, and shorts. Going all out with a suit and tie when meeting with a tech angel investor will also give the wrong impression that you're too stiff and formal.

Social Proof
Not to be confused with leveraging social/peer pressure to mislead a prospect with false choices or manipulate them into favoring a specific decision. For example,

- Claiming an item is the most popular product (even if it isn't).
- Suggesting that many people prefer it (even if it isn't true).
- Pressuring you to get multiple stakeholders on the call together.

It's acceptable to use social proof as long as you are being honest in doing so. You can only get so far tooting your own horn. Instead of telling, show them who else is at the table. People are more willing to trust you if they can see that others have also trusted you and not been let down. Are there any notable or recognizable current or former customers you've worked with? How about reviews from third-party websites? Do you have customer reviews or testimonials?

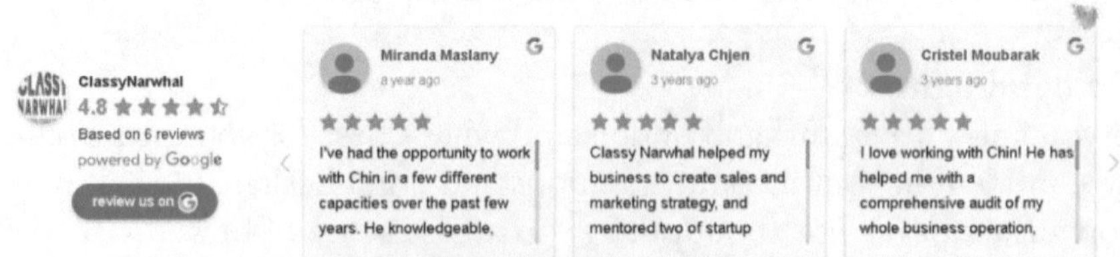

(Reviews on my website: https://classynarwhal.com/ pulled from Google)

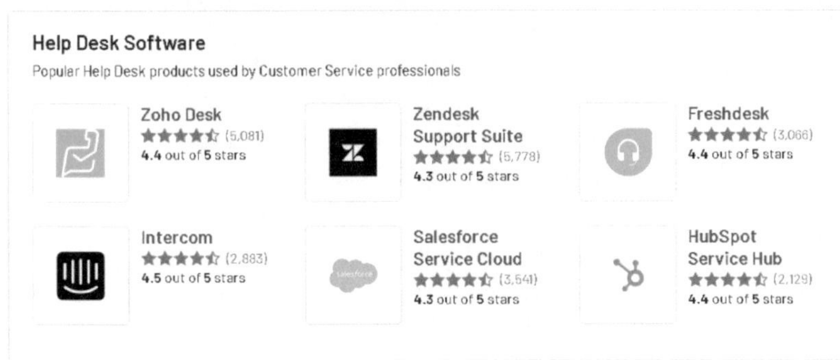

(Recommended software vendors on G2)

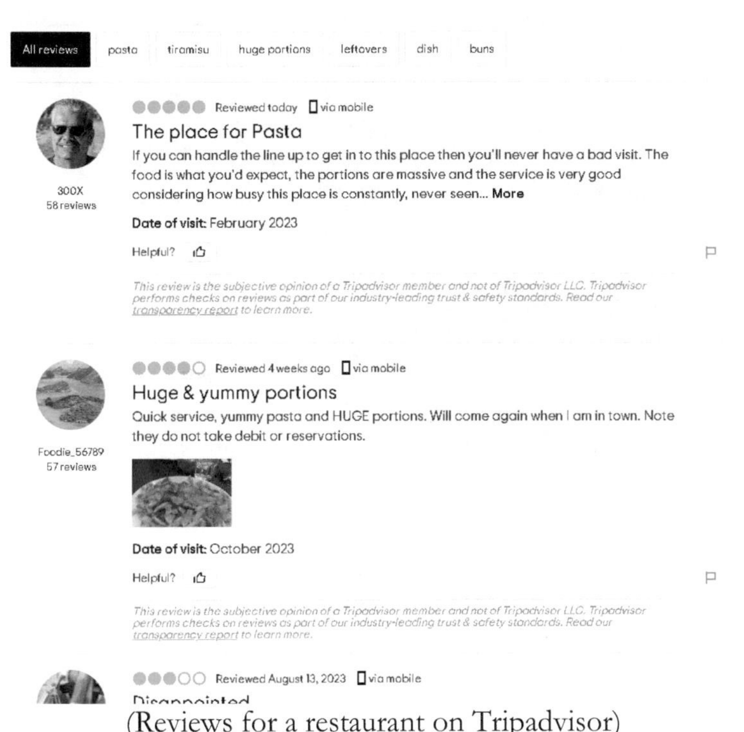

(Reviews for a restaurant on Tripadvisor)

It's OK to be vulnerable.

In the Empire Builder's Podcast, Episode 140: Building Trust, Steve and Dave share a really good example that I'll paraphrase:

> Steve had a client who was a used RV dealer. They were struggling to sell an old RV previously used as a hotbox and strongly infused with marijuana smoke. It wasn't selling because they were afraid of coming clean about it, but once they did and said *"If you're a marijuana smoker, you can't wreck this"*, it sold fast!

Being honest and transparent about your weaknesses or flaws isn't just acceptable; it's better! If you seem too perfect, customers don't feel like they genuinely know you, that you're not being completely honest with them. In social psychology, this is known as the Pratfall effect.

Give Trust

Others will trust you if you first trust them. We feel safe and more comfortable opening up when others are willing to take that risky leap with us first. Steve and Dave also shared in that previously mentioned podcast episode the example of warranties or return policies chock-full of conditions. Policies like these suggest you don't trust your customers, and you're worried they will abuse it. Yes, a handful will try to take advantage; however, the trust you earn by first giving trust will empower many more people to take the leap and purchase your offerings.

Shared values and beliefs

If your organization has clear values or a stance on a particular topic, that's a good thing. Yes, it may alienate some prospects, but those are likely not the type of people you want as your customers anyway. Boldly communicating your values and beliefs will help those who share them identify you as members of their tribe. They will more readily trust you because they understand that you share their interest and ethos.

ASSIGNMENT

Be Likable

1. List some potential greetings that create the opportunity for more interesting conversations that will help you learn a little more about your prospect.
2. Are there questions you can ask to invite them to share passionately about a common ground topic that you're also equally passionate about discussing?
3. Notice one thing you admire about the next three people you meet and tell them about it.

Build Trust

1. What can you highlight about yourself to establish credibility? Your personal experience with the problem/solution? First-hand experience with other customers?
2. What can you highlight about your company? Happy customers, Reviews, thought leadership, advocacy, etc.

Notes:

(A)SSESS

Now we begin to shift towards understanding our prospects, less on a personal level, but more for understanding if they are a fit for our offerings and if so, how they might benefit from them.

(A)SSESSMENT comes in 2 forms:

1. Research
Don't be lazy; research your prospects before the interaction. Understand as much as you can about them in relation to your offerings. The more you know about them, the less you have to ask in conversation. To qualify them: Use the BANT framework (page 129).

Here are sample considerations that will help enhance your understanding of how to present to them:

- Who are their competitors?
- What should success look like for them?
- Are they on par with their peers?
- What alternative solutions are they currently utilizing or looking into?
- What is the trend in their market or industry?
- What might they be motivated by?"

2. Relevant Questions
These are questions you need them to answer to provide insights into how they might use your solution. Their responses will reveal opportunities for you to emphasize specific features, upsell, or cross-sell (page 198). To accomplish this effectively, we must proactively plan for and deliberately ask the right questions, rather than expecting prospects to already know what they want or need.

"If I had asked people what they wanted,
they would have said faster horses."
– Henry Ford, Ford Motor Company

Prospects can articulate their problems, but they often lack a clear vision of the ideal solution. It's our responsibility to discern what suits them best based on their unique situation.

For instance, if you are selling cell phones and you're trying to highlight the motion photo feature:

Normal Questions:	• How do you currently use your phone to take pictures? • What do you like to photograph? • How do you capture that perfect moment during a sports match?
Better Questions:	• Do you have kids? • Do you play sports?

The first group consists of questions directly related to the camera's features. Although useful, they can be limiting. The second group is better because it helps you uncover benefits and values that multiple other features could speak to.

If they say they have kids, you could now say:

> *"You mentioned having kids; let me show you a really cool feature in this phone"* (Paraphrases and acknowledges their point to demonstrate you're genuinely paying attention to their needs.)
>
> *"I'm frequently tasked with photographing my nephew and his family at gatherings. As you know, it's always a challenge to perfectly capture those magical moments when they're squirming, blinking, or distracted by every little thing."* (Demonstrates relatability through common ground, defines the problem, and highlights a Value that the prospect cares about – capturing those magical family moments.)
>
> *"The camera on this phone features a special motion photo setting that operates by recording a short clip before you press the shutter button"* (Feature)
>
> *"It enables you to review and select the best image without the concern of potentially missing a moment or if someone blinked or looked away at the wrong time."* (Benefit)

> *"Additionally, it's waterproof, so you won't have to worry about washing your device after your little ones get their dirty hands on it. I can also walk you through setting up parental controls to childproof your device."* (Elaborating on other relevant features now that you have a better understanding of your prospect's lifestyle.)

So how do we ask good questions?

Use open-ended questions

These are questions that can't be answered with a simple yes, no, or a single word. They encourage the prospect to share more, helping you better understand their needs. Open-ended questions minimize back-and-forth dialogue and foster a more natural conversation by making it feel less like an interrogation.

"Do you…" questions are closed-ended. Turn them into open-ended questions by adding the *5Ws and H* to the start of it.

> *"Who do you…"*
> *"What do you…"*
> *"Where do you…"*
> *"When do you…"*
> *"Why do you…"*
> *"How do you…"*

Quantify Value if possible

Work with your prospects to define success Key Performance Indicators (KPIs) and benchmark metrics before vs. after. This enables you to easily highlight progress and helps them more clearly realize the value and impact of your solution once they've started using it. It improves retention and also makes it a lot easier for you to turn them into case studies or testimonials should they permit.

> *"What would solving X do for you?"*
> *"How is this problem currently impacting your team?"*
> *"How do you currently measure success?"*

Uncover their interest, motivations, and desires

What is their current reality?

What challenges, obstacles, and implications are holding them back?
How does it match up to their vision of the desired future?
How will your solution bridge aid in bridging that gap?

For B2B scenarios, this payoff or reward can manifest not only as a benefit to the business but also personally, in the form of professional accolades or a promotion.

Dig deep with 5 Whys

Sometimes, prospects may become fixated on the superficial symptoms of their problem and overlook the underlying root cause. If your solution effectively addresses this root cause, consider highlighting it early in the conversation. This helps prospects gain a clearer understanding of the relevance of your solution.

Drawing inspiration from lean manufacturing, the 5 Whys technique, introduced by Taiichi Ohno at Toyota Motor Corporation, is an excellent starting point. It encourages us to think critically and challenge both our assumptions and those of our prospects by digging deeper. For example,

The machine stopped working.
Why?
There was an overload that blew out the fuse.
Why?
The bearing was not sufficiently lubricated.
Why?
The lubrication pump was faulty.
Why?
A strainer wasn't reattached after servicing it and some scrap metal got in.

In troubleshooting, it's common to overlook the root cause and instead address only the symptoms, mistakenly thinking the issue is resolved. Without tackling the root causes, the problem is likely to resurface. The 'Why' questioning need not always be 5 times; it could be more, or less. Ultimately, it's about challenging yourself to explore further

Why isn't the only vocabulary at your disposal; use all the 5Ws and H mentioned earlier to dig deep. Here's what it might look like in a sales interaction:

> SDR: *You're experiencing fulfillment issues with your current manufacturer. How does that translate to your business?*
> Prospect: *The slower turnaround means our customers have to wait much longer before they can receive the products they ordered.*
>
> SDR: *And how do you believe that impacts your bottom line?*
> Prospect: *We end up wasting a significant amount of time and money processing returns or answering inquiries about the status of their orders. It's distracting our team from leaning harder into sales or marketing efforts and eating into our profit margins.*
>
> SDR: *How much would you estimate you spent on processing refunds alone last year?*
> Prospect: *Probably a little more than $10,000 (Quantify Value), and that doesn't even account for all the headaches and time wasted.*

What problem does this problem solve?
5 Whys helps us uncover the root cause; however, in certain cases, we might want to broaden both our and our prospect's considerations beyond the current manifestation of solutions. For instance, if your wheelbarrow breaks down:

If we only focus on fixing the wheelbarrow, our solutions might be limited to improvements in wheel design, handle grip, or material durability. While these changes can make the wheelbarrow more efficient, they are within the confines of the existing paradigm of material transportation.

By asking, *"What problem does this problem solve?"* we shift our prospects from seeking incremental improvements to exploring transformative solutions.

Underlying Issue Identification: What fundamental problem does the wheelbarrow address? It's about the manual transport of materials.

Explore Alternatives: If we dig deeper into the need for manual material transport, we might realize that the wheelbarrow, while effective, has its limitations.

Think Beyond the Wheelbarrow: What if we reimagine material transport entirely? Could there be alternative solutions that don't involve pushing a wheelbarrow? Perhaps a system of conveyors, drones, or automated carts.

Innovative Solutions: By questioning the necessity of the wheelbarrow itself, we open the door to more innovative solutions. For example, a modular, self-driving cart system that can carry heavy loads efficiently, or a drone-based delivery system for materials in hard-to-reach places.

This approach aids us in challenging our prospects to reconsider the nature of the problem and explore innovative alternatives beyond the existing framework. It encourages breaking free from conventional thinking and considering unconventional, yet potentially more effective approaches.

As you (A)SSESS your prospects,

Listen
For what *they* want, not what *you* want to hear: Not only in sales, we often listen with the intent to respond, constantly contemplating what to say next or how to connect our points to the other party's words. This distracts us from being fully present in the conversation, from genuinely listening, and empathizing with the people we're speaking to.

80/20: 80% listening, 20% talking. Give your prospects space to share, don't jump the gun by pitching. The only thing you're doing at this point is asking questions and acknowledging their responses.

Acknowledge, don't interrogate
If the conversation follows the pattern of Question → Answer → Question → Answer, it can quickly start to feel like an interrogation. Acknowledging makes the assessment flow more like a natural conversation. Paraphrase or summarize, especially when a lot of information is being shared.
Besides showing them you're actively listening, acknowledging ensures

you're interpreting what they're saying correctly. Due to confirmation bias, we tend to listen to what we want to hear and tune out the rest.

Write things down!
Taking notes has become such an under-practiced virtue, which is exactly why it gives a strong positive impression on prospects when they see that you care enough about them to write down and track the details. Let the other party know you're going to be taking notes, so you don't come across as distracted or multi-tasking.

And do it, even if you think you have a great memory, not for the sake of appearing attentive, but because we often overestimate ourselves. Besides helping us remember what our prospects are saying, it also has the added benefit of enabling us to "let go" and be present in the conversation instead of constantly trying to cache and remember all the nuances.

Listen for the sake of understanding, not for the sake of replying.

Never assume.
If you're uncertain about anything, it's okay to politely ask for clarification and admit your ignorance. Doing so doesn't make you any less intelligent; instead, it shows that you care enough to learn. It's better to clarify than to stereotype or make potentially incorrect assumptions, which could jeopardize trust and harm the relationship.

ASSIGNMENT

List down 10 questions that might help you uncover your prospect's needs. You don't have to ask ALL of them in your conversations; they will be a few possible options available to you depending on who you're speaking with and what you're trying to learn about them.

Notes:

♦♦♦

(R)ECOMMEND

We shouldn't initiate conversations with our prospects by delivering a pitch. It is only appropriate to transition to our recommendations only after we've developed a good understanding of our prospects. An effective way to start this transition is by acknowledging and summarizing everything we've learned about their needs and situations from the (A)SSESSMENT.

"Based on what you've told me…"

This reminds the prospect that you're paying attention, provides them with an opportunity to correct any misunderstandings, and signals that the solution you're about to share is relevant and meets their needs.

NEED VS. WANT

While they may sound similar, it's important to understand the nuanced difference between the two to effectively communicate the value of our offerings. The "Drill vs. Hole" is a classic example that illustrates this point:

You don't *want* a drill; you *need* it because you *want* to drill a hole. To take it even further, you desire a hole because you *want* to hang a family portrait or customize your house to your taste. The drill is a means to an end.

It's important to understand our prospect's motivation, why they want the problem solved, to address this *want* or "end". By doing so, it allows us to better position the *need* (our offering). Prospects are not interested in the features of your solution; they care about how it benefits them. They buy into the outcomes. What do you enable them to achieve or become? Focus on that.

Sell them what they want,
give them what they need.

Oversimplified for stark contrast, but here's a Drill vs. Hole example:

Addressing the *Need*:

> *"Introducing our state-of-the-art drill. This powerful 20V cordless tool can reach up to 750 rpm and features a versatile 24-position clutch. It's engineered for precision and efficiency, making your drilling tasks a breeze. With its advanced technology, you'll have the ability to create holes of various sizes for practical purposes in carpentry or DIY projects."*

Addressing the *Want*:

> *"It's exciting to transform your living space to reflect your unique taste! Creating the perfect setting for your home improvement plans is easier than ever with this drill. It can effortlessly handle various materials, be it drywall, wood frames, or steel plates, with its 20v motor that can go up to 750 rpm.*
>
> *For convenience and accessibility, it's also cordless and comes with two removable 20000mAh batteries, ensuring you always have the power to work with.*
>
> *If you aren't already aware, another significant issue many homeowners run into when doing their own improvements is wearing out their screw heads. This makes it challenging to remove the screw if they choose to reposition their furniture. The 24-position clutch on this drill allows you to calibrate the torque so that it doesn't overtighten or damage the screw head."*

This doesn't only apply to selling in conversation. For a marketing example, look up Google's Parisian Love advertisement on YouTube.

In the ad, the prospect's problem is a superficial need: a quick and efficient way to search for information. They did not create an ad that directly pitches Google's search features and various ways it could be used. Instead, this ad revolves around the underlying "why" for a specific use-case: the story of this user in his journey to court a lady and eventually move there to start a family (the want). In the process, as a byproduct, it highlights the various ways Google search could be used.

Notice that the "hero" of this story is the user, NOT the company or their offering.

"Your customer is the hero of the story, not your brand"
– Tim Yates and Donald Miller, creators of the StoryBrand framework

Of course, it's best if you can speak to your prospect's motivations. However, as we see here, even without doing so directly, by focusing on the *want* instead of the *need*, it already drastically humanizes your solution and makes it much more relatable. This is an essential element for engaging storytelling that will strike a chord with your audience.

Facts tell, stories sell.
Show, don't tell

Here are a few more quick examples:

Solution	Need	Want
Calculator	Solve math problems more quickly.	Be more productive at work.
Doctor's prescription to avoid having a heart attack	Eat healthier foods and exercise more. (People don't want to hear what they *need* to do, even if they know it's necessary)	Spend more time with my grandchildren. (To effectively inspire change, we need to address the *want*)
Listerine	Get rid of bad breath.	Woo a potential partner.

Don't stop at articulating the problem your solution solves. Recall 5 Whys (page 24) and dig deep to address what truly matters to your prospects. Help them connect the dots and identify with the problem if they aren't already aware of it.

For visual learners, here's an illustration to paint a clearer picture:

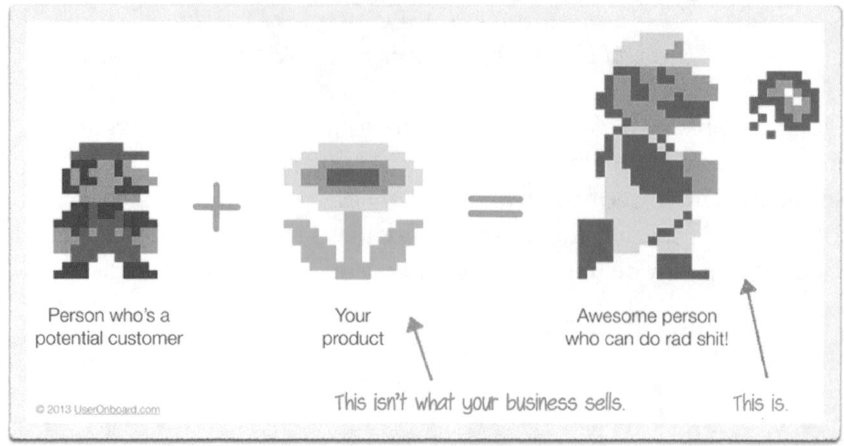

(Features vs. Benefits
depicted with an illustration of Mario by UserOnboard)

Prospects don't care about your product; stop selling the fire flower. They only want it because it turns them into an invincible, fireball-throwing Super Mario.

UVP/USP: DIFFERENT VS. DISTINCT

Articulating this *want* is what is known as the Value Proposition of your offering. In existing literature, it is commonly referred to as the Unique Value Proposition (UVP) or sometimes as the Unique Selling Proposition/Point (USP). This emphasis on uniqueness or competitive differentiation is overrated. It's entirely possible to run a successful business without being the only one in the market. We've mentioned before when we discussed copy-paste businesses: as long as there's demand, there's room for supply. However, it is helpful to have an angle, especially if you're in a crowded marketplace with numerous competitors.

If you operate a copy-paste business, consider how you might explore distinctiveness and differentiation. Here are three non-mutually exclusive ways to explore that:

Distinctiveness
In the realm of branding: catchy designs, colors, sounds, or memorable catchphrases. This approach primarily falls under marketing or strategic management and makes no claim of being better or involves specific positioning. It is effective when individuals encounter your visual and audible brand, either in-person or online, and works best when your brand identity is associated with more than just your solution.

Although it enables you to "stand out" amidst a sea of generic competitors, it is only marginally effective and highly dependent on your budget and ability to imprint with as large an audience as possible.

Differentiation Through Reason
Even if you aren't unique, you can still claim to be better or different through association with positive qualities or specialized performance. Of course, everyone claims to be "better" than their next-door competitor. The crucial aspect here is to strategize how or in which specific area you aim to excel.

Being specific doesn't confine you; in fact, less is more. Trying to do too much hurts your brand and dilutes your reputation. It's hard enough to be well-known for one thing, let alone many. Don't try to be an everything company. Instead, focus and be clear. What is your main offering? The others are your upsell or cross-sell. Diversification is a luxury reserved for those who have already established a solid reputation.

Examples include,
Ellevest: The financial company built by women for women (positioning for a specific demographic).

The Honest Company: Safe, effective products for our families and yours (qualities: safe, sustainable, doing business ethically and inclusively).

Ink LLP: Strategic counsel to high-growth companies and those that build them (specialization in working with emerging companies that have dramatic scaling ambitions, from inception through to exit).

Tylenol: For back pain vs. for arthritis both contain the exact same ingredients.

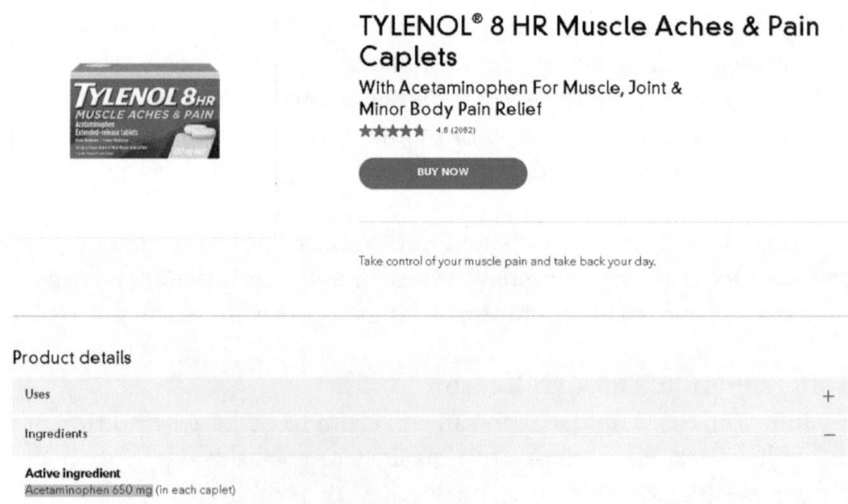

(Tylenol Muscle Aches & Pain,
Active Ingredient: Acetaminophen 650mg)

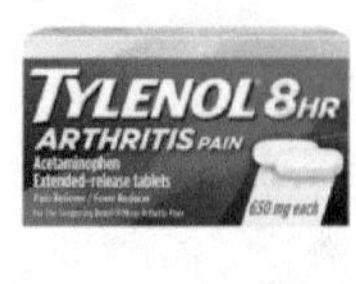

TYLENOL® 8 HR Arthritis Pain Relief Tablets

For Extended Release Arthritis & Joint Pain Relief, 650 mg Acetaminophen

4.8 (1606)

BUY NOW

From the #1 Doctor Recommended brand for pain relief and fever reduction, TYLENOL® 8 HR Arthritis Pain Tablets provide fast-acting, temporary relief of minor arthritis pain. Each TYLENOL® 8 HR arthritis pain relief tablet contains 650 mg of acetaminophen and features a bi-layer design with two layers of effective pain relief - the first dissolves fast and the second lasts up to 8 hours to ease minor arthritis pain.

Intended for adults 18 years and older, this oral TYLENOL® pain reliever is safe when used as directed and can also reduce fever and relieve other minor body aches and pains.

(Tylenol Arthritis, Active Ingredient: Acetaminophen 650mg)

Yet you're more likely to reach for one over the other if that specific condition applies to you and even claim one is more effective than the other (placebo effect). Is this manipulative? I don't think so, unless they are making baseless claims for which they aren't effective. If something does indeed work for various scenarios or users, claiming it "does it all" can inadvertently lead to it being perceived as a fraudulent miracle solution akin to snake oil. Specificity assists prospects in self-identifying and in more readily accepting that the solution will address their particular problem.

BookedIn: A Canadian company that does a good job of applying specificity. They have specific landing pages which they use to advertise for different use cases.

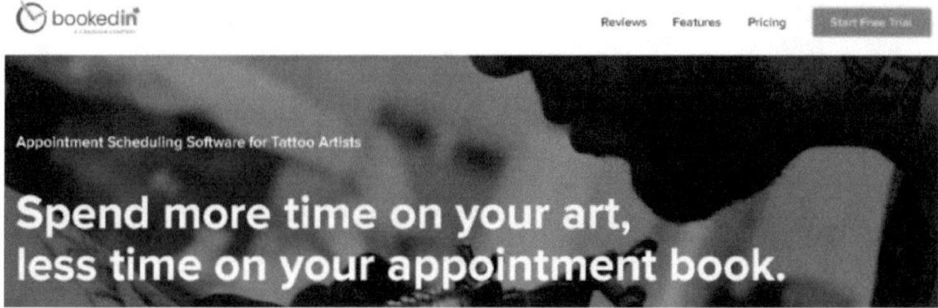

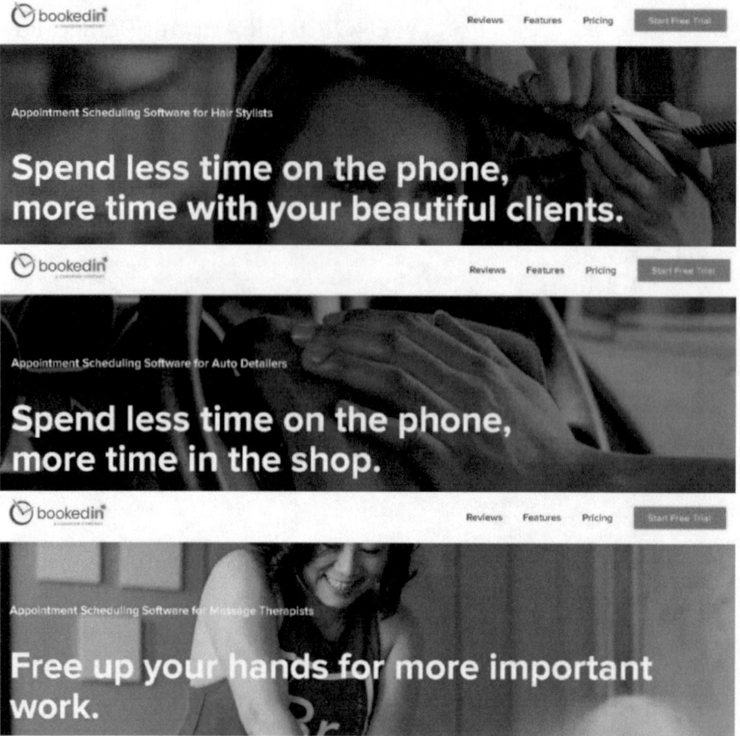

Instead of competing against countless others using price, customer service, or claims of better results, another option is to use risk reversal (page 187) to find some white space by stacking immense value. Ryan Chute from Wizard of Ads explains it in his blog post: https://wizardofads.org/whats-your-perfectly-fair-competitive-advantage/. Some examples include

- Free lifetime oil change
- Lifetime manufacturer warranty
- Waiving setup fees if a prospect signs up for X months.
- 1- year full refund or exchange. No questions asked.

Set yourself apart by offering something that competitors are unwilling to do.

Bonding Over Shared Values and Community
This is when consumers choose to buy from you because of your

brand's personality, values, or the sense of belonging or expression of personal identity they experience through the proxy of your brand.

Recreational Equipment Inc. (REI) Co-op is one such example. By positioning themselves as a co-op, they emphasize their focus on shared values (outdoor equity, climate action) rather than solely maximizing shareholder value.

Another example is when consumers choose to buy locally, even when there's no distinctiveness or differentiation in the product. They're choosing to do so to support a fellow local entrepreneur and behave in accordance with their values and beliefs.

Each of the above points is valuable on its own, but their impact is greatly amplified when applied simultaneously. While it's possible to achieve this by accident, why risk it when you can *intentionally* apply all three of them together? In some cases, it may be easier to show instead of tell. Refer to the Viral Engine (page 147) for ideas on enabling your prospects to experience your offering firsthand before making a purchase.

Also read: https://classynarwhal.com/how-to-leverage-hidden-differentiation-to-outperform-your-competitors/

FEATURE-BENEFIT-VALUE (FBV)

When you lead with features, your (R)ECCOMENDATIONS come across as a prescriptive pitch and tends to be jargon-heavy. Don't educate prospects, argue with facts, or overwhelm them with data or statistics. Instead, use analogies to relate concepts to what's familiar to them. Here are some examples:

Instead of	Try
This air conditioner is rated at 7,000 BTU	This air conditioner is strong enough to keep you nice and cool in a single-bedroom
It contains 20g protein	That's equivalent to 3 eggs' worth of protein
It has 5GB of storage	Famously: "1000 songs in your pocket"

Better yet, relate those features to direct benefits that speak to your prospect's values. We make purchase decisions based on our values and a desire for our actions to reflect ourselves. It is for this reason that some are ardent Apple advocates while others stand by Android, despite both companies offering products with nearly identical features.

Apple represents ease of use and a secure experience. There is an unspoken level of quality and status associated with their brand, along with the elegant design of their products. On the other hand, Android adopts a more open-source approach, conveying freedom through better customizability and control.

Feature-Benefit-Value is a framework you can deploy to relate the features of your solution (*need*) to the desires of your prospect (*want*). For each feature you have, brainstorm the different potential benefits (which likely motivated the inclusion or development of those features in the first place). Beyond benefits, consider the overarching values they speak to. Connecting these dots helps us better communicate the thought and care that goes into the creation of our offerings and how they are relevant to the prospect we're speaking with.

Value here does not refer to monetary value or a good bargain; instead, it pertains to the underlying personal values that drive your prospect's behaviors. It's what they care about.

Here's a visual example:

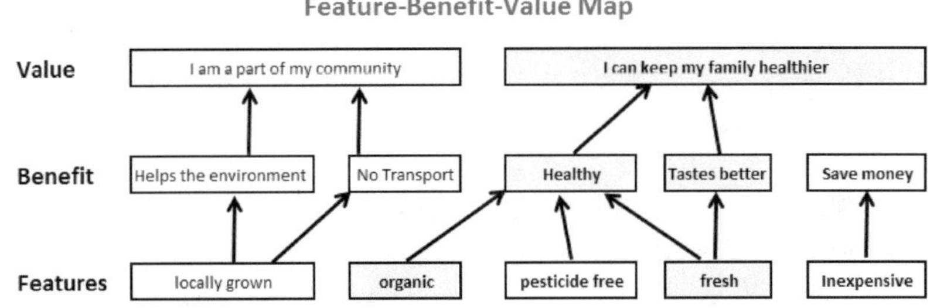

Refer to the sample dialogue about a phone's motion photo feature, previously mentioned under "Relevant Questions" in the (A)SSESSMENT stage (page 21), for another example.

Here are a few more examples:

> *"You mentioned you like taking pictures at night (acknowledging their want). This particular camera has the longest shutter delay, allowing more light to be captured (feature). This enables you to take clearer pictures at night (benefit). With that, you'll never miss capturing a valuable nighttime memory again (value)."*

> *"You mentioned you often download movies through torrents at home (want). I believe the Hi-Speed broadband package will be the best for you. With that package, you get download speeds of up to 128 Mbps (feature), allowing you to download an average movie in less than 15 minutes (benefit)! This means you'll waste less time waiting and spend more time enjoying (value)."*

> *"Not a lot of people know this, but given what you've shared about the bad experience your building's strata has had with their previous snow removal and salting contractor (want), you'll probably appreciate that we offer our clients the real-time ability to decline service (feature) if you disagree with our assessment based on the day's weather report or if you wish to handle it yourself on those days. This extra layer of control and flexibility prevents unwanted, unnecessary visits (benefit) and helps strata councils save money (value).*

If you're finding it hard to distinguish Benefit from Value. A simple way to put it is:

> **Benefit = how the feature will directly solve their problem.**
> Typically articulated in terms of money (save/make more), energy (requires less), or time (saved).
>
> **Value = how the solution will change the prospect's life or enable them to express their personal values.**
> Typically expressed as positive motivators through identity, sense of purpose, or adventure/surprise. Or as an alleviation of negative motivators such as fear, shame, or guilt.

If you need to educate your prospect, you can also highlight how other customers have used specific features and relate them back to your prospect's personal values using FBV. For example:

> *"Since you mentioned that delivering exceptional customer service (value) is important for your business, it's worth noting that many businesses setting up marketing campaigns often overlook the experience that follows. XYZ company used our calendar booking system (feature) to maximize the number of inquiries that translate into actual booked meetings (benefit). This will be crucial in designing a great customer service experience (value) as it ensures inquiries aren't left unanswered."*

When you're recommending, you're not discussing every single feature of your solution. Avoid rambling on about features that have no relevance to what your prospect has said. Instead, select the most relevant ones you believe could be beneficial for your prospect's particular situation and share that information with them. Also notice in the sample responses above, you should lead with what they care about, not your features.

As you improve your skills in (A)SSESSING, listening, and taking notes, reiterate benefits and values in the prospect's own words where possible, not yours. Subtle nuances in language can make a difference. I know of an entrepreneur who adjusted the copy for his social media training program from "Freelancer" to "Digital Nomad" and observed a significant (approximately 20% increase) in conversion. Avoid industry labels and use language that your prospects identify with.

The "Don't Mess with Texas" campaign is another great example. The state was able to successfully reduce littering by about 72% between 1987 and 1990 by communicating in a tone that resonated with their target audience (18-35-year-old men, who they identified as the demographic most likely to litter). Had officials adopted the more notoriously polite approach, e.g., "Please stop littering," it probably wouldn't have been as effective. It has since gone on to become a statement embraced by Texans as a quintessential part of their identity.

ASSIGNMENT

Your FBV: List 3-5 features you'd like to highlight about your solution.

- What are some underlying or direct benefits?
- What values do these benefits reflect? Conversely, which features were derived from your company values? For instance:

Our customers care a lot about privacy (Value) → We provide enhanced security authentication (Benefit) → which utilizes 2-factor authentication and 256-bit encryption (Features)

Sustainability is one of our core values → To reduce the plastic that gets into the waste stream (Benefit) → we upcycle and make our soles from reused plastic (Feature).

Notes:

Notes:

PSA VS. PAS

In needs-based selling, SDRs also often unconsciously PSA:

1. Identify the prospect's **P**roblems.
2. Pitch **S**olutions.
3. These prospects then go off and research **A**lternatives on their own. When you aren't involved in this research, you don't get a chance to address how you're different or better.

Instead, involve your prospect as a fellow collaborator when investigating potential solutions. Don't be afraid to discuss alternatives; presenting options doesn't necessarily increase the likelihood that they will choose an alternative over you. They're probably already considering that alternative, or if not, will do their research and find it after speaking with you. Even if they don't, they might still become aware of a more suitable alternative after choosing your solution, leading to buyer's remorse. This can be even more detrimental as it jeopardizes their relationship with you and could even result in negative reviews.

If there is an alternative solution that is indeed better for them, there's nothing wrong with referring them to it. They might not have been your ideal customers anyway, and operating with integrity will pay off in the future when they are eventually better suited for your solutions. Even if they didn't make a purchase, they may still refer others who are a good fit since they had a positive experience with you. PAS:

1. Identify **P**roblems.
2. Identify the different ways to solve them: Engage prospects in evaluating **A**lternatives, providing yourself the opportunity to address concerns, objections, misconceptions, or frequently asked questions before they arise.
3. Position your **S**olution as the best option amongst those available.

Don't make Public Service Announcements (PSA),
be a team player and PAS.

When discussing alternatives, avoid bash competitors. It makes you look petty, and be prepared, they'll bash back if they catch wind of it.

Refer back to page 33 for ideas on competitive framing, positioning, and articulating your Unique Selling Proposition/Point.

Here are some additional tips to improve your (R)ECOMMENDATIONS:

B2B is still H2H
Even if businesses pay, people are still the ones doing the buying. Get to know your target stakeholder(s) so you can appeal and tailor your recommendations to them.

Don't give them the fish, teach them how to fish
Especially if you are a service-based business, don't rush into fixing and prescribing, even if it's what your clients want from you. If they already know what to do or what they want, they can usually find their own way. You are simply a means to an end, a commodity.

Observing and addressing the symptoms of an issue is basic; prove yourself invaluable by exposing them to the underlying root causes, even those of which they may not be conscious. Prospects will truly value you when you can help them see opportunities or challenges from a new perspective, point out blind spots and incorrect assumptions, assist them in foreseeing issues they may not have predicted, or provide meaningful direction when they feel overwhelmed and disoriented.

As a consultant, I often encounter clients seeking quick fixes, urging me to step in and sell on their behalf. However, I wouldn't have reached my current position if I had taken that approach. Instead, I guide them to see the bigger picture – identifying the roots of their cash flow issues, establishing recurring and predictable processes, or realigning their brand and target audience. This prevents them from facing a similar cash crunch that led them to seek external help in the first place.

Teach, Don't Preach

At times, you'll engage with prospects who are unaware of their problems. Raise awareness about industry norms, and if they're lagging, emphasize how you can assist in catching up or getting unstuck. To accomplish this effectively, ensure they are willing to acknowledge where they are, their pace, and their intended timeline during (A)SSESSMENT.

Show, Don't Tell

If you have an experience that will truly wow them, sometimes the quickest way is to let them try it out. If you have a physical product, place it in their hands and allow them to try it! A demonstration (demo) of a great solution is far superior to a polished pitch. However, don't interpret this as sales being able to take a backseat if you have a great offering. Merely handing your solution over to prospects for them to tinker with on their own doesn't constitute an effective demonstration. Instead, pinpoint the features they care about and highlight them in a demonstration, rather than only talking about how great the solution is. If your prospects are hesitant to schedule a live demo, consider making it easier for them by offering a free trial. Enhance the experience by providing video tutorials for specific features you know they would find valuable.

Don't underestimate the power of relationships

Invest in the long run. In business, we establish artificial boundaries: daily, weekly, quarterly, and annually, to facilitate better reporting of results. While some initiatives yield immediate results, others require more time to bear fruit. Don't underestimate the significance of ethical and value-aligned behavior, especially in the context of building relationships. I have witnessed both firsthand and with my clients, prospects circling back years later or making significant referrals despite not converting immediately.

Collaborate

The sales process tends to be smoother when prospects feel a genuine connection to their solution, which can be achieved by allowing them to contribute to its development in a meaningful manner.

(E)NGAGE

All systems check, thrusters (E)NGAGE! It's time to turn your prospects into official customers. This is the section in sales that, if done incorrectly, causes both you and the prospect to feel manipulative, pushy, or greasy.

But before we take that next step, ensure everything aligns. At this point, we should have confirmed BANT.

BUDGET: Available
AUTHORITY: decision-maker identified
NEED: Problem agreed to
TIMELINE: Understood

For instance, unless you can demonstrate a clear benefit justifying the breach of their contract, you shouldn't attempt to close a deal with someone who is interested but has expressed an unwillingness to change solutions until their current contract expires (misalignment on **T**IMELINE).

BUYING SIGNS

Assuming we've verified alignment on BANT, how do we know if we've sufficiently convinced our prospects of the value of our offerings and if they're ready to take the next step to purchase? Buying signs, while not definitive, are potential indicators that signal our prospects are ready. Here are some examples:

Physical	Verbal	Virtual/Behavioural
• Leaning forward • Smiling • Nodding • Hand	• Agreeing • Positive words • Delighted tones	• # of times an email is opened • The extent to which an email is circulated within the organization (gauged by the # of opens from different IP addresses)

hovering around their wallet • Pulled out their wallet! • Mimicry		• Engagement on the website (time spent on the website, which pages were visited, how often they revisited, etc.) • Using a trial

Some of these may be painstakingly obvious but are often easily overlooked in the heat of the moment. I'm not suggesting you actively elicit them from your prospects. Instead, it's about being mindful and noticing when they are exhibited.

Mimicry, also known as mirroring, is one example; it occurs when an individual exhibits the gestures, speech patterns, attitudes, or behaviors of another. For instance:

- If the salesperson is nodding, the buyer nods along.
- If the salesperson has their arms crossed, the buyer does the same.
- If the salesperson leans forward, the buyer does so too.

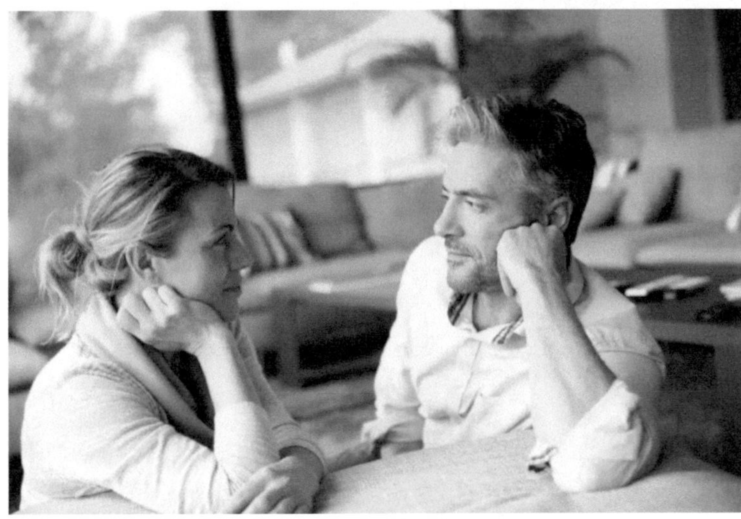

Mirroring is a subconscious psychological phenomenon that occurs when we desire to be liked by the other person. We do so unconsciously to be perceived as similar, signaling our agreeableness.

It is manipulative to intentionally and consciously mimic your prospects in an attempt to accelerate rapport. You should avoid it not only because it's unethical, but also because this inauthentic form of mimicry is noticeably artificial and awkward. Prospects will notice, and it's a big turn-off that can instantly kill the interaction. If you aren't intentionally mimicking but notice they're subconsciously mimicking you, then that's a positive buying signal. Recognizing this does take some experience and attentiveness, and it's what I'm suggesting here.

For the virtual/behavioral examples in the table above, CRM tools like Salesforce or HubSpot make it possible to track our prospect's actions even if we can't observe or hear them. Further details on how this is achieved are explained when I discuss CRM (page 327).

ASSIGNMENT

Do some people-watching! Go to the mall and mindfully observe people. Notice how they behave when they're ready to make a purchase. You can do this at the food court or in a store.

Observations:

Observations:

TRIAL CLOSE

As mentioned, buying signs help but aren't definitive. For more certainty that our prospects are ready to (E)NGAGE, we can perform a trial close to test the waters.

Trial closing is the only time we should be asking close-ended questions in the sales process. How does it work? By asking some questions that, when answered with a YES, signal that our prospects are in the right mental state to make a purchase.

For example:

- Do you understand everything I just said?
- Do you like this product?
- Do you believe this will solve your problem?

Yes! Yes! Yes!

If the prospect is agreeing to everything, you probably have the green light to ask for the sale. It's not about intentionally positioning statements to reduce the likelihood of them saying NO, nor should your goal be to turn every NO into a YES. NOs are as valuable as YESes

NO is associated with Protection
YES is associated with Commitment

Instead of pressuring people to say YES and commit to taking action, you can also move the interaction forward by making it comfortable for them by allowing them to say NO.

"Are you still interested in signing up?"
Vs.
"Have you given up on this project?"

With the second example, prospects would be more comfortable advancing the conversation because saying YES doesn't suggest locking themselves in, and saying NO provides them with an opportunity to explain their delay without feeling pressured to commit to anything.

Using a trial close before an actual closing statement also allows us to more naturally inquire why if we receive a NO response.

Compare:

"Do you think this is the right plan for you"
Vs.
"Let's get you set up. Are you ready to make a payment?"

With the former, inquiring about the NO will feel less pushy, as it suggests you're trying to find the best possible fit with your prospect's best interest at heart. With the latter, probing into it feels a little pushy, as it's already the final step, and your curiosity here could be easily misinterpreted as self-serving.

OVERCOME OBJECTIONS/CONCERNS

Because it's impossible to filter (page 128) your prospects perfectly, inevitably you will occasionally run across objections that can't be overcome. If someone is indeed not a fit, don't push it. It's better to let them go with a good experience instead of forcing them into a bad experience. But for those who are indeed a fit, objections usually stem from false beliefs, typically from one of these categories:

False Belief	Examples
Means: This is not the right way to…	• I don't believe social media is the right channel for my business. • I don't believe taking a course is an effective way to learn; perhaps, it's better to learn by executing first-hand.
Internal: I don't have what it takes	• It's too complicated. • If it doesn't deliver the promised results (risk), it will reflect poorly on me. • Successful implementation might render my role redundant. • It's not my style, or I can't pull off wearing that dress.
External: I'm limited by something outside of my control	• Now is not the right time. • I don't have enough capital to invest in this project. • My spouse would never agree with this.

At times, even if everything is done right, a prospect may still present an objection. So, what do you do when they say NO? If it's not already obvious, NO isn't the end of the road. It does not mean they aren't interested in your solutions and never will be. A NO could be a definitive end if we haven't done a good job qualifying our prospects. However, if the prospect is qualified, it often instead indicates a concern was not adequately addressed, and we simply need to take a detour.

If it isn't explicit, try to understand the concern underlying their objection. Avoid projecting your beliefs onto others; it may not always be a pricing issue. Harboring a false bias may lead to over-justifying pricing without paying enough attention to other benefits. Is it really too expensive for them? Did you perhaps forget to mention a key feature they care about? You risk alienating your prospect by trying to close the deal without first satisfactorily addressing all their concerns. They're not ready yet. Your flow should be:

They say NO → Overcome Objection → (R) ECOMMEND (again) → Trial Close/Close (again).

All objections are reasonable and justifiable. You're not trying to *kill* (page 289) objections. Don't deny them or try to prove your prospects wrong. Instead, here's another **C.A.R.E.** acronym you can apply:

CONFIRM & **C**LARIFY

1. Ensure you're not misunderstanding or misinterpreting by repeating it back to them.

2. Try to understand if there is an underlying issue, concern, false belief, or misconception that is not being explicitly communicated or is hiding behind this excuse of an objection. Uncover these by questioning or asking your prospects to elaborate. For example:

Vague objection: *"I don't think this is the right time for a project like this"*

Possible responses to **C**ONFIRM or **C**LARIFY:

> *"When do you believe this would be more appropriate?"* – Asking them to elaborate
>
> *"Are you worried that working with a consultant is too time-intensive?"* – False belief about the means?
>
> *"Do you think your team is still too small for this?"* – Internal false belief?
>
> *"Are you concerned that investors are away and unresponsive during the holiday season?"* – External false belief?

What if they're dancing around it and not providing a clear answer? This is the only place in the sales process where I would recommend making an assumption. For instance,

One of the most common objections is *"I'll think about it"*

Assumption: *"What is it you're not sure about? Is it too expensive?", "Do you not like the color?", etc.*

Any assumption you make will help you uncover the real objection. If it is incorrect, the prospect will often gladly correct you. If it is correct, it'll help quickly identify their concerns.

Their possible response could be,

> *"No, it's not too expensive; I just need to talk to my spouse about it"*

To which you could reply along the lines of,

> *"No problem, feel free to jump on a call or take a picture of it to send to them"*

3. Lastly, determine whether this is the only objection or if there are multiple.

ACKNOWLEDGE it

Align yourself with them by empathizing and validating their opinion and objections. You don't necessarily have to agree with them, but you need to communicate that you understand why they perceive it as such and how they've developed that belief. Denying will only further antagonize them.

RESPOND

Because everyone's offering and degree of flexibility is different, it won't be possible to address every type of objection. I'll include realistic hypothetical examples here to give you ideas on how you might address some of your objections.

Instead of BUT, use YES, AND.

If you've affirmed their objection but begin your response with BUT, you're denying their perspective or insinuating they are wrong. Even if you're not doing so intentionally, it will make them unconsciously defensive. YES, AND further validates their concern and opens the opportunity to dive deeper into it.

Reframe

If the objection stems from a false belief or misconception, your goal is to provide new information that will shift their perspective. Using the previous objection example:

> *"Are you worried that working with a consultant is too time-intensive?"* (**C**ONFIRM & **C**LARIFY)

Potential response:

> *"Many rightfully perceive that working with a consultant is time-consuming* (**A**CKNOWLEDGE). *This is because most consultants are incentivized to draw out their projects since they bill by the hour."*

Notice the response doesn't open with a but… this is a type of YES, AND.

> *"We've intentionally priced our services based on the scope of work to motivate our consultants to be efficient."* (Reframe)
>
> *"Furthermore, by operating on a result-oriented retainer fee, it ensures we aren't cutting corners just to complete a project quickly but are equally vested in your success."* (Addressing another potential objection in advance)

ENSURE

Lastly, verify whether what you've presented adequately addresses their concern to their satisfaction. If not, continue to explore why they don't think it does or if other potential concerns haven't been addressed.

COMMON OBJECTIONS + POTENTIAL RESPONSES

PRICE

"It's too expensive"
"It's out of our budget"

One of the most common objections you'll hear. This could be a legitimate unsolvable issue if you are targeting the wrong prospects (page 128) that lack the budget for your offerings. If it's not the case, it usually arises because the value of your offering isn't adequately justified.

Another reason it's common is because pricing is understandably often deferred to the end of the interaction. This is done so that you have the opportunity to justify the value of your offering before putting a tag on it. Rarely will you lead your recommendation by discussing pricing, as it might cause prospects to become defensive and unconsciously find ways to invalidate your justification of value if it induces sticker shock.

How to address:
1. Avoid projecting your biases and assumptions on your prospects - what you can't afford isn't the same as what others are willing to pay. If it's worth it, they will pay for it.

2. Do not avoid the pricing question if the prospect does bring it up earlier in the conversation. Beating around the bush will only make you look more suspicious as if you're trying to hide something. Instead, embrace it as an opportunity to better explain your offerings.

> If it is more expensive than the competition, explain why; it will help remove that objection.
>
> If it's less expensive, do the same and discuss how you maintain quality yet can afford to charge lower prices. This helps alleviate their concerns about it being too good to be true.

3. It's also common to find yourself in situations where a prospect wants to lead the conversation with pricing without first understanding

your offerings. In those situations, it's important to align their expectations and understanding of pricing vs. scope or quality of work. Here's what it might look like in a potential conversation between an SDR for a video production company and a difficult prospect who, in a simple-minded manner, wants to know how much it costs without first having a clear idea of what sort of video they want to make.

> SDR: *"Could you tell me about what your video needs or your budget?"*
> Prospect: *"Just tell me how much it'll cost!"*

Empathize with why they might be defensive right out the gate and unwilling to share a budget or what they have in mind.

> SDR: *"Happy to. We often encounter many prospects who are hesitant to disclose their project or budget because they're concerned that agencies will try to bill them at the highest rate possible if they're aware of their budget. Our rates are fixed, so that doesn't apply to us."*

Explain why you need that information and help them understand what inputs are necessary to achieve their desired outputs, such as the scope of work, duration of the video, or amount of editing, which will influence the final pricing of the project.

> SDR: *"I'm only asking because I need some context to evaluate the best option for you. If you have a limited budget, there are limitations to what we can create. If you have specific needs, it might require us to get creative with how we approach filming or production to achieve the desired outcome within the allocated budget"*

It may be especially helpful to use an appropriate analogy to better explain to a prospect who is unfamiliar with your type of services.

> SDR: *"It's just like walking into a car dealership asking for the best car. 'Best' is subjective, I would be remiss to showcase an expensive luxury car if what you're looking for is a reliable and spacious SUV for your family needs. A car dealer would be doing a poor job if they showed you the most expensive option available, I would be doing the same if I merely designed a quote based on your maximum possible budget."*

4. Either way, don't be apologetic. It's not priced "badly". There is no such thing as the "right" pricing that will satisfy everyone.

5. Demonstrate and quantify the value or ROI of your offerings if you haven't already.

6. Avoid discounting (page 227) for the sake of lowering prices. Doing so does not justify the value and instead reduces the perceived value, giving the impression that you were overcharging to begin with and are now desperate to close a sale.

> *"I hear you; it IS expensive, and we've intentionally decided not to discount our services because we want to pay our employees a living wage and ensure that we deliver a top-quality product. That said, if you don't need all the features, I'm happy to recommend some alternatives, even if it isn't one of our offerings."*

Remember, the goal is to help them, not to sell at all costs. It's ok to refer them to a competitor, especially if they are not an ideal customer.

7. Highlight the cost of maintaining the status quo. In terms of lost opportunities (additional revenue they might have been able to capture), time wasted, or extra money spent in other ways that they might have overlooked. Downgrading to a lower offering is only recommended if they have a hard budget, and you potentially overestimated their needs. Ideally, your solution should be worth the price.

If you quantified value (page 23) during (A)SSESSMENT, using the previous example: *"How much would you estimate you spent on processing refunds alone last year?"*

> Response: *"Based on what you spent on processing refunds last year, that works out to be about $5,000 a month. Our solution is only $300 per month. Even if it only cuts the number of refunds you process in half, that's still a savings of $2,500-$300 = $2,200 per month!"*

TIME

"We don't have the capacity for this right now"
"Follow up with me in the new year"
"I don't have time right now"

This communicates a lack of urgency on their part. Pressuring them with scarcity tactics, like limited-time offers, won't do you any good and will instead come across as pushy. We'll delve into urgency in more detail when we discuss Closing (page 75).

How to address:

1. If it is indeed a legitimate objection, they will be able to readily provide a reasonable explanation if you ask them to elaborate. For example:

> *"We're processing a high volume of orders before Christmas and our team is taking some time off in the last week of December. We're interested but won't have time to look into it until the new year."*

2. If they're using it as an excuse to deflect you, or if you have a good reason to prove to them that their issue is more urgent than they realize, this is where reframing comes in. For example,

> *"Entrepreneurs looking to fundraise often underestimate how long it takes to find investors and secure capital. Don't wait until you only have 3 months of runway left in your bank; it's too late by then. It actually takes an average of 6-12 months to close a round. Why? Assuming you haven't raised money before: 1-3 months to get your paperwork, the right terms, valuation, and due diligence assets in order. Another 2-3 months to find and start building relationships with investors (you don't simply reach out and directly ask for money! It's like asking someone you just met to get married on your first date!). Finally, another 3 months from officially opening your round to negotiating all the cheques across the line. If you need to have more capital before April next year, you can't afford to wait until January/February to only start learning about the process."*

3. Reduce the scope of the project if it is too broad or intensive to begin with.

4. Ask for a smaller time commitment.

5. Or demonstrate the ease of implementation.

FIT

"I don't think that's a problem for us"
"I was hoping it could do X"
"This doesn't apply to us"

If you've properly qualified (page 128) them, it indicates they are unaware of the problem or aren't making the connection between your offering and its ability to solve their problem.

How to Address:
1. It doesn't mean they aren't interested; it means they need to be educated. Demonstrate the success their competitors or similar companies have had with you, and discuss the unintended consequences of not addressing the issue that they might not be aware of.

If it's brought up because you do have the feature they're looking for but did not discuss it during (R)ECOMMENDATION:

> *"Thanks for asking! I forgot to demonstrate that…"*

2. If it's something you don't have, either because it hasn't been built yet, or if your company consciously decides they don't want to solve for it for whatever reason, you can still justify why you believe it isn't a deal-breaker:

> *"Great point; it's been brought up multiple times by some of our users as well. It's on our product roadmap and we should be releasing an update soon to include it / We're considering adding this feature if we get more requests for it…In the meantime, here's a workaround/integration to achieve the same functionality."*

> *"Here's how other customers accomplish that…"*

> *"We don't offer that, but many of our customers use this (different external) solution and find it greatly compliments our solution."*

> *"No, it doesn't do X. It's interesting that you bring it up; I've had many other customers raise the same issue but find that they don't actually need it*

> *because our solution does Y for them, rendering the need for X unnecessary."*
>
> *"We don't provide the ability to adjust lighting and colors in our photo editing tool; instead, we offer popular preset filters. While this does limit control over finer details, our customers appreciate it because it significantly speeds up the editing process while still offering the option to modify images to their preferred style."*

PRIORITY
"It's not a priority for us at this moment"

They have the problem, but perhaps it isn't important: a nice-to-have, not a need-to-have.

How to Address: Identify their top priorities and show how your solution helps them accomplish those goals.

CREDIBILITY
"I've never heard of you/your company"
"I'm not quite sure I believe what you're saying"
"I doubt it can really do that"
"I'm not confident it'll give me the results I'm looking for"

How to Address: Leverage social proof (page 16) from existing clients: stats, case studies, and reviews.

UNTARGETED
"This is not relevant to my job title/me"
"I can't make this decision"
"I need to discuss this with my team first"

How to Address:
1. Learn about their decision-making process (page 136) and ask for an intro to the right decision-maker (page 132).

> *"Sorry about that. Who is normally responsible for these types of decisions in your organization? If you see value in this, would you mind facilitating an introduction?"*

2. Improve your targeting.

3. If you've properly qualified them as the decision-maker, they may still raise this objection to deflect or procrastinate. In this case, offer to assist them with that conversation by facilitating the discussion with all the necessary decision-makers.

4. If the decision-maker has already bought into it and simply needs to convince the rest of their team. Ask them about what is relevant, the common concerns, and what the other parties care about. This will allow you to provide them with the right information to have those conversations or personalize your outreach if you're going to be the one speaking to them.

> *"I need to speak to my spouse about this first"*
>
> Response: *"If you'd like, feel free to give her/him a call. I can assist with answering any technical questions you might not be too familiar with."*

SATISFIED (with their current solution)
"If it's not broken, why fix it?"
"We're already using/with (competitor)"

This is not as bad as it sounds because it indicates they recognize a need or the problem and are already addressing it through other means.

How to Address:
1. Ask about their experience with their existing solution to identify what's important to them and to discover any differences or improvements they might be interested in.

2. Because they know you have a personal motivation to address this, it can come across as preachy if you're self-justifying. Avoid this by sharing the opinion of a potentially less biased third party. For instance, highlighting, if available, a customer who used their solution and transitioned to yours. Discuss the advantages they've observed since switching or other problems your solution has been able to help them address.

3. Encourage them to compare the experience with a trial or demo.

> *"That's to be expected ☺ It is, after all, a problem many others face, so it's unsurprising that there are many alternative providers in the market. We're still confident our offering is much better. No pressure to switch, but if you'd like to compare it with what you're already using, I can set you up with a trial account or show you a quick demo. That will help you decide if it's a better fit or not."*

4. If they are bound by a contract and if it is feasible, consider offering credits to compensate for the costs associated with breaking the contract.

OVERCOMING OBJECTIONS VIRTUALLY

If your entire sales process doesn't involve any meetings, which is possible and common for low-ticket (typically <$300) offerings, it can be a little harder to pinpoint what's holding them back. The quality of your **R**ESPONSE will depend heavily on your ability to track their behavior online. Ensure you're integrating analytics to readily identify prospects that are falling out of the funnel and where they are falling out.

Here are some ideas:

Behavior	How to frame your Response
Signed up for a trial account, and extensively used it, but hasn't upgraded to a paid account.	What's their experience? How are they using your product? How satisfied are they? What else do they wish it could do?
Visited your pricing page multiple times but did not take any further action.	Would they like a guided walkthrough or demo to see it in action?
Downloaded or created an account but hasn't used your solution.	Is there something they're trying to do but can't figure out how?
Added an item to their cart but did not check out.	Highlight your commitment to making your offerings as accessible as possible and your willingness to discuss alternative payment options (e.g. installments, deferred payment, etc.) or your free return policy/guarantees.

PERSISTENCE WITHOUT BEING PUSHY

Persistence is key to selling, not because you're trying to strong-arm someone into a sale, but often because it's easy to get derailed and prospects often hold personal biases or some of the false beliefs we discussed. If you truly believe your solution will add value to your prospect, don't back down at the first sign of resistance.

Remember, kindness vs. niceness (page 7). If a prospect is avoiding something they should be confronting, it's important to expose them to the truth of their situation. Lead with their best interest at heart. You aren't being manipulative if the solution you're selling is truly to their benefit. It's okay to encourage them and you're not being pushy when suggesting they do what's best for themselves, to maximize their potential, especially if they're holding themselves back due to unreasonable fear or personal doubt. Have them consider: What could the future look like if they don't adopt your solution? What opportunities are they missing out on?

Recall: Challenger Sales Mindset (page 5)

A good rule of thumb is to not back down unless you get at least 3 NOs. If you're not doing at least that, it's highly likely you're not doing the bare minimum to ensure you're providing your prospect with the necessary information to make an informed decision.

When I say 3 NOs, I'm not suggesting you call or email your prospect repeatedly if you aren't hearing back. That's harassment. Nor am I suggesting you ask for a sale over and over again, even if they're declining.

"Insanity is doing the same thing over and over again
and expecting different results"
– undetermined quote often misattributed to Albert Einstein

(Comic by Cathy Thorne: Sales Call Technique)

Find different angles or ways to approach it. For example, if you're attempting to cross-sell (page 199) accessories for a car:

Bad

Waiting until the end to present accessories, then responding to objections consecutively, one after the other:

> *"So which accessory would you like?"*
> *"Are you sure you don't want any?"*
> *"What if I gave you a discount?"*

Even though they're worded differently, it still comes across as desperate.

Better

Suggesting them throughout the interaction:

> During (R)ECOMMENDATION: *"Based on your lifestyle, here are some accessories that might go well with your car. Take some time to check them out while I set up your paperwork"*
>
> During Closing: *"Have you decided on an accessory yet?"*

In response to an objection: *"Are you hesitating due to the cost? We do have a few bundling options that might save you some money"*

In both cases, three attempts were used to close on the cross-sell. The second one feels more comfortable and less pushy (despite still being persistent) because we're circling back on a suggestion instead of simply reaffirming their decision. Making an assumption and offering options also makes discounting in the second example less like a desperate attempt to get them to commit.

Another common example is observed in how many people follow up on email communication:

Bad

"I sent an email last week and you've yet to reply, are you interested?"

"Sorry to disturb you again, have you seen my previous email?"

"Just wanted to follow up to see if you had the opportunity to review my previous message"

"Since you haven't responded, should I assume you're not serious about this opportunity?"

"I noticed you haven't taken action yet. Don't miss out! Our offer is expiring soon. Act now!"

"I've reached out multiple times, and it's disheartening not to receive a response. Did I do something to upset you? Please let me know."

"Hope you've had a chance to review the information I sent over. I wanted to highlight…"

"By the way, did you know [interesting industry facts or news]? I thought you might find it interesting"

Better

If you follow up via email, give them the benefit of the doubt by assuming they missed your previous email:

> *"My email might have gotten buried in your inbox over the weekend, just giving this a bump to float it up"*

Better yet, reach out through a different channel by calling them or sending a LinkedIn message:

> *"Sent you an email, but I'm not sure if it's the best way to reach you. Thought I'd try calling/ sending a message in case you're not in your inbox as often."*
>
> *"Not sure if my email landed in your promotions or spam folder. Thought to send you a message here just in case"*

If you have the right mindset but feel that following up is starting to feel pushy, don't force it. If you're feeling uncomfortable, the prospect probably is too. Don't pressure them any further. Actions that don't align with your values come across as inauthentic and will be easily picked up by prospects. It's a big turn-off when they sense you're trying to sell, not help.

If you aren't adept at reading your prospects and understanding underlying concerns that aren't explicitly stated, you could also accidentally come across as pushy. I've found that some people on the autistic spectrum might find this particularly challenging. Here are some additional tips that may help:

UNDERSTAND YOUR PROCESS

There's a saying that it takes an average of 5-7 touchpoints before prospects are ready to close. This doesn't mean you're doing the same thing 5-7 times, expecting the same results. Don't pitch the same way twice.

Some of these touchpoints could be marketing-related or may have occurred before their interaction with you. They include, but are not limited to, some of the following:

- Hearing about you from a friend
- Seeing an advertisement
- Visiting your website
- Reading one of your emails

- Reading a post on your blog
- The call with you
- A follow-up email you sent
- Your second meeting with them

It's important to understand your process and what's been communicated so you don't accidentally end up repeating yourself, leaving them with a pushy impression. It may be possible to address some of those objections in other ways, which brings us to the next point…

PLAN AND PRACTICE

With so many potential objections, it's important to predict and prepare potential responses to them in advance. Answers you come up with on the spot are often not going to be particularly good answers. Even when an objection seems illogical or unfounded, providing a weak justification can be perceived as desperation, leaving an unwanted impression that you are untrustworthy or unknowledgeable, thus jeopardizing the sale.

This is where roleplaying and coaching comes in. Practice potential responses to various objections with your team. Seek feedback to improve your responses and make them less defensive.

NINJA MOVE: ADDRESS OBJECTIONS BEFORE THEY ARISE

For instance, if quality is a common objection, discuss misconceptions about the quality of your solution during the (R)ECOMMEND stage. If it's already been addressed, when you move to (E)NGAGE and close, it will no longer be an objection.

STICK WITH YOUR PROSPECTS

But not in an annoying and clingy way. You drive the bus; don't expect them to. Lead the follow-up and guide the process. Be there for them through their conflicts. Hold them accountable to their timeline and goals (which you should identify and have them acknowledge during (A)SSESSMENT).

For example, prospects will often say *"Just email me the details"* as an excuse, only to ignore your email and never reply.

You could respond with:

> *"Sure thing. Just to ensure I send you the right information and don't overwhelm you, is there anything specific you believe is a priority or major concern?"*

This way, you're sticking with them and, at the same time, making it easier and more personalized for them.

Another common deflection is: *"Send me an email and I'll find a time in my calendar"*

Respond with:

> *"Of course, just to confirm I have the right email, it's your XXX@YYY.com email, right?"*
>
> ...
>
> *"Just to make sure I send over some reasonable options, is there a day that works best?"*
>
> ...
>
> *"Is morning or afternoon best?"*
>
> ...
>
> *"Awesome, I happen to be free next Thursday at 3pm. If that works for you, I'll send over a calendar invite as a placeholder"*

Notice in this exchange that despite sticking with them, it doesn't come across as pushy. This is because you're doing so in a way that makes it easier for them. If they aren't interested, you're not cutting off their "escape" or deliberately making it difficult for them to say no. Most engagements stall not because prospects aren't interested, but because there's too much friction in the process.

FOCUS ON THEIR NEEDS

Remember, customer service > sales. Don't be afraid to turn prospects away, it doesn't make you or your solution look bad. Instead, acting with integrity reflects well on yourself because it suggests you aren't pushing for a sale purely for the sake of profit.

ASSIGNMENT

1. What are some of your common objections?
2. How could you address them? Remember to discuss them with your prospects when you're (R)ECOMMENDING so they won't be raised later.

Notes:

NEGOTIATIONS

Prospects may attempt to negotiate, even if there isn't any real objection. If they do, it suggests that they are interested in your solution, but may be seeking a bit more, either to maximize value (who doesn't love a good bargain?) or because they have a legitimate restriction and would appreciate some flexibility.

If you're not the business owner, and many factors appear to be standardized or inflexible, remember, *everything* is still negotiable. Having less flexibility in specific scenarios can streamline your offerings, but should a VIP prospect express interest, there's always the option to escalate the matter to upper management or the owner(s) for approval.

Also, although price is often the most commonly negotiated factor, don't assume it's your prospect's biggest concern. Many other terms and conditions can also be negotiated. For instance, offering a bigger discount in exchange for a longer-term commitment, adjusting the duration of the contract itself, payment terms, features/services included, cancellation policy, etc. As mentioned, avoid discounting if at all possible as it devalues your offerings.

The SCARF framework, introduced by David Rock in his research paper titled "SCARF: A Brain-Based Model for Collaborating with and Influencing Others", highlights what matters to our prospects during negotiation. The acronym SCARF stands for:

STATUS
CERTAINTY
AUTONOMY
RELATEDNESS
FAIRNESS

STATUS
What is their sense of positioning in the negotiation? Challenging or proving them wrong can threaten their sense of status. While it may be necessary to challenge your prospects at times, you can avoid threatening their sense of status by recognizing the validity of their perspective. It also helps to adopt a collaborative approach rather than

a prescriptive one as you (R)ECOMMEND solutions. This can be accomplished by seeking their advice to tailor your solution for them or by collaboratively drafting a proposal.

CERTAINTY
Is risk aversion and pattern recognition at play. This is why people prefer transparent pricing over ambiguous "contact us for a quote" statements.

Be explicit, transparent, and clear about both the process leading up to the sale and the onboarding process once they become a customer. If possible, highlight and offer guarantees, or mitigate risk (page 187) by reducing the scope of the project.

AUTONOMY
No one enjoys being manipulated; we all desire a sense of control and feel more in control when presented with more options. Due to this, the process of selling a solution inherently induces a sense of threat for a prospect, as it involves narrowing down their choices to your proposed solution."

In the manipulative world of sales, this is often observed in the guise of false choices (The Decoy Effect). For instance, creating multiple packages: entry-level, medium, and premium, to create the illusion of choice, even though you are aware that entry-level is too basic for most prospects and the premium level is unnecessary. Instead of doing that, being collaborative, as previously mentioned, will help your prospects regain a sense of control. Be clear you're 100% there to help, even if they decide not to go with your solution. Openly discuss alternatives and be gracious if they decide to go with your competitor.

RELATEDNESS
Do they perceive their relationship with you as "us" vs. "them"? Negotiations induce stress because we believe the other party prioritizes their interests over ours. When this perception exists, we seek to maximize our own value, potentially at the expense of a loss for the other party.

Turn the win-lose mindset into a win-win mindset. Demonstrate that you're on their side and genuinely care about their success. I'm a strong advocate of Usage-based Pricing (page 192) because it signals a vested interest in your prospects' growth and success. If you "walk the talk" and use your own solution, communicate that as well. This way, prospects can readily see that your actions align with your words and that you're a user, like them.

FAIRNESS

Do they feel that this is comparable to market value, within their expected range, or they're being treated equally as a prospect, without any favoritism?

If you have a premium solution more expensive than many others in the market, fairness can still be communicated by clearly justifying the value of your solution. If you happen to be selling in a group setting, make it clear you aren't providing preferential treatment.

Also read: https://classynarwhal.com/bad-advice-on-sales-negotiations/

CLOSING

Assuming everything checks out, your prospect should be convinced and ready. The last and final step that separates them from becoming a customer is the Close. I won't be going into closing techniques in this book as there is a wealth of existing literature on the topic. However, since most are manipulative, we'll focus instead on understanding *how* to close ethically and authentically.

CLOSING MINDSET

There is a significant amount of stigma and pressure associated with selling, much of which originates from poor management and the incentivization of inappropriate behaviors. If you find yourself in an organization guilty of this, the most crucial step you can take is to define yourself as a customer service agent rather than an SDR.

If you've followed the right markers leading up to this point, your prospect *should* already want to buy what you're selling. It's unfair to the prospect if you're not offering to close. Consider it this way: you have a solution to fix their problem, and by not offering to help them, you're withholding something they genuinely want! You should be the one that makes the ask; it's not their responsibility. A wonderful analogy from my sales mentor, Shannon Ward, Chief Growth Officer at Genus Capital, helps illustrate this:

"Not asking for the sale is like attending someone's birthday party with a gift, enthusiastically describing how amazing it is. Then, after a fun night, leaving without handing it over. Since you're the one in possession of it, it's only polite that you offer, they shouldn't have to demand it."

If you don't ask, the answer is almost always …[silence].

Prospects expect you to guide the interaction and close the deal; not doing so is poor service. Again, draw strength from kindness rather than niceness. Don't avoid closing because you're uncomfortable with it. Often, this discomfort arises from within, stemming from having the wrong mindset, not because you're using the wrong approach and being manipulative. Discomfort is good; if you feel discomfort, it means you care and don't want to be manipulative. If you're a manipulative person, you probably wouldn't find anything uncomfortable about this at all.

It's only pushy if you're moving to close before observing the appropriate buying signals or addressing all their concerns. Otherwise, it's important to recognize that prospects may enter into your funnel at different stages. Some may have already conducted their research and are ready to purchase when they come into your store. In such cases, it's acceptable to bypass the C.A.R. (**C**ONNECT, **A**SSESS, **R**ECOMMEND) phases and proceed directly to **E**NGAGING and Closing. These interactions will feel transactional, and that's expected. Some prospects prefer a quick in-and-out approach, seeking efficiency. Attempting to manipulate them to do otherwise signals that you don't respect their time and decision-making autonomy.

1. Confidence in Closing

You'll feel uncomfortable if you bear the perception that selling is manipulative. No amount of coaching will help you if you don't first embrace the mindset that, by selling, you are providing a service to your prospects by helping them get what they truly need. Accepting this is the first step to closing with confidence.

Confidence is important because it is contagious. A lack thereof will make your prospects second-guess their decision, even if your offering benefits them (an uncertain prospect will never say yes). They'll start to wonder if there are hidden caveats you might be concealing to secure the sale, unintentionally creating an atmosphere that suggests manipulation (even if you aren't trying to!). This not only holds them back from committing to the purchase but also increases the likelihood of them experiencing buyer's remorse.

Buyer's remorse should be avoided if at all possible. It's worse than a prospect deciding not to purchase. When a customer comes back for a refund, it requires additional time, resources, and effort to process. Or worse, if they decide to keep it while stewing in regret, it sullies the experience and could lead to a negative review.

If you genuinely care about your prospects, pay equal attention to making their sales experience as comfortable as possible by confidently communicating and closing. For example:

"So would you like to get this?"
Vs.
"Based on your needs, this is the option I recommend for you. Are you ready to sign up?"

The latter communicates more confidence because you aren't second-guessing the right option for the prospect. It's not an assumptive close but an informed recommendation; you're simply checking if they're ready to move ahead with the purchase.

2. Give them space
I've witnessed many SDRs talk themselves out of a sale they would have probably otherwise closed. It's important to lead the interaction and follow-up; however, avoid over-justifying as it may come across as desperate.

Give your prospects the space they need to digest your (R)ECOMMENDATIONS and deliberate. Don't worry, if your solution is indeed the best for them, they'll come back to you.

3. Don't oversell
Similar to the point above, if the prospect has already committed to the purchase, stop selling the same thing. They're already convinced; overjustification will give your new customers the wrong impression that you're trying to divert their attention from a flaw in your offering.

Don't confuse this with cross-selling (page 199). It's still okay to offer complimentary offerings, as long as you aren't continuing to pitch the primary offering you've already closed.

URGENCY IN CLOSING
Is often used to pressure prospects into taking immediate action. Urgency itself is sometimes necessary, as some prospects tend to procrastinate taking action, even to their detriment, even if they are already convinced of the value of your offering.

They may be waiting for a sale or promotion, thinking they would save more by purchasing at that time, failing to consider that they may be losing out on more by not switching sooner. Or perhaps they're leveraging time in hopes of compelling you to sweeten the deal.

In any case, some form of urgency is helpful if applied correctly. Sadly, it often isn't.

1. Sleazy Inauthentic Urgency
is when a company creates a false sense of urgency to pressure the prospect into closing. Example include:

- When a company claims a sale is "ending soon" but continues to offer the same discount for weeks or even months. Sales and Promotions are overused. Consumers become desensitized if you're perpetually having a sale and come to expect that as your normal price.

(Sale! Sale! Every thing is on sale all the time!)

- Companies that claim a product is "running out" or only "available in limited quantities" despite having sufficient inventory.
- Early-bird pricing is also often a form of inauthentic urgency, especially when there isn't any added value to justify purchasing earlier.

2. Real Authentic Urgency
On the other hand, is when there is a genuine reason for prospects to act quickly. For example,

- If you're selling tickets to a concert and there are only a limited number of seats available due to the size of the venue, compounded with high demand because it's for a popular band. This creates authentic urgency. Prospects know if they don't buy their tickets now, they may not be able to get them later or may be left with less-than-desirable seating options.
- Truly having limited inventory due to production constraints.
- Needing to enroll participants by a certain date for a live course, program, or event with a clear starting date (as there are often accompanying logistical resources like venue, materials, and necessary facilitators that need to be ironed out before it begins).
- Limiting your capacity to work with too many clients because you lack the resources to serve them at your standard of quality.
- Early-bird pricing is acceptable and not manipulative if you properly incentivize it by providing additional limited value-added benefits. For example: The first 100 tickets get an autographed poster, or the first 50 purchases during an event will be entered into a lucky draw to win a prize.

Incentives can be a great way to reward your customers, deepen your relationship with them, and cultivate loyalty. The best kinds are related to your offering and genuinely desired by your prospects. Random swag or cash isn't recommended as they are transactional.

3. Internal/Intrinsic > External/Extrinsic Motivation

Although inauthentic urgency may drive sales in the short term, it will ultimately harm a company's reputation in the long term. Prospects dislike feeling pressured into buying and are unlikely to return to a company that uses sleazy sales tactics.

On the other hand, authentic urgency can create a sense of excitement and anticipation. If used correctly, it can help create a positive experience for your prospects, leading to them becoming loyal and returning customers.

External motivation isn't always bad; it still works when applying urgency, as long as it is done with integrity. Even so, it's more effective to focus on internal motivation. To further elaborate:

External Motivation
Drives the prospect to take action but comes from the environment. It is controlled by you – the organization. Examples include the previously mentioned limited inventory, limited seats for your course, program start dates, or product availability dates.

> *"This promotion ends in 3 days. Since you're here today, you might want to get it before it's too late."*

They do have an effect, and it's not wrong to use them, but ensure you are authentic in doing so and transparent about why. There is one exception: external motivation in the form of incentives inversely correlates with referrals (page 171).

Internal Motivation
Is when prospects are driven to take action due to their personal desire to accomplish or resolve something by a certain time. Focusing on these self-acknowledged factors, instead of externally imposed deadlines and limitations, empowers your prospect with a sense of autonomy.

To apply this effectively, you'll have to first identify and understand *their* timelines. Do so by asking timeline-related questions in the (A)SSESS phase. For example:

> *"By when are you hoping to resolve this?"*
> *"How soon do you want to see <x> result?"*

When Closing, remind them of their timeline and hold them accountable. For example:

> *"You said you wanted ___ by ___ date. To achieve that, we'll need to start by ___ because it will take ___ weeks to migrate your data, ___ weeks on average for training, and ___ weeks for your employees to familiarize themselves and begin to efficiently use the new platform."*

If you haven't already been exposed to it, the Gap Selling methodology by Keenan emphasizes identifying and addressing internal motivations. Gap Selling is about recognizing and understanding the "gap" or discrepancy between the current state of the prospect and their desired future state: the goals, aspirations, and desired outcomes that the prospect aims to achieve. This gap becomes the focal point for discussions and serves as the motivation for the prospect to take action.

The offering is then positioned as the solution that bridges the identified gap. Urgency is incorporated by highlighting the negative consequences of inaction, quantifying the benefits of the solution (the sooner they act, the sooner they can benefit), understanding the prospect's timeline to achieve their desired outcomes, and reinforcing the value of time.

4. Avoid Fear Mongering

Avoid employing manipulative sales techniques that promote instilling Fear, Uncertainty, and Doubt (FUD) in your prospects to coerce them to change, or die. Inciting panic only breeds distrust, and it might even inadvertently cause people to associate your brand with the negative emotions you evoke in them. Instead, captivate and impress your prospects by demonstrating the possibilities they can unlock with your solution.

CLOSING WITH AN ASK

You should close every interaction, but that doesn't mean you should pressure everyone to buy. Closing doesn't only come in the form of confirming the purchase. If you are aware the prospect isn't ready yet, you could use some of the following closing statements to conclude your interaction:

> *"Can I contact you for more questions? (then get their email if you don't already have it)."*

> *"Who else should I speak to about this?"*

> *"Can you send me more information so that I know which features you would be interested in seeing during our scheduled demo?"*

LEARN TO ACCEPT REJECTION

All said and done, rejection is an unavoidable part of sales. Some prospects will never end up making a purchase, even if you've done your best to address objections. Sometimes, it's not even about you. They might be making unreasonable demands, have contrasting values or beliefs from you/your organization, or show no interest in collaborating or compromising. It's better to walk away than be stuck in an unhappy relationship.

Because it takes a mental toll on you over time, it's important to be mindful of your relationship with rejection and how it's affecting you. Here are some helpful pointers:

1. Don't take it personally

It's hard to account for every variable. Sometimes, there are circumstances beyond your awareness or control that prevent your prospects from committing. You may also face unfair or unjust rejection based on discrimination or unconscious biases related to gender, race, sexual orientation, religion, etc.

2. Don't begrudge it

I'm not saying "let it be"; we all should take an active stance to call out and rectify discrimination. Instead, when I say don't begrudge it, I mean you shouldn't let it define your self-worth. It doesn't make you any less of a person. Don't fall into a negative spiral of inaction or kill your potential simply because someone else doesn't agree with you. Find ways to make the most of the situation, and find other avenues. If you have the energy to lament, turn it instead into productive action and make the best out of it. As they say, "If life gives you lemons, make lemonade". Define yourself by how you react *after* being rejected.

3. Embrace and expose yourself to it instead of avoiding it out of fear

All too often, we hold ourselves back from even trying because we're paralyzed by the potential of rejection. It's better to have tried and learned than to never have ventured out. Misplaced and disproportionate fear may even lead us to inaction in situations where we might not have faced rejection in the first place.

In psychology, learned helplessness refers to a condition that develops when a subject is exposed to repeated rejection and pain. The subject will start to believe they lack control over the situation and will resign themselves to accept continual rejection and pain, even if new alternative options become available. Here is a simplified explanation of the iconic (and inhumane) experiment that initiated research into this theory:

> A dog is placed in a cage and subjected to repeated electric shocks. It comes to learn there is nothing it can do to avoid these shocks. This same dog is now placed into a new cage with a partition that it can hop over to avoid the shocks. The dog simply lays down passively and whines when shocked. The dog is defined as having acquired learned helplessness at this stage.

New research in the past few decades has shown that this theory has it backward; in fact, our default belief is that we are powerless. Through exposure, we learn that we actually have control over certain elements and will change our behavior or try new things. The keyword is exposure. If you aren't exposed to those learning opportunities or to the hidden reasons that explain why you were rejected, you won't realize that you have more control over life than you expect. Check out Jia Jiang's TED Talk, "What I Learned from 100 Days of Rejection", for some great advice.

4. Slow down
Don't run at the first sign of rejection. There is often an opportunity to further explain yourself.

5. Approach with curiosity
Be sincerely curious, not for the sake of trying to overcome every possible objection, but to understand. People are often willing to explain if you ask "Why?".

If you are sincerely curious and aren't trying to be manipulative, people won't stonewall you; they will open up to you and share their perspectives. Perhaps they're saying NO because they don't understand what you're asking? They're on guard and skeptical because what you're offering sounds too good to be true? They are interested but now is not the right time? Or they don't need it but they know someone else who might (and would be happy to connect you)? You'll never know if you don't expose yourself to the opportunity to learn by asking WHY.

6. Recognize that you've been helpful
Every interaction is meaningful, even if it doesn't result in a sale. If you focus on adding value, your prospects should walk away better educated and informed about options, regardless of their decision to make a purchase.

7. Focus on the relationship
NO now doesn't mean NO forever. They may return to purchase in the future or even provide referrals if they had a good experience and value the relationship they've built with you.

8. Seek peer review
It can be challenging to distance ourselves from the outcome and objectively understand what happened during the heat of the moment. Colleagues and mentors may be able to offer a different perspective that will help us better internalize or learn from it.

9. Supportive NOs
And if you ever find yourself in a situation where you need to be the one doing the rejecting, you can make it easier to say NO by supporting them in your rejection. Do so by pointing them in the right direction for resources, alternatives, and further advice.

B2B Closing Tips
Avoid sending a proposal before reviewing it with your prospect in a meeting or call. This often results in prospects going cold, making it difficult to determine what they are unsatisfied with.

It's best to guide prospects through a proposal first and send the document to them *after* as a formal record. This provides the opportunity for you to clarify if something was missed and emphasize that you're flexible in adjusting the proposal to better meet their requirements

Practice Makes Perfect
As with everything, knowledge without application will only get you so far. Build muscle memory through roleplay and direct experience with your prospects!

ASSIGNMENT

What are some good closing statements you've heard? They don't have to be sales-related; they could be in any situation where someone is trying to persuade someone else to do something. For example:

Persuasion	Closing statement
Come to my party	Ali and Jia Min have already confirmed and it wouldn't be the same without you!
Trade my snacks with yours	Let's trade, that way we both get to have more variety!
Join us for a hike	I have space for 1 more person in my car, let me know by Tuesday this week to save your spot.

Notes:

Notes:

♦♦♦

(E)XPECTATIONS (SET + MANAGE)

It's not over! Sales doesn't end with the Close. Because your prospect's time and attention are limited, you'll often only get to focus on key features that are relevant to your prospect's needs when (R)ECOMMENDING. Now that your prospect is officially a customer, you can afford to leisurely explain the finer details that are also important for them to know. Details such as:

- Setting up their account, product, or solution.
- Onboarding and how to use some of the other common features
- Implementation process
- Your return/refund policy
- Warranty
- Customer support channels, processes, or how to troubleshoot common issues

This process of explaining and further educating your customers plays a key role in setting and managing their expectations. It is so important that it justifies an entirely separate section for itself. The acronym I used should really be C.A.R.E.E. with two E's (**E**NGAGE + **E**XPECTATIONS), but that wouldn't make it pretty.

EXPECTATIONS DEFINE EXPERIENCE

Your happiness or disappointment with any and everything is directly related to the expectations you have before experiencing it. This not only applies to sales but to everything in life, including food, travel, and romantic relationships.

If you have high expectations and it doesn't meet your expectations	=	You are disappointed
If you have low expectations, and they are exceeded	=	You are delighted

My realization of this comes from a silly personal experience:

I was invited by some friends to watch the first Transformers movie when it came out. Advertising at that time wasn't as prevalent as it is today, and I hadn't bothered watching any of the trailers. Going into the cinema, I had no idea what the movie would look like. Not only did I have zero expectations, I actually had a negative expectation: I expected it to be total crap! Previous live-action remakes of animated films were terrible. I couldn't imagine how they could use computer-generated imagery (CGI) to make vehicles transform into robots in a cool way; I thought it would be silly.

Fast forward 2 hours and 24 minutes, I was pleasantly surprised! I did not expect the style of animation, the interesting designs, and the storyline that came with it. It isn't one of my all-time favorite movies, but because there was such a difference in expectation going in and coming out, it became one of my most memorable and delightful moments. I came to realize the power expectations have over our happiness. It shapes how we perceive occurrences in our lives as positive or negative.

For this same reason, we're often disappointed by sequels. Creators attempt to replicate the success of the original by copy-pasting, but since we've already been exposed and developed a new baseline, we've come to expect all the usual bells and whistles. Merely meeting that expectation is neutral; creators need to constantly reinvent the experience if they wish to exceed expectations and create another hit (I don't envy that challenge and truly respect those who are successful in overcoming it). With a mediocre storyline and nothing novel, all the budget in the world for cars and explosions couldn't save the Transformer sequels from flopping.

OVERPROMISE, UNDERDELIVER

Don't oversell to close a deal; remember, the goal isn't to "close a deal"! Instead, focus on helping your prospect by adding value, and the deal will naturally fall into place. If you overpromise, you'll only end up underdelivering.

If you claim to have the "best" product, warranty, team, level of service, or support, it comes across as false bravado and is seen as manipulative. Prospects will question your need to exaggerate and wonder if your solution isn't excellent enough to stand on its own. Besides, everyone already claims to be the best…or so they say. Making the same claim doesn't help you stand out and instead makes you more generic. It's overused and no one believes it.

Worse yet, if you're already at the top, there's nowhere to go but down. Any minor flaw, or if you do indeed have a great solution but fail to meet their expectation because they misinterpreted something, will lead to disappointment.

~~UNDERPROMISE~~, OVERDELIVER

However, I'm not suggesting you underpromise and sell yourself short either. So, what should you do if you sincerely believe you excel in a particular area? Is there a way to humble brag?

1. Show, don't tell: If you're running an ad, instead of cheesily saying *"We operate with integrity"*, demonstrate integrity by telling a short story about a time when you went out of your way to do the right thing for a customer.
2. Another way is to leverage third-party reviews or let your customer testimonials vouch for you instead. After all, it sounds insincere when you're tooting your own horn.
3. Otherwise, the other option is to focus on overdelivering. Create memorable experiences by identifying areas in their buyer and user journey where you can exceed their expectations.

MITIGATE BAD EXPERIENCES

As we now know, bad experiences arise from poorly managed expectations, when the real experience falls short of what one expects. Since no solution is perfect, complaints are inevitable, regardless of the effort we put into polishing our offerings before release. However, bad experiences can still be minimized by ensuring we're clear on what we can or can't do.

Be honest about flaws or shortcomings in your solution. Admitting to them isn't a sign of weakness. Prospects are realistic, and as long as it's reasonable and justified, they will appreciate your transparency and trust you more.

If they find out now that it's not a fit for them, it's OK, and it's not too late for them to back out. Don't force the sale or deliberately omit information, even if you only discovered after closing that a potential deal breaker was overlooked. Don't assume they won't find out! It's better to be upfront and process a refund now than to wait for them to experience a nasty surprise that would necessitate a return for a refund or lead to negative reviews.

Storytime:
My second corporate job was in 2012 for WIND Mobile (which has since been rebranded to Freedom Mobile and acquired by Shaw, and later, Shaw itself was acquired by Rogers). At that time, WIND was a new, independent Canadian telecommunications carrier that introduced low-cost unlimited plans (back in the days when calling, texting, and data all had strict usage-based tiered pricing).

Although WIND was much more affordable, they had limited coverage. Reception was reliable in the city but often failed in certain areas. When engaging with potential customers, we were trained to address basic coverage to ensure they had reception at home and work. After closing the sale, we would conduct a more detailed analysis of other places where they commonly use their phone, such as their parents' or in-laws' places, schools, and travel destinations. We would take the time to properly educate customers on how roaming works, roaming fees, and how to disable or enable it for emergency use. This approach significantly helped reduce unpleasant surprises when they received their monthly bills.

If the customer realized, for example, *"Oh no! It doesn't work at my parents' house"*, we wouldn't push the sale and would process a refund if they had already purchased. Otherwise, we were also taught to inquire more deeply to determine if that was a logical objection: How often are you really there? Do you use your phone much when you're visiting? Do they have Wi-Fi? Ultimately, it wasn't about arguing for a sale, but sincerely supporting the prospect in determining if the cost savings and unlimited value were worth some of these restrictions.

Comparing my experience at WIND with my first job at Bell (for those unfamiliar, Bell is one of the incumbent telecommunications carriers in Canada and boasts the largest nationwide coverage), we were trained to dismiss objections that compared us to these smaller, more affordable carriers. We would often criticize their poor reception and emphasize our excellent coverage. Despite that, there were still coverage blackspots in some areas, and because we had positioned our coverage as the best, customers would frequently return, angrily complaining that they didn't have reception when they were out camping, hiking, or because they were charged unexpected roaming fees. Through good expectation setting, WIND was able to turn a weakness into a positive experience, and I found myself dealing with far fewer angry customers compared to when I was working at Bell.

Side note and fun history tidbit: Yes, Bell Canada was co-founded by Alexander Graham Bell (as was AT&T in the US), the individual credited with the invention of the telephone.

PROACTIVELY EVALUATE EXPERIENCE

For every complaint you receive, many others likely go unvoiced. Don't wait for customers to complain (reactive) before taking action to resolve an issue. Instead, proactively check in with customers on their experience and solicit feedback. This allows you to address shortcomings in your solution, tackle user experience challenges, and catch issues before they escalate, potentially creating a negative experience for many of your other customers.

If you do catch something early, don't stay silent and hope no one else notices. Never make assumptions; silence doesn't always indicate a smoothly oiled machine. Ensure you're meeting, if not exceeding, their expectations. Even if you're unable to resolve an issue right away, the simple act of acknowledging it and mentioning that you're working on resolving it is better than waiting for customers to complain. If you wait till then, they're already dissatisfied.

Storytime:
As a new homeowner, I took on the role of strata council president in the first year of our newly developed apartment. We terminated our caretaking/janitorial company less than 3 months in. All of this could have probably been easily avoided had they proactively solicited feedback from residents instead of waiting for cleanliness issues to be raised as complaints through the council.

A year later, before to our Annual General Meeting (AGM), a similar issue arose, leading us to switch our property management company. The decision stemmed from our previous property manager frequently abruptly ceasing to respond to emails. In an attempt to address this, I took the initiative to advise him on potential improvements. The council was understanding and reasonable, empathizing with the need to take time off for personal issues or to maintain work-life balance. We strongly encouraged him to provide advance notice or set up an out-of-office (OOO) auto-response for his email inbox if he was away.

Unfortunately, none of these suggestions were implemented, and he persisted in periodically ghosting both the council and residents of our building. I raised the concern not only with him but also with the property management company itself. However, by the time they took action to resolve the situation and assign our building to another property manager, we had already initiated the quotation process and selected another vendor. Remaining with them would have been preferable, and they could have retained our business if they had approached the situation proactively rather than reactively.

FOLLOW UP

It demonstrates care for the customer beyond the transaction. Define what ongoing communication beyond the sale should look like:

- When might you follow up?
- How often?
- What channels will you use to reach them?
- What channels are best for them to reach you, depending on the issues they face? For example, when or why to call vs. email.

Personalize your follow-up, whether it's through an in-person meeting, a call, or an email. An automated follow-up merely meets expectations; it is the bare minimum. A real, human, and personal follow-up is increasingly rare and will truly leave an impression on your customers.

The last time a manager personally called me to follow up on a purchase (not to ask me to fill out a survey) was back in 2014! I had bought a new handbag from Coach for my girlfriend (now my wife), and the store manager personally called to check if she liked the gift. As you can tell, that simple personal touch left a lasting impression (or I wouldn't be writing about it). It was rare back in 2014 for retail to follow up with a personal call like that, and it's even rarer now.

When you follow up, do so sincerely to check in with *them*, not for your own benefit. It's okay and a smart thing to follow up to get feedback or ask for reviews, but have that as your secondary objective. While you already have their attention, here are a few other ways to make the most out of the interaction:

Review Performance
Assess whether your solution is delivering on its promises. If possible, quantify and measure the progress or improvements since they started using your offering. Compare these results with the benchmarked metrics you may have obtained while quantifying value during the (A)SSESSMENT phase (page 23).

Readjust Expectations
If anything has deviated from what was promised or isn't going to plan, work together with your customer to adjust the proverbial "expectation bar". Educate or explain why it has moved or was set higher than it should be. Tempering expectations helps curb disappointment when their real experience falls short, while also making it easier for you to surpass that bar and delight them.

Get Feedback to Improve the Buyer's Experience, But Avoid
Using surveys with *"Did our SDR do X?"* type closed-ended questions. They feel highly scripted, presume that a good experience requires that exchange to have happened, and are impersonal.

Nor should you ask *"Anything you would like to add?"* or overly general *"How was your purchase experience?"* type questions, as customers will typically respond with *"nothing"* or *"good"*.

Open-ended questions are good for feedback, but they need to be framed so that the receiver understands what type of feedback to focus on. They should convey that you're sincerely trying to improve and aren't merely going through the motions to be polite.

For instance, I've lost count of the number of times a restaurant server has asked, "How is everything?" only to hear someone reply, "Good" and then immediately go back to badmouthing the meal or experience once the server is out of earshot.

Better ways to communicate sincerity in the solicitation could be:

> *"We're testing a new menu/recipe and would really love some honest and unfiltered feedback. How was your butter chicken?"*

> *"We're looking to improve our store's experience by implementing new training for our servers. Was there anything your server could have done better?"*

Of course, not every customer appreciates being interrupted during their meal or even afterward to talk. People also often default to being "nice" and are reluctant to provide harsh comments, especially in public. You can make it easier and more comfortable for them to voice their feedback by offering an email for them to write to. Doing this, instead of giving them a link or QR code to fill out a survey, helps maintain that personal touch. The personal solicitation also communicates sincerity better than a paper slip left on the table for feedback.

Ask for Reviews, Testimonials, or Referrals.
Now is as good a time as any to ask. They've likely achieved that positive milestone and are often willing to reciprocate if they are having a good experience so far.

INTENTIONALLY DESIGN EXPERIENCES

Magical moments don't happen by accident. Take a page out of how Disney approaches distracting people from queuing. Mindfully observe the distractions if you ever get the chance to visit; they are all purposefully designed to distract guests and keep them entertained. From the screens that narrate the story of the ride you're about to embark on to the cosplayed characters.

How can you intentionally do the same? With the music or message you might play for someone on hold during a call, how you respond to emails, or your customer onboarding experience.

ASSIGNMENT

1. Identify three touchpoints where you could exceed your customer's expectations.
2. Define what customer success means. What *should* an excellent experience look like? What is a neutral experience? Anything short of that requires attention.

To take it further, let's hear from Brian Chesky, co-founder, and CEO of Airbnb, as he discusses Airbnb's "11-star experience" in his interview with Reid Hoffman on Episode 1 of the Masters of Scale podcast.

> *"We basically took one part of our product and we extrapolated: what would a 5-star experience be? Then we went crazy. A 5-star experience is: You knock on the door, they open the door, they let you in. Great. That's not a big deal. You're not going to tell every friend about it. You might say, 'I used Airbnb. It worked.' So, we thought, 'What would a 6-star experience be?'*
>
> *A 6-star experience: You knock on the door, the host opens and shows you around. On the table would be a welcome gift. It would be a bottle of wine, maybe some candy. You'd open the fridge. There's water. You go to the bathroom, there's toiletries. The whole thing is great. That's a 6-star experience. You'd say, 'Wow I love this more than a hotel. I'm definitely*

going to use Airbnb again. It worked. Better than I expected.'

What's a 7-star experience? You knock on the door. The host opens. Get in. 'Welcome. Here's my full kitchen. I know you like surfing. There's a surfboard waiting for you. I've booked lessons for you. It's going to be an amazing experience. By the way, here's my car. You can use my car. And I also want to surprise you. There's this best restaurant in the city of San Francisco. I got you a table there.' And you're like, 'Whoa. This is way beyond.'

*So what would a 10-star check-in be? A 10-star check-in would be The Beatles check-in. In 1964. I'd get off the plane and there'd be 5,000 high school kids cheering my name with cars welcoming me to the country. I'd get to the front yard of your house and there'd be a press conference for me, and it would be just a mindf**k experience. So, what would an 11-star experience be? I would show up at the airport and you'd be there with Elon Musk and you're saying: 'You're going to space.'*

The point of the process is that maybe 9, 10, 11 are not feasible. But if you go through the crazy exercise, there's some **sweet spot between 'They showed up and they opened the door' and 'I went to space.' That's the sweet spot. You have to almost design the extreme to come backward***. Suddenly, doesn't knowing my preferences and having a surfboard in the house seem not crazy and reasonable? It's actually kind of crazy logistically, but this is the kind of stuff that creates great experience."*

- What would your 5-star experience look like?
- Better yet, what about 6, 7, 8, 9, 10 stars?

Notes:

EXPECTATIONS AND HAPPINESS

Not a sales-related section, but while we're on the topic, even the age-old question of how to live a happy life can be boiled down to expectations. I'm personally agnostic, but a lesson I've learned from Buddhism comes to mind: Suffering stems from desires and attachment.

Attachment as a Form of Expectation
We become overly reliant on an outcome or experience. Holding a notion of how situations should unfold and incorrectly associating achieving or obtaining it with a sense of security, pleasure, happiness, satisfaction, fulfillment, or completeness. This expectation can be a source of anxiety and disappointment if the outcome doesn't align with our desires, leading to cravings and suffering.

When we are attached to a certain person, situation, or possession, we resist the natural impermanence of life and the inevitability of change. Expecting things to remain constant when they never will leads to suffering.

Attachment also manifests as an identification with possessions, relationships, or roles. We come to expect that these external factors define our identity and sense of self. When these external factors change or are lost, suffering arises due to the unmet expectations tied to identity. For instance, someone may incorrectly expect and associate the possession of a luxurious car with a sense of success. Losing it would result in grief as their sense of self-worth or identity as a successful person is threatened.

Buddhism encourages the cultivation of contentment (santutthi) as an antidote to incessant wanting. Recognizing and appreciating what one has in the present moment, rather than constantly seeking more or different experiences, leads to a sense of inner peace. This can be achieved by acknowledging and letting go of rigid expectations, understanding the transient nature of experiences, and embracing the present without being overly attached to the past (comparing what we have with what we had) or the future (living in anticipation of certain outcomes). By doing so, we can reduce suffering and find a deeper sense of contentment that is not dependent on external circumstances meeting unrealistic expectations.

But! If you're a lifelong learner with a growth mindset like me, are you doomed to a life of unhappiness? While expecting less makes you happier, this principle doesn't apply universally. It may bring bliss in the short-term, but ignoring long-term consequences is risky. Would it be better to experience a moment of joy and then die tomorrow? Or endure some pain to enjoy months or years of happiness afterward?

> *"It is better to be a human being dissatisfied than a pig satisfied;*
> *better to be Socrates dissatisfied than a fool satisfied.*
> *And if the fool, or the pig, has a different opinion,*
> *it is because they only know their own side of the question."*
> *– John Stuart Mill, English Philosopher*

You've heard sayings like *"Eliminate all desires"* or *"If you want to be happy, stop trying to be happy"*. These suggest that happiness contradicts ambition; if you desire more or aim high, you won't truly be happy because you don't learn to appreciate what you already have. This interpretation is incorrect. You can aim high, yet still enjoy the journey and be happy with what you have, even if you don't hit your targets.

This is where words, semantics, and language make all the difference. Instead of "Eliminate all desires", think "Eliminate all *expectations*". Remove all expectations you have attached to an outcome.

> To desire is to want, to wish for.
>
> To expect is to look for, to look forward to, to have a previous apprehension of, or to anticipate.

Children are joyous not because they lack desires, but instead because they lack experience. Without experience, they have nothing to look forward to, no previous apprehensions, and they don't anticipate anything. They have *no expectations.* Therefore, when something happens, they live it in the purest moment. As they grow, they start to learn and build experience. Initially, with limited experience, children have low expectations. When something happens that exceeds their expectations, they are delighted. However, as they accumulate experience through consistent exposure, they begin to solidify their expectations. If something happens and it fails to meet their expectations, they are disappointed.

Framing it as expectations instead of desires helps explain why:

You can still be ambitious and yet be happy
If you aim high but don't hold any expectations of what the journey to your destination will look like, you'll better enjoy the journey.

You can still be a happy philosopher
Don't pursue knowledge holding the belief that this is how things *should* be. Instead, be open and marvel at what you learn in the process.

Accident victims can live happier lives than lottery winners
(https://bit.ly/4dbPrCY)
Eventually, the thrill of winning the lottery will wear off. If all experiences are judged by the extent to which they depart from a baseline of past experience, gradually even the most positive events will cease to have an impact as they are absorbed into the new baseline against which further events are judged. Thus, as lottery winners become accustomed to the additional pleasures made possible by their new wealth, these pleasures are experienced as less intense and no longer contribute much to their general level of happiness. Expectation breeds a sense of entitlement. When you compare your current situation with an idealized or desired state and believe you deserve something more but fail to get it, it only leads to disappointment.

Mindfulness, being present, and living in the moment = happiness
When you're in the moment, there is only *now*. There is no "what if?" or expectation of the future. There is no "it should have been" and no comparative expectation with what happened in the past. Without expectation, you are left with only *being*. When you are simply being, everything exceeds your expectations, and that makes you happy!

Expectation even explains how the 100% rule of fully committing affects satisfaction and happiness

Take relationships as an example. Options are usually a good thing. With choice, you have the ability to choose the "best" possible match/outcome. However, like many other things in life, most of you theoretically have unlimited options when it comes to relationships. It becomes crippling when we avoid fully committing to a relationship because we think "There are other available options out there, there must be a better fit". Sorry to burst your bubble, but there is no such thing as a perfect or destined partner! That is a fictional fairy tale. Look at enduring relationships around you. The strength of a relationship comes from the unwavering commitment each person gives to the other. It's normal to fantasize about others; however, if you are unable to commit to a relationship, you won't end up in a strong one and be truly satisfied. I'm not a professional relationship coach, but here is what I've learned:

- It isn't bad to have high standards. I'm not saying you should settle for subpar.
- Date a little before you commit. It'll allow you to differentiate between what's good, bad, and a fit for you.
- Once you've found something that fits your criteria (or closely), there's value in accepting and learning to settle for what you have instead of endlessly pursuing an unachievable standard of perfection (don't harbor unrealistic expectations).
- When you're ready to commit, remove yourself from the dating pool.

Besides relationships, expectations of "what could be" that stem from unlimited choices also affect us in many other ways: The more houses you see, the less satisfied you will be with your final purchase. The more job applications you receive, the less satisfied you'll be with the candidate you end up hiring. It is prevalent to the point that there exists an entire field of mathematical research dedicated to this topic known as Optimal Stopping.

EXPECTATIONS ARE GOOD TOO

Expectations aren't all bad. It's unrealistic to say that we can rid ourselves of all expectations. Humans are creatures of meaning, constantly seeking patterns in various aspects of life. Expecting is a central part of how we learn and grow, and is both a normal and a necessary aspect of our lives.

This is also reflected in the Buddhist concept of the Middle Way, which advocates avoiding extremes. Buddhism doesn't advocate for the complete elimination of all desires and expectations, as some can be wholesome and contribute to well-being. For instance,

Motivation + Growth: Expectations serve as motivators that spur growth and improvement. They give us a sense of purpose and direction. Contentment and a complete lack thereof lead to a sedentary mindset and lifestyle.

Planning and preparation: We can't make plans without attaching some sense of consistency to predicted outcomes. While we shouldn't expect outcomes to always be consistent, it's practical to make predictions with a reasonable level of certainty. This helps us set priorities and take proactive steps to influence our lives.

Positive Anticipation: Anticipation itself can also bring excitement, joy, and a sense of accomplishment if we relish it in the present without becoming overly attached to the actual outcomes. For example, looking forward to a vacation, a celebration, or a personal achievement can enhance the overall happiness associated with these events.

Relationships and Communication: Clearly communicating and expressing our expectations in relationships helps each other understand what we expect from one another. Being clear about these expectations and sharing what we expect helps contribute to a healthy relationship, reducing disagreements or disappointment that stem from one party silently harboring unmet expectations of the other.

The Middle Way encourages a balanced and mindful approach to expectations, avoiding both indulgence and extreme asceticism. It isn't about the complete abandonment of expectations, but instead, it involves acknowledging and accepting what is, what we have, and what we expect.

EXPECTATIONS AND HUMOR

The comprehension of expectations can also enlighten us on humor. We laugh at a punchline or a pun because it is something that makes sense yet is unexpected. Said best in this article by Sam McNerney: https://bigthink.com/articles/the-science-of-expectation-using-humor-to-understand-creativity/

> *"Despite their surface diversity, most jokes are built using the same set of blueprints: they lead us down a path of expectations, build up tension, and at the end, introduce a twist that teases our initial expectations in a clever way. Humor arrives when we figure out how the punch line both broke and fulfilled our expectations. When this occurs, we experience mirth, the reward of successfully connecting the dots of a joke. It's the "a-ha" moment of comedy, or what we feel when we "get" it."*

For this reason, it's difficult to replicate humor, and it has become increasingly challenging to create funny content in today's digital landscape where everyone has been exposed to different variations of the same joke and can predict what comes next.

These are a few of the many lessons sales has taught me about life, and I thought it meaningful to share it with you as well. On the sales front, understanding this helps us better manage our customer's experience and also helps build resiliency. Attaching anticipated outcomes to our interactions makes it easy for us to feel disheartened when prospects walk away. It's also challenging not to take rejection (page 82) personally, given our conditioned expectation of acceptance as an integral part of our identity.

♦♦♦

C.A.R.E. OVERVIEW

Returning to our main topic: C.A.R.E. is a framework that can be employed not only for the overall process of leading your potential customer toward conversion but also for enhancing every small interaction within that journey.

Here's how C.A.R.E. appears in the customer journey for various types of solutions:

	B2B	Website	Retail
C	Introduction, the initial outreach email	Everything you see above the fold (before needing to scroll), testimonials	Storefront, window displays, signage, store layout, how you greet prospects
A	Discovery Call	Survey, quiz	Questions you ask
R	Demo, trial	Product page	Demo, sample
E	Proposal, contract, pilot, onboarding	FAQs, CTA, checkout process, confirmation email	Checkout, setup

C.A.R.E. within an intro email:

C	The subject line, how you address them, readability at a glance, tone of voice.
A	Context of how you found or got connected to them, why you're reaching out to them
R	What's in it for them (WIIFT), why they might want to continue to engage.
E	How you make the ask to get them to continue engaging or provide more information.

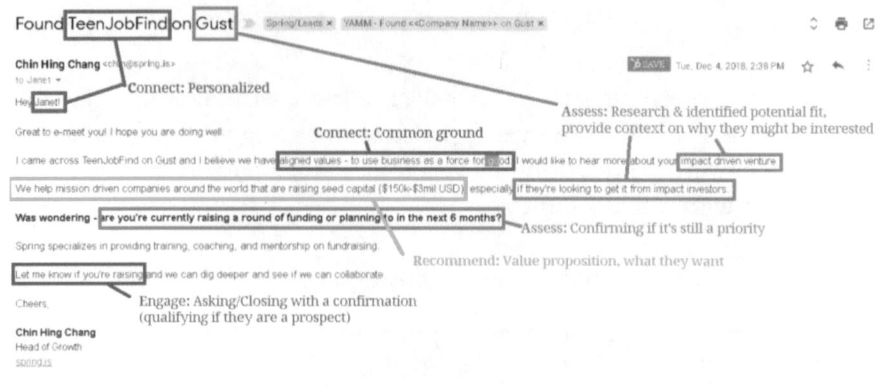

ASSIGNMENT

Craft your sales "script" or playbook using C.A.R.E. – create different ones for a call, your website, an email, or other channels.

If you've followed along with the previous assignments, this should be as simple as compiling all your assignments under the C.A.R.E. section into one document.

Additional Resource: https://bit.ly/how-to-write-a-sales-script

ACCOUNT MANAGEMENT

C.A.R.E. can also serve as a framework to assist with de-escalating customer complaints.

CONNECT	**Credibility + Trust** You're the right person who can resolve their issue.
ASSESS	**Listen, Understand, Empathise** The 5 Whys technique (page 24) is an effective method for uncovering the root causes of their dissatisfaction, ensuring you address the underlying issues rather than superficial symptoms.
RECOMMEND	When responding, avoid: • *"I don't know/ understand"* (signals ignorance and inexperience). • *"It's not within my power"* (deflective and doesn't solve the problem). Instead: • *"Good question, let me look into it"* (you don't have to have all the answers, but you need to confidently communicate that you can get them). • *"Could you clarify… / let me confirm if…"* (don't make assumptions). • *"Here are a few things we could do/ try"* (focus on what you can do, not what you can't). **Acknowledge: their problems, feelings, and frustrations** All too often, we jump into prescribing and problem-solving, thinking it's the right course of action, believing it will resolve the complaint, and assuming it's what the customers NEED.

When, in fact, we should be listening, holding space for our customers, and letting them vent, because sometimes that's all they WANT.

I'm guilty of doing this myself with my wife. Sometimes, she vents about a bad customer interaction at work. The consultant in me reflexively starts troubleshooting, brainstorming solutions, or trying to find reasons why the customer may have behaved that way. Yet, all she really wants is to vent to someone willing to listen and receive affirmation of her feelings of frustration.

I am not being misogynistic; this applies to both genders and is not exclusive to women.

Apologize

You should rectify their problem if possible. However, sometimes, fixing the issue or obtaining a reimbursement or credit isn't what they truly want or care about. Sometimes, all they want is an honest and sincere apology.

As obvious as it may seem to be an appropriate and polite way of responding to complaints, many organizations have policies that discourage apologizing. They worry that it could be used against them as a form of admission of guilt.

There's a fascinating Radiolab episode, "Apologetical", which delves into this topic, discussing apology legislation designed to encourage open communication and resolution by ensuring that a simple apology is not taken as an admission of guilt. As they discussed in the episode, there are clear business benefits to apologizing: it significantly reduces the likelihood of customers filing lawsuits.

Whilc it docs havc thc cffect of minimizing the financial damage of your mistakes, I'm not suggesting you use the apology as a mere tool. Instead, I'm emphasizing that it's okay, and in fact, beneficial to apologize if you sincerely wish to express it. At the very least, you can still apologize for them having a bad experience, even if it's an unfounded complaint that isn't your fault or your company's.

Offer alternatives + collaborate on a solution
Your understanding of what your customer desires as recourse may not be accurate. Engage and involve them to better tailor your resolution to their satisfaction. Some customers may make unreasonable demands, or, in some cases, a problem or dissatisfaction may not be resolvable. Adopting a collaborative approach will ensure they still walk away from the exchange with a positive experience. For example,

"I can't refund your entire bill; however, I can apply a credit for the full amount that will go towards your next bill"

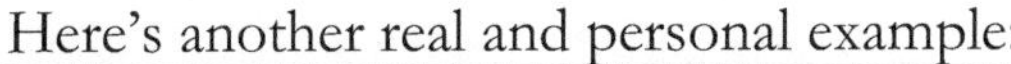
Here's another real and personal example:

	(Chin paddling towards English Bay on his Kokopelli Packraft) I purchased a packraft (a durable and lightweight inflatable boat) from Kokopelli back in 2020. The model I selected had dual chambers, meaning the front and back of the boat were separated. I considered this feature important due to a previous experience with a cheap inflatable boat from Intex. In that instance, I found myself panicking in the middle of a lake when a leak sprouted. Opting for a model with two inflatable sections seemed like a wise decision; in the event of a leak in one section, the other would still keep the boat afloat. After using it about 2-3 times, I began to notice a slight leak in the baffle (the section that separates the front and rear chambers), essentially turning it into a single-chamber boat. I contacted them about it, and here was my experience: 1. They were highly responsive and promptly offered to cover the shipping cost for its return. In the event it couldn't be fixed, they also proposed a replacement. 2. It turned out the issue was unrepairable due to difficulty in access. They called me directly, clearly communicated, and explained the problem and constraints. Unfortunately, sending me a new boat of the same model was not an option as this particular model had been discontinued. 3. They offered various options and were open and collaborative in seeking a resolution. I didn't

	want a new boat because I specifically chose this model for certain features and sizing. I conveyed my preference to keep it and proposed that I would be satisfied if they could provide two of their waterproof/airtight dry bags. These bags could serve as backup buoyancy chambers, given that my Tizip model allowed me to open up a section of the boat for storage. They agreed to this solution. 4. They sent it back with expedited shipping and even exceeded my expectations by including several additional free accessories: a large carry bag, bow bag, and pressure gauge cap for the inflation valve. All in all, they turned what could have been a negative experience into a highly positive one, making me a big advocate for their brand.
ENGAGE	**Exceed expectations in how you respond** It's even possible to turn errors into opportunities and transform complaining customers into raving advocates, how? By going above and beyond to deliver an exceptional customer service experience. John DiJulius shared in his book "What's the Secret?: To Providing a World-Class Customer Experience" about the time he left his charger behind at The Ritz-Carlton Sarasota. The very next day, he received an air package containing his charger along with a note that read, *"Mr. DiJulius, I wanted to make sure we got this to you right away. I am sure you need it, and, just in case, I sent you an extra charger for your laptop."*

	This is one of many fables showcasing the legendary level of service at Ritz-Carlton. Read the famous story of Joshie the Giraffe (https://bit.ly/Joshie-the-Giraffe) or of how Ritz-Carlton Bali went above and beyond to source specialized eggs and milk for a family whose son had a food allergy (https://bit.ly/Ritz-Carlton-Bali). They make this possible by empowering their employees to craft these magical experiences on their own. Ritz-Carlton employees are authorized to spend up to $2,000 a day to resolve any guest problem. **Ensure** Your proposed solution satisfies them. If not, continue exploring other relevant options they might be open to. **Further educate + set new expectations** Whatever resolution you provide to your customer, it's a good idea to take this time to reset expectations, ensuring that a similar complaint won't arise. Educate them on what to expect with their new solution (whether you provided a different offering, downgraded, or even upgraded).

Try not to take complaints personally. Often, they arise from issues that are outside of your control – such as pricing, a poor design experience, or unforeseen service or inventory interruptions. Even if a mistake was caused by misinformation you provided, the blame isn't solely yours to bear. Training or perhaps standard operating procedures (SOPs) could be improved. Ultimately, mistakes are bound to happen; what's more important is that you aren't intentionally misleading people.

Read this post: https://www.qualtrics.com/blog/customer-service-examples/ for some excellent tips and real-world examples to inspire how you might enhance your customer service experience. Here's a quick summary of key points from that article:

- Large gestures aren't always necessary; small gestures can still make a big impact if they're unexpected.
- Proactively express that you appreciate and care about your customers.
- Meet them where they are by making it easy for them to reach you.
- Do not avoid communicating an issue, hoping nobody will notice it. Instead, proactively acknowledge it. This preemptive approach doesn't make you look bad and will eliminate most complaints because the issue is no longer unexpected.
- Today's customers don't merely want products or services; they care about the experience.
- Actively engage and involve your customers in improving your offerings, and recognize them if you move forward with adopting their suggestions.
- Focus on cultivating advocates instead of influencers, despite their smaller reach. By prioritizing real everyday people over celebrities, it makes your brand more relatable and authentic."

ASSIGNMENT

Use C.A.R.E. to create a script for responding to customer complaints:

CONNECT	What can you communicate to highlight credibility and build trust?
ASSESS	What questions can you ask to understand their problem? What are some prompts to dig deeper? Are you digging into underlying causes or false beliefs?

RECOMMEND	Confirm/Clarify. Acknowledge/Apologize. Provide suggestions/collaborate on a solution.
ENGAGE	Exceed expectations. Ensure it's resolved. Further educate + set new expectations.

2: BUSINESS STRATEGY & PROCESS

Setting the right foundations to grow and scale

Everything in this section is primarily for managers and business owners.

The right strategy and design take much of the work out of sales. Let's shift gears to explore how you might adjust your approach and offerings to better facilitate sales, revenue, and even organic growth.

MARKETING VS. SALES

Sales vs. Marketing are arbitrary terms we've made up to delineate roles, responsibilities, and activities in our business. *The prospect doesn't care.* It doesn't mean these terms are insignificant, but it's important to remember that the lines are often blurred and some sales-related activities or campaigns could also be viewed as marketing, and vice-versa depending on how each organization has drawn those boundaries.

Your prospects are on their own journey. Your sales and marketing efforts are the guide that will help them achieve their desired outcome. They should work in tandem, and teams should avoid pointing fingers or antagonizing the opposing department.

INBOUND/OUTBOUND/PUSH/PULL

Marketing is generally, but not always, inbound. Inbound is about getting prospects to come to you (instead of you reaching out to them: outbound).

That said, certain outbound activities might also fall under the responsibility of your marketing department:

- Prospecting (a.k.a. List Building, page 346): creating a list of prospects, identifying potential decision-makers, and obtaining their contact info.
- Lead generation: through campaigns, events, website pages, etc. To attract and gather a list of qualified leads to be directly contacted or nurtured until they're ready to buy.
- Boothing at conferences and collecting information from interested people.
- Creating and distributing lead magnets: tools, guides, templates, books, etc. that aid with identifying your prospect's intent.

Within Marketing, there's also Push vs. Pull Marketing:

Push Marketing
Is when you take your company/offerings to the prospect, increasing exposure and awareness. Is interruptive, you're trying to get prospects to notice you:

- Ads (online, TV, Radio): some people argue that Ads are pull, but I disagree. It's interruptive.
- Visual merchandising (retail displays).
- Product placement (movies, influencers).
- Direct sales (promoting at a tradeshow, selling face-to-face).

Pull Marketing
On the other hand, attracts prospects to you. This could be achieved through building your reputation, trust, and customer loyalty by:

- Becoming a thought leader through content marketing.
- Designing strong referral (page 170) programs.
- Good account management (page 107) to ensure customers return and repurchase.
- SEO.

Wait, I'm confused now…inbound, outbound, push, pull?! So what?

Use the right activities in the right places. Some work better or are less effective based on where your prospects are in their buyer's journey (page 235). Depending on what you already have in place, you may want to revise your activities/campaigns if you're doing too much of something or prioritizing the wrong type of campaigns that aren't best suited for your business or the solutions you have to offer.

Here's a matrix comparing activities and recommendations between Inbound vs. Outbound and Push vs. Pull. Target percentages of time for activities are suggested starting points for new businesses and subject to variation depending on your offerings (I'll explain more about what to prioritize when we discuss Growth Engines, page 146).

	INBOUND	**OUTBOUND**
PUSH	• Getting prospects to come to you • Interruptive	• You getting in front of prospects • Interruptive
	E.g. Ad for a webinar	E.g. Cold calling, Email Outreach
	So What? • Work best for solutions (highly visual, ergo easily marketable) that are either innovative, not in a crowded competitive marketplace, strongly differentiated, or easily communicable with words. • Might also work if prospects are aware of their problem but might not have considered your type of solution. • Low priority if you're none of the above or if your solution needs to be *experienced* first before they understand how it's better. • Target 20% of your time.	*So What?* • Most effective when you know these prospects are highly qualified and ready to buy or highly discontent with an existing provider. • An activity in which you can control your output. Results can be consistently predicted based on activity. • Target 40% of your time. • Good sales techniques are key.
PULL	• Getting prospects to come to you • On their own accord	• You getting in front of prospects • On their own accord
	E.g. Blogging, SEO, Publishing a book	E.g. Boothing at trade shows, Google Pay-per-click (PPC) Ads

	So What? • The long game. ROI of time spent or monetary investment into these activities isn't usually immediately quantifiable. • Important for building reputation, brand, and thought leadership. • Target 20% of your time.	*So What?* • Great if you know where to target them and what to say to catch their attention. • Generally, the highest and quickest rate of conversion. • Unfortunately, it's limited because it's challenging to control when or how often people search for you. • Target 20% of your time.

ASSIGNMENT

Evaluate your current activities

1. Are they the right activities for your solution or context?
2. Are there other channels or campaigns you believe are effective but have been avoiding?

Notes:

Notes:

TYPES OF SALES

Let's look at some of the different forms of sales. Not everything will apply to you but it's worth exploring because there are strategic concepts here that might influence how you sell your solutions.

Direct Sales
Direct to consumer. Not to be confused with "direct marketing". Direct selling takes place when salespeople reach out directly to prospects, whereas direct marketing involves a company marketing directly to the prospect without going through an agent, consultant, or retail outlet.

E.g. Peddling/1-on-1 Demo/Website

The benefit of direct selling is you control the process and branding. You have a full say on what your SDRs can or can't do and how they should or shouldn't position your offerings. They can be categorized as:

> *Single level:* Buy from A, sell to B.
>
> *Multi-level (a.k.a. MLM or network marketing):* Buy from A, sell to B, and earn commission from the sales of recruited salespeople below them.

MLM is still considered "Direct" as they are working directly for you, not a separate 3rd-party selling on your behalf.

There's a lot of negativity associated with MLM. The structure itself isn't good or bad, poor implementation is the problem. I've seen organizations do MLM well with the proper structure and training. MLM is also an internal term, feel free to call it something else if there's too much negative baggage associated with it.

Channel Sales
When you have a 3rd-party selling on your behalf.

E.g. Franchising/reseller/dealer

Pros	• Lower overhead, let them do the selling for you. • They already have a network of prospects (that you might not have easy access to) + distribution figured out. o Allows for massive expansion and increased exposure.
Cons	• You have less control over your prospect's buying experience. • The reseller has their own best interest in mind, not yours. o Their bottom line is *profit.* • Slow to start as they have different priorities and need to be convinced of the ROI: not only monetary (if they have to purchase inventory) but also time + effort needed to train and familiarize their SDRs with your offerings.

A good and strategic channel partner should ideally sell similar solutions to similar buyers and align with your values and your brand identity.

If channel selling is your intended distribution model, I still highly encourage starting with direct selling. Why? Direct selling will help you:

- Understand your sales model, who to target (the right decision-makers to approach), and how to best articulate your offerings. Don't expect a channel partner to hit the ground running, you should be equipped to train them on the above.
- Gauge product-market fit. Amazing partnerships won't save you if your solution isn't what prospects are looking for. If you've already proved product-market fit before approaching channel partners, it makes the ROI conversation a lot more convincing as they can readily see how your solution will increase their profits too. It's less risky for them to sell an offering with strong demand vs. one that is unproven in the market.

Remember, their priority is selling, not creating demand. You still have to do marketing and drive traffic to them.

Once you've decided to pursue channel partnerships, ensure you commit to it. Don't compete with your partners. It can be tempting to also sell your own solution, but channel partners don't like it when you're competing with them and become less committed to promoting your solution(s) or might even discontinue their partnership. Doing so gives short-term revenue but works against building the leverage of the channel. Instead, invest in supporting your partners by providing them with training, tools, news, updates, and resources that will help them better sell your solutions.

B2C

If your solution is low-priced, low-margin, or consumer-centric, your activities should be weighted more toward marketing rather than sales. Why? Because, as I've mentioned, sales is resource intensive.

That said, even if you have the above, you can still benefit from selling. Affiliate/referral partnerships, wholesaling to retail or distributors, and MLM (recruiting commissioned salespeople) are sales activities you can explore even if you're B2C. It's harder to control results that come from marketing, whilst you can directly control the volume of your sales activities and will usually see immediate results from it. Like Channel Sales, do Direct Sales to start before leveraging 3rd-party resellers.

B2B

Consider H2H (Human to Human). Remember, even if companies are paying, people are the ones doing the buying. There are 2 main ways to approach it, neither is "wrong" or "right":

- Some B2B solutions are sold at a high price.
- While others directly target individual users within an organization and are priced lower to facilitate quicker conversion and higher volume of purchase.

For the former, there is an added layer of complexity because organizations have more complicated purchasing processes. Approval generally requires more stakeholders and it takes longer to build relationships with all of them. Unsurprisingly, there's also a smaller pool of leads if you're going after organizations instead of individuals. Implementation and adoption are more complicated as you're trying to create bigger change or have multiple people learn something new and adjust their existing workflows.

Some quick B2B tips:

Get acknowledgment of where they are (timing) and the problem(s) they are facing.
Some prospects aren't aware that they have a problem or are missing out on opportunities. Educate them on the industry, what their competitors are doing, and what milestones should look like relative to similar businesses at a similar stage of growth. Show them that they're falling behind (if that's the case). Highlight how you can help bring them to the next level.

Don't underestimate the power of relationships.
Know your target stakeholders and their *personal motivations* (e.g. getting a promotion, recognition for a new initiative, saving time, etc.); appeal to these motivations.

ASSIGNMENT

1. What should "good" milestones look like for your prospects? Identifying these will give you a benchmark to assess if your prospect is "below average".
2. What questions can you ask to evaluate their timing and where they're currently at?

Notes:

Notes:

QUALIFYING CUSTOMERS

When should you involve Sales? Sales is generally one of the most resource (time, effort, financial) intensive departments. Salespeople are (and should be) your highest-paid employees because they're the lifeblood of your company.

If your solution is less than $300, you shouldn't need Sales. Marketing should be sufficient and most prospects should be able to decide to purchase without having to first speak to someone. "Sales" in these companies is generally more customer service oriented, primarily to address questions or concerns. It doesn't need to be in-person and could be in the form of live chat, call center, FAQs (Frequently Asked Questions), or email support.

Marketing is where you can still afford to do things at scale, sales are when the details matter, when you need to focus on building a personal relationship. You should aim to have sales only engage when a prospect is *qualified.*

Here are the two main factors to consider:

1. Fit

Your "ideal" customer, ideal can be in a variety of ways:

- Easiest to work with.
- Potential for future projects.
- Strong reputation for social proofing.
- Converts the quickest.
- Has the problem and is actively considering solutions.
- Most readily see your solution as the right (differentiated) solution for them in the market.

Define the demographics, psychographics, or sociographics markers that characterize your ideal customer.

Demographics

Qualities of a specific group of people

For B2C (Business to Consumer): age, gender, geographic region, race, income, education, etc.

For B2B (Business to Business): years in operation, size of company (# of employees), $ capital raised, industry, etc.

Psychographics
Classification according to attitudes, motivations, aspirations, values, interests, hobbies, and other psychological criteria.

Example values: comfort, safety, sense of belonging
Example aspirations: status, success, recognition

Sociographics
How your market behaves socially (not just social media). What solutions are they currently using? Channels they're on? How do they make decisions? What language do they use to define the problem?

Example: A sustainable soap company I know of found that Tesla users (sociographic marker) were also a good target customer because they share similar psychographic markers as their ideal customers.

2. Intent
Beyond identifying characteristics that help you qualify your ideal customer, are you also capturing data that tells you if they are exhibiting purchase-ready behaviors?

For instance: Researching competitors, looking at your pricing page, asking for a quote, or jumping on a consultation/demo call.

BANT
This previously mentioned acronym is a popular and recommended framework for qualification that captures both fit + intent. It works for both B2B and B2C and stands for:

BUDGET	• Does it fit within their expectations?

	• Can they afford it?
AUTHORITY	• Are they the right decision-maker? • Does this organization/prospect have characteristics (demographics, psychographics, or sociographics) of my ideal target customer?
NEED	• Do they have the problem or acknowledge they need it right now? • Are they exhibiting behaviors that indicate they are looking for a solution?
TIMELINE	• Are they ready to buy? Or are they merely exploring something for the future? • When do they hope to see changes or improvements? When do they hope to accomplish certain results? • Does it match their purchasing cycle?

It's equally important to identify red flags and disqualify non-ideal customers so you won't waste your time and effort pursuing unproductive leads:

During my time managing incubation programs at Spring Activator, the red flags (there are exceptions, but generally these were pretty accurate) I identified in their prospects were:

> *Students*: Even if passionate, would often abandon their business idea upon graduation. Got debts to pay right?
>
> *Lifelong learners*: dubbed such not because of their growth mindset, but because they only consume yet never take action on their business. Learning is important but it isn't everything! Don't use it as an excuse to procrastinate building your solution or pursuing customers.

ASSIGNMENT

1. If you haven't already, take the time to define Fit and the characteristics of your customer persona.
2. How can you identify and capture Intent-related behavior for your prospects?

Notes:

Having a clearly defined customer persona(s) helps salespeople not only identify who's a fit to engage with but also how to best tailor their messaging to them. It even helps marketing decide who to target and which channels to focus their efforts on.

USERS, DECISION-MAKERS, ADVOCATES, (AND GATEKEEPERS)

Creating customer persona(s) for consumers is straightforward and the buying process is a lot simpler. There are typically 3 main consumer profiles:

Users
Advocates (a.k.a. Influencer)
Decision-makers (a.k.a. Customers or Buyers)

They could all be separate, or be the same person too. It's important to pay attention to this as your marketing/sales language might change depending on who you're speaking to.

Example: A company I worked with developed a ring that would help young women determine if their drinks were spiked with date-rape drugs. In their situation:

	Persona	Messaging/Motivation
Users	Young women, typically 20s-30s, active night lifestyle	Discrete, fashionable
Advocates	Could also be the young women, their parents, or even clubs, pubs, or schools	Avoid liability issues, a safe community/space
Decision-makers	Parents/Spouse	Protect, safety, care

Businesses, similar to consumers, also have Users, Decision-makers, and Advocates. In addition, there's 1 other role to be aware of: the Gatekeepers (a.k.a. Approvers or Blockers). They don't have purchasing authority but can potentially slow down or block the sales process. Learn about who they might be and what their considerations and concerns are.

E.g. If you're selling sales tracking software:

	Persona	Messaging/Motivation
Users	SDRs	Save time following up with leads, close more sales
Advocates	Sales Managers	Track performance, coach your team
Gatekeepers	IT	Integrate with current tech stack, address security concerns
	Finance department	Within budget
	HR	Change management and training on new software
Decision-makers	CEO/VP Sales	Clear ROI, aligns with strategy

Typically, as organizations grow larger, there is less overlap between roles, while in smaller organizations, some individuals may take on multiple responsibilities. Your goal is to explore and understand who needs to get involved and where. It may differ from organization to organization, but you should be able to find commonalities in prospect profiles (which entail similar purchasing processes) within certain groups or industries. For example:

Companies with a small team of less than 50.
Medium companies with 250-500 employees.
Larger companies with over 1000 employees.

If you're new to selling in a particular sector or have an innovative/uncommon solution, consider beginning by engaging with all potential stakeholders. Approach this as you would a customer discovery process, aiming to learn as much as you can. Each stakeholder is likely to provide valuable insights.

I had the opportunity to work with Bryan, the founder of LifeBooster, a health and safety analytics company using AI and wearable devices to identify risks in the workplace to prevent injuries before they occur. He designed a solution for industrial workers that would alert them of potential injuries related to posture, movement, vibration, and heat stress.

> When he initially began researching his market, he approached COOs, Safety Executives, and Operation Managers, assuming they were the decision-makers, which turned out to be correct. By speaking with them, he gained insights into typical purchasing and procurement timelines in their industry, which helped significantly shorten their sales cycle. However, he discovered that they often require pressure from their workers' union to take action.
>
> Next, he contacted unions to gain their support. During this process, he discovered that unions serve as Advocates. They provided valuable insights into the implementation and approval procedures. Furthermore, he realized unions would only take action if workers were interested in using the solution. Given its IoT nature, he also had to secure the cooperation of IT (Gatekeepers) and site managers to integrate it into their systems and workflows."
>
> Finally, he engaged with the workers and gathered extensive feedback on aspects such as design, comfort, usability, and compatibility of his device. For instance, the device needed to be compatible with existing personal protective equipment and in many cases was not allowed to transmit any radio signals. These insights led to critical design considerations and enabled sales with Fortune 100 manufacturers.

All in, he ended up talking to over 250 individuals in his discovery process. Some of which eventually ended up becoming his customers.

ASSIGNMENT

Regardless if you're B2B or B2C, who are your potential

1. Users
2. Advocates
3. Gatekeepers
4. and Decision-makers?

Notes:

B2B PROSPECTING MAP

On the other side of the fence, when speaking to companies, the most common complaint I get is "SDRs don't understand and respect my buying process".

There are 2 common entry points into organizations:

Top-down: When there is strategic alignment which incentivizes the decision-maker to instruct management or users to explore your solution further.

Bottoms-up: When users or advocates rave about your product to management.

Understanding an organization's purchasing process can become complex when multiple stakeholders are part of the equation. This B2B Prospecting Map (view on next page) will help you chart out the right decision-makers and understand the fastest path to getting in front of the right people, especially if you're dealing with an industry you're not familiar with.

As you work through the prospecting map, notice that I'm encouraging you to reach out to *multiple* individuals within the organization that you're targeting. You don't have to contact all potential individuals simultaneously; begin with the one you believe is most likely to respond first, if they're unresponsive, move on to reach out to others. Your objective is to understand the most efficient entry point and determine the key individuals involved at various stages of your sales process. For example, you might find having the technical gatekeeper, manager, and CEO present in your product demo greatly accelerates approval as you won't have to book separate meetings to redo the same demo or pitch.

After utilizing this tool to create your map, a helpful follow-up step is to familiarize yourself with their approval procedures and budgeting timelines.

Role	Agent	Motivations	Email/Call 1 Desired Outcome: Schedule a discovery call Tool used: Calendar scheduler			Email 2 Desired Outcome: Follow-up if no response			Sales call Desired Outcome: Book a live demo Tool used: Testimonials, Case studies			Demo Desired Outcome: Sign up for Trial Tool used: Features, Product demo/Presentation			Proposal Desired Outcome: Pilot program/rollout Tool used: Pricing	
			Response	Duration for response	Comments	Response	Duration for response	Comments	Response	Duration for response	Comments	Response	Duration for response	Comments	Response	Duration for response
User	Sales rep	Improve close rate, gain more commission	Yes	2 days	Interested, need to test it first	-	-	-	...							
Advocate	Sales Manager	Improve performance of sales team	No	3 days	Not convinced of value	-	-	-								
Approver (Technical)	CTO	Will it integrate with our existing CRM/Marketing tools?	No	3 days	No reply	Yes	2 days	Speak to CEO about it, not me								
Approver (Budget)	CFO/Controller	Do we have the budget for it in this quarter?	No	8 days	No reply	No	7 days	No reply								
Decision Maker (Strategic)	CEO	Will this tool scale with us?	Yes	2 days	Interested, check with the sales reps and managers	-	-	-								

ASSIGNMENT

If you sell B2B, **make a copy** of this B2B Prospecting Map template: https://bit.ly/B2B-Prospecting-Map to draft a potential outreach workflow vs. different stakeholders (you won't have edit access as this is a public template).

Because it's best viewed horizontally with the many columns, here's a version with it cut into multiple tables:

Role	**Title**	**Motivations**
User		
Advocate		
Gatekeeper		
Decision Maker		

…

…

Contact 1 Desired Outcome:		
Response	Duration	Comments

…

…

Contact 2 Desired Outcome:		
Response	Duration	Comments

Here are 2 key concepts that greatly impact B2B sales. They apply in B2C too but carry more weight for high-ticket (expensive) solutions which are more common in B2B. These concepts were taught to me by one of my mentors: Mike Winterfield, founder of Active Impact Investments, former COO of Traction on Demand (acquired by Salesforce), and former President of Randstad Canada. They'll not only affect how you sell but more importantly, what you sell.

THE DECISION THRESHOLD

is an arbitrary and subjective mental threshold, which if exceeded, will trigger the decision and motivation to make a change. Everyone's threshold is different and influenced by their personal values, interests, and objectives which are also all weighted differently. It sounds complicated but it's quite binary.

To put it simply, people change when:

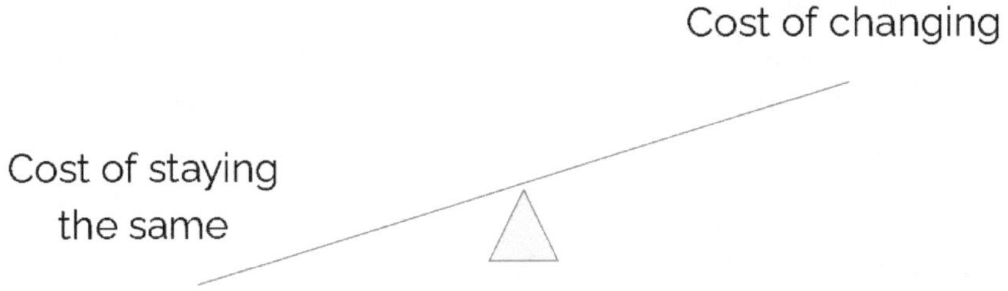

This diagram should illustrate it better. Like a teeter-totter, if the cost of staying the same (left) outweighs the cost of changing (right), people are willing to make the switch. This isn't a purely logical exercise; emotional perception also carries weight in this equation. Here are some factors that influence the

Cost of staying the same:

- Risk of competitors stealing their customers.
- Fines/penalties for non-compliance (your solution helps with).
- Frustration, challenges, and difficulty with their current method for solving the problem.
- Time wasted.
- The financial cost of doing it the old/manual/slow way.

- Lost opportunity.

Cost of changing:

- Price.
- Tedious approval process/chain.
- Learning curve for the new solution.
- Resistance to adoption.
- Risk aversion.
- Fear of the unknown (or unfamiliar).
- Complications with existing workflow, process, and tools.

Hence, to sell someone and get them to change, you can either

1. Emphasize and elaborate on the cost of staying the same.

- Uncover needs, highlight how pressing their problem is, their inconveniences, the cost of inaction, or missed opportunities. Show them how your solution will alleviate it.
- Alternatively, paint a picture that helps them envision how much better their situation could be (their ROI for switching).

Or,

2. Make it as easy as possible for them to change.
It's often easier to focus on highlighting ROI (missed opportunities) or pain because it can be accomplished through adjustments in sales or marketing messaging. Although this is important, selling into a business can be expedited by minimizing the pain of changing instead of focusing solely on the pain of staying the same. Think about it: The lower the cost of change, the lower the required pain threshold to tip the scales. Minimizing the pain of changing, however, can be tricky if you are unable to influence executives or managers who ultimately define your offerings.

Now that we understand the Decision Threshold, we can discuss the closely related concept below which targets #2: Make it as easy as possible for them to change.

THE THIN-EDGE-OF-THE-WEDGE

Like a door wedge. What "small thing" can you offer to get your foot in the door? Explore how you can start a working relationship with your client in the quickest and simplest way possible without involving too many decision-makers. When the cost of changing (or it is low risk to try or sample) is low, they'll require less persuasion to take the leap.

Below are some ideas and examples.

Ideas:

- Selling a smaller report/audit/assessment instead of a large implementation project.
- Offering a free trial.
- Lowering the risk of adoption with guarantees.
- Offering a more basic version of your solution.
- Doing a pilot program with a smaller department, region, or for a limited time, instead of rolling it out company-wide. Pilots reduce the risk by reducing the scope and scale of implementation. Give them a chance to see how this will play out in their organization first.

Real-world examples:

- Traction on Demand (acquired by Salesforce) sells Customer Relationship Management (CRM) and Enterprise Resource Planning (ERP) implementation services (primarily Salesforce). As you can imagine, CRM/ERP implementation is one of the most complex services to sell because migration requires tight integration with all other existing systems, organization-wide changes in behavior, comprehensive training to facilitate adoption, and is usually relatively expensive. Instead of opening a sales interaction by offering their implementation services, Traction offers their prospects a low-cost operations assessment report. This report would evaluate their existing processes, highlight recommendations and areas for improvement, and potential solutions or tools (including Salesforce) that aid with it. This report alone was valuable, even if they decided not to work with Traction for implementation.

It contained practical insights that companies could use, was much cheaper than committing to an expensive, comprehensive implementation project, and could be more easily approved by an individual decision-maker. Over 80% of companies that got an assessment report would close into a more formal implementation project.

- RunGo, a turn-by-turn running app that provides directions for your route, recently pivoted its focus to hotels. They now offer it as a tool for hotel guests to explore the cities they are visiting. When Craig (the founder) was pitching to hotels, he discovered the ideal price was $5,000 and nothing more. Why? Exceeding this amount would require approval from the head office. This slowed down the sales process. At $5,000 or below, local branches could approve implementation without needing to escalate to higher management. Understand your customer's buying process by collaborating with the advocate you're speaking with so you can expedite the sale.
- Mailchimp, the popular email marketing platform offers a free tier if you have <1,500 contacts. Usage-based Pricing (page 192) is tiered based on # of subscribers if you exceed it.
- Tempur-Pedic, one of the most highly recommended mattress brands in America, actually started with pillows. While this is an oversimplification of their origin story, these pillows were essentially miniaturized mattresses for your head!
- HubSpot offers their CRM for free and upsells HubSpot Marketing & Sales (which is also priced in tiers based on # of contacts in your CRM).
- Calendly offers freemium accounts where you can create 1 calendar type. Other premium features for team calendars are unlocked through upgrades.

ASSIGNMENT

Take a moment to evaluate your current offerings. How can you better highlight the cost of staying the same vs. reduce the cost of changing (think Thin-Edge-Of-The-Wedge) to make it easier for your prospects to convert?

Notes:

STARTUP SALES + CUSTOMER DISCOVERY/DEVELOPMENT

Most startups begin with 80% marketing, 20% sales. Not because that's the right approach, but because that's the easy approach. Selling is difficult and we avoid situations and tasks that make us uncomfortable. It's easier to start with marketing because you don't have to face direct rejection and can easily fool yourself into feeling productive through busywork. Being busy and being productive aren't the same.

Instead, if your business is new, you should focus on a sales-heavy approach. Not only because it helps generate the immediate cash flow necessary for survival but because sales help you learn the most about your market and your customers.

If you're familiar with the Lean Startup methodology, you've heard of "Customer Discovery/Development". Early sales are a form of customer discovery (Read Running Lean by Ash Maurya and The Lean Startup by Eric Ries if you'd like to learn more about it). Many entrepreneurs are comfortable conducting customer discovery interviews, but once they feel the need to sell, they crawl into their defensive shells. The misconception here is that many believe

Customer Discovery = Asking + Listening

Sales = Telling + Selling

Truth is, they're not separate, they're a continuation. You only happen to stop at asking + listening in the early days because you don't have anything to sell yet.

The second important thing to realize is that everything doesn't have to happen in a single interaction/conversation (and often won't). Once you accept that, the pressure is off the table and you can focus on truly understanding the prospect and receiving feedback. When doing customer discovery, you're encouraged to focus on listening not pitching, to learn about what's in their head before seeding ideas or soliciting feedback. Your objective is to understand their challenges and identify the root cause/motivations (page 24) of their problems (instead of addressing superficial symptoms). It's the same as the (A)SSESSMENT process taught in needs-based selling methodologies.

As a startup, you're trying to figure out your ideal customer, market, or decision-maker, their buying process, their objections, the main selling points or features of your solution, and the right price for it, etc. There's no better way to do that than by speaking to a prospect face-to-face and hearing them describe their problems, opinions, objections, and concerns in their own words.

You can't do that with marketing. It's more of a 1-sided conversation. If you put out an advertisement and see a lack of success, it's hard to tell if it's because of the wrong copy (messaging), because you're advertising to the wrong audience, or because your solution doesn't actually solve their problem.

Starting with sales helps you learn more about your prospects and gain the knowledge you need to shape marketing. If you start with a heavy focus on marketing, you're hitting the ground running with a lot of untested assumptions.

Once you've established

- A decent brand reputation,
- Worked out the kinks of *problem-solution fit*: are you going after the right problem or target customer? Is your solution solving it the right way? Are you using the right messaging and words your prospects resonate with?
- *Product-market fit*: are you using the right channels? Is there actual and active demand?
- *Business model fit*: are your unit economics/prices sustainable?

You can then aim to move back towards the ideal 80% marketing, 20% sales ratio (ideal mostly because sales is resource-hungry). When you've established a reputation, marketing can do most of the nurturing, qualification, and even conversion (if possible), and you can turn your sales engine into an onboarding/admissions/customer support process.

GROWTH ENGINES

In his book, The Lean Startup, Eric Ries introduces 3 main models of user and customer growth for any business: PAID, VIRAL, and STICKY.

These strategies are not independent and can be applied in parallel. However, it's important to identify your primary growth engine, as it will yield the best ROI and produce results more quickly. Also, you don't need to attempt everything simultaneously.

Here is a table with explanations and examples for each:

Growth Engine	Explanation and Examples
PAID	A form of push marketing. Interruptive, designed to get prospects to notice you. Works well if prospects *easily understand the inherent value of your solution without needing to experience it first.*
	Most common in the form of advertisements. Product placement in movies and booths at trade shows also falls under Paid.
VIRAL	VIRAL isn't about content that gets distributed widely. VIRAL is primarily a reference to how something gets spread from person to person, like a virus. And like viruses, Eric mentions, the spread is *not optional.* Suitable if your solution *needs to be experienced firsthand* in order to understand its value, is in a *competitive market, and it's hard to communicate how you're different*, or is something that *prospects aren't aware* of.
	Consultants, coaches, agencies, and education programs most commonly fall under this category.

	Other examples include: a new flavor of wine, a life-changing personal development program, a level of service that exceeds expectations, doing thc samc thing but with better quality, a new technology, or a novel/innovative/better way of solving a traditional problem.
STICKY	Growth through retention and increased word of mouth. *Solutions that generate recurring revenue* benefit the most from focusing on this engine.
	Examples include memberships (gym), subscriptions (Netflix), refillable products a.k.a sunk money consumables (Brita replacement water filters), rentals, and products that require servicing (car).

Let's skip PAID since it primarily pertains to marketing-related initiatives and take a closer look at VIRAL and STICKY.

VIRAL ENGINE

Eric differentiates viral growth from word-of-mouth (organic), in his words:

> *"Distinct from the simple word-of-mouth growth… Instead, products that exhibit viral growth depend on person-to-person transmission as a necessary consequence of normal product use. Customers are not intentionally acting as evangelists; they are not necessarily trying to spread the word about the product. Growth happens automatically as a side effect of customers using the product."*

However, it's important to distinguish between VIRAL vs. word-of-mouth (I'll elaborate more under the STICKY ENGINE, page 163). I would like to introduce a framework here because there are elements in it that will give you ideas for designing offerings that share themselves.

STEPPS

What makes a campaign viral? Why do some social media posts or news receive more attention and discussion than others? What motivates people to share? Jonah Berger's STEPPS framework from his book "Contagious: Why Things Catch On" is an excellent tool for increasing shareability or referability. It's not limited to designing marketing campaigns; it can also be directly integrated into your offering.

SOCIAL CURRENCY	What makes the sharer look good and want to spread the word?
TRIGGERS	What keeps it top of mind and keeps them talking?
EMOTION	Induce sharing through a heightened sense of arousal.
PUBLIC	Make opinions and behaviors visible. If people can see it, they will want to imitate it.
PRACTICAL VALUE	Adding value to the receiver.
STORIES	Incorporate a narrative.

Let us go through the STEPPS below and a few examples for each. If you're interested in a more in-depth exploration and additional detailed examples do consider reading Jonah's relatively short book.

A quick reminder from Jonah before we dive in:

"Influencers help, but alone, aren't sufficient… You're truly viral if you can get the average person to want to talk about you."

SOCIAL CURRENCY
Consider how you can:

- Define the inner *remarkability* of your solution or campaign (giveaway competitions or free upgrades).

- Make people feel like insiders who have *exclusive* information no one else has (closed or private invitation-only groups tend to grow more quickly than open or public groups that anyone can join).
- Invoke a sense of *scarcity*.
- Or give them *status* (people love to brag) through gamification: quantify performance.

TRIGGERS
Should happen often, in close proximity to your offerings, and shouldn't already be strongly associated with something else.

Examples from the book include the Kit Kat slogan, 'Have a break, have a Kit Kat,' which associates the snack with break time, and Budweiser's 'Wassup?' ad (https://youtu.be/HDB2pA76yfw), which associates the beverage with the slang commonly used by male Generation Xers at parties.

(Budweiser's 'Wassup?' ad)

EMOTIONS
A heightened state of arousal can lead to increased sharing. Marketers, as well as salespeople, frequently opt to evoke positive emotions or highlight the pleasure and benefits of their offerings, rather than resorting to negative emotions or emphasizing pain. They fear doing so

associates their brand with negativity and potentially deters customers.

However, individuals perceive benefits differently. A tool that saves time might appeal to one person as an opportunity to dedicate more time to their health, to another as a chance to be more productive, and to yet another as an opportunity to spend more time with their family. Conversely, pain is often more relatable.

Negative emotions can be employed effectively both to increase sharing and to more persuasively engage our prospects, provided we understand how to do it correctly. The key lies not merely in informing them that your solution alleviates their pain. Instead, you must guide prospects through a transformative journey: assist them in recognizing their pain, demonstrate how your solution addresses it, and lead them to their desired state of pleasure. This approach allows you to be associated with the transformation rather than the pain.
In Jonah's book, he shares the key discovery that it's not about positive vs. negative emotions; instead, sharing is correlated with how arousing an emotion is. For example, contentment is positive but non-arousing, whereas frustration (voicing complaints) is negative but arousing. Content that speaks to the latter is more likely to be shared.

That said, I'm not suggesting fear-mongering (page 81). Instead, I want to encourage you to leverage emotion by focusing on the *why* (both objectives and motivations) that underlies what your customer is trying to accomplish with your solution. Why is your solution meaningful to them? What does it empower them to achieve?

Google's "Parisian Love" ad (https://youtu.be/nnsSUqgkDwU) is a great example.

PUBLIC

Is about increasing visibility. This creates social proof and further drives adoption. If thoughts and beliefs are private, you organize an event, or if your solution is used transiently, consider how you might generate visible *behavioral residue.*

Examples include the ALS Ice Bucket Challenge, "I voted" stickers, and "Sent via iPhone".

PRACTICAL VALUE
Focuses on the receiver but may also overlap with **S**OCIAL CURRENCY which emphasizes the sharer. How can you help the receiver make better or more confident decisions, save time, save money, earn more money, avoid costly mistakes, or have a good/better experience? The key here is to be specific. If it's too general, people will struggle to think of who to share it with.

For instance, a guide on choosing shoes vs. a guide on choosing ballerina shoes. Despite targeting a narrower audience, the latter will get shared more as readers can readily identify who would benefit from it.

STORIES
Are shared more than facts. Discover compelling stories and integrate them into your campaign. These narratives could revolve around your customer's journey to empowerment with the help of your solution, your company's origin story, or your impact story (highlighting the lives you are positively affecting through your #dogoodbusiness).

Publicity stunts may get you a lot of attention but the story gets blurred as they are shared and passed along. The Evian Roller Babies (https://youtu.be/ni8GI5NxPu8) and Progressive Insurance Radio Ad (https://youtu.be/Yz4lUXpeI_U) are some examples of bizarre attention-grabbing campaigns not connected to a compelling story. Despite garnering high viewership, they are ineffective because people may remember the ad but often forget the associated brand.

(Evian Roller Babies)

Instead, a good story should be related to your solution and ensure that your brand remains a key part of what sticks. Google's Parisian Love ad mentioned before, Dove Evolution (https://youtu.be/KN2yunRynks), and Bertha Benz (https://youtu.be/vsGrFYD5Nfs) are some excellent examples of storytelling that seamlessly associate the brand with the message.

(Dove Evolution Ad)

Case Study: Dropbox

Dropbox is a well-recognized example of the VIRAL ENGINE of Growth. In their early days, they began with traditional paid marketing but found little success. Despite this, user acquisition continued to thrive. Upon closer inspection, they realized people struggled to grasp their novel way of file sharing through the cloud. Traditional ads couldn't effectively convey the value of their platform. Instead, growth was driven by users telling their friends how amazing it was. As a result, they abandoned their traditional marketing efforts and focused instead on making it as easy as possible for their users to spread the love.

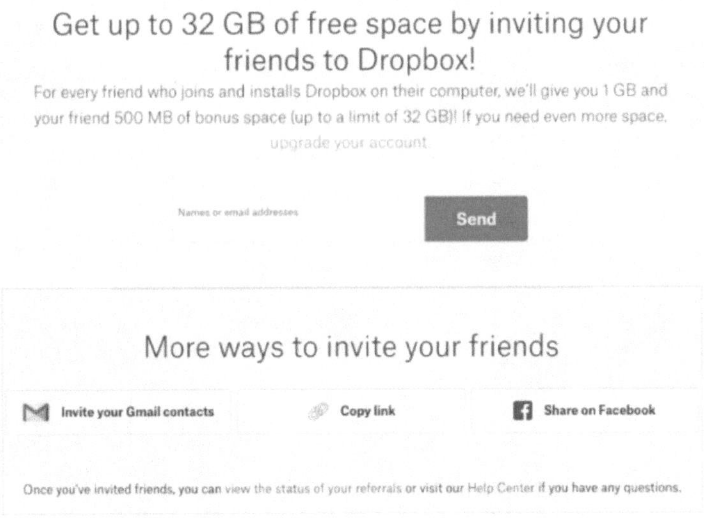

Get up to 32 GB of free space by inviting your friends to Dropbox!

For every friend who joins and installs Dropbox on their computer, we'll give you 1 GB and your friend 500 MB of bonus space (up to a limit of 32 GB)! If you need even more space, upgrade your account.

Names or email addresses

Send

More ways to invite your friends

Invite your Gmail contacts

Copy link

Share on Facebook

Once you've invited friends, you can view the status of your referrals or visit our Help Center if you have any questions.

(Screenshot of Dropbox's referral page)

Notice the benefit to the sharer (**S**OCIAL CURRENCY) + the receiver (**P**RACTICAL VALUE). They also made it easy to share (simply enter their email and hit send, integrating Gmail contacts, copy the sharing link with a simple click of a button, sharing to Facebook). Finally, they make it easy for you to follow up on the status of your referrals.

Other notable key lessons from his book include:

- You don't necessarily need to include all elements of STEPPS to go viral, but in general, the more you include, the better
- It doesn't only apply to ad campaigns; virality can also be built directly into your offerings. Some examples include: Please Don't Tell (a speakeasy cocktail bar in New York City), Duolingo (the language learning app), and Election Ink. All of which have directly built elements of virality into their product and service offerings to increase shareability.

ASSIGNMENT

What are some elements from STEPP that you can incorporate into your solution or campaigns?

Notes:

Here are some additional ideas:

Buy 1, give 1
If you have a solution that people need to first try or experience to understand what makes it special, you could run a "buy 1, give 1" (not "get 1") campaign. In this campaign, you would apply a model similar to a pay-it-forward campaign. Instead of giving prospects an additional product when they make a purchase, you have them give away a free product to someone nearby. By doing so, you're integrating referability directly into the transaction, encouraging them to advocate on your behalf and feel good while doing so.

Free Service for an Introduction
Offering a free service in exchange for a brief introduction or explanation. If you have an emcee or translator training program, you could offer a free emcee or translator for an event in exchange for a few seconds or minutes to acknowledge your company.

This gives the prospect a free service, gives you publicity, and is a live learning experience for your emcees. Triple win! It also enables you to show, rather than tell, by allowing attendees to witness the quality and experience the difference first-hand.

Automate exposure
"P.S. Get your free e-mail at Hotmail" was inserted into the signatures of emails sent by those who used their service (before they were sold to Microsoft). It increased visibility (**P**UBLIC) and helped them explode! They got 1 million sign-ups in 6 months, hit the 2 million mark 5 weeks later, and had 12 million users about 18 months after launching. Eventually selling to Microsoft for $400 million. The modern-day version of this is "Sent from my iPhone". PayPal is another example Eric mentions in his book. When you send money to someone using PayPal, they are automatically exposed to it.

Network effect of social platforms (Reddit, LinkedIn, etc.)

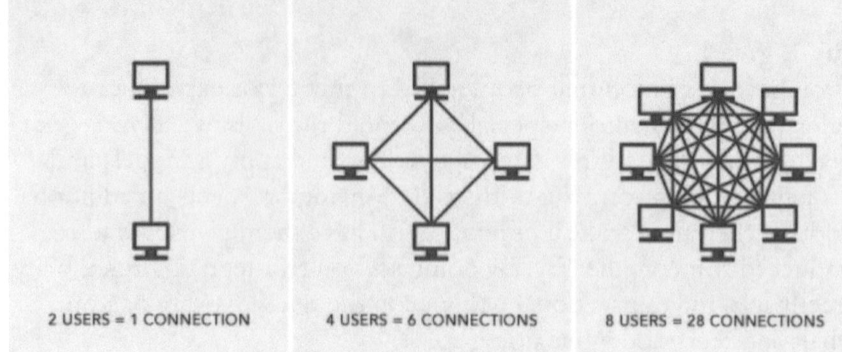

(Network Effect: Source Unknown)

The more people are on it, the more others want to join. This is to avoid missing out and because the platform becomes more valuable when there are more people in your network already using it; this happens because there's an increased amount of content from people you're interested in and more opportunities for introductions.

Be strategic and selective about your ambassadors

Fashion brands like Nike, Spanx, and Eileen Fisher, as well as brands that leverage status such as GoPro, Bang & Olufsen, and Tesla, also exemplify viral growth as a byproduct of usage. Prospective customers are influenced by the desire to purchase when they observe current customers using these products (**P**UBLIC).

It's not about gauging your customers or encouraging unsustainable fast fashion, I share these examples here instead to encourage you to be strategic about how you position your brand, who you choose to go after, and how you can make your offerings more visible.

EXPERIENTIAL SELLING/MARKETING

Marketing, as we traditionally think of it, is paid advertising and social media. These mediums are only effective IF it's easy to communicate the value of your offerings through words and imagery. This is only possible IF you have a very clear (who it's for, what the outcomes are, how it works) and unique (clearly differentiated from the many alternatives) offering.

Unfortunately, although we all think we are different or better and communicate it well, it's rarely the case. This is especially true for many service businesses, whereby clients only best understand the value and quality difference in our offerings by experiencing it first-hand.

Words and imagery aren't sufficient and convincing enough to capture and articulate experiences. Hence, organizations with these types of offerings tend to get most of their deal flow through referrals or word-of-mouth instead. Put yourself in your prospect's shoes. How would you choose between product A or B, or consultant A or B? They all toot their own horn and claim to be the best, but you still wouldn't trust them. You would make your decision based on:

- Reviews or testimonials, especially if you see something positive said by someone you know and trust.
- Being referred or recommended by someone in your network.
- Having "tried" before you buy, such as attending an event, workshop, or booking a consultation session run by the organization that left you with a positive impression.

The former 2 are indicative of you making your judgment based on the experience of others, and the latter on your personal experience. Ergo, show, don't tell. Instead of trying to communicate the value of your offerings, consider how you can give people a means to experience it.

Stop wasting your time (and money) on traditional paid marketing. You might be sticking to it because you believe it is predictable: The more money you put into it, the more leads you get. That's not always true. You could make a lot of noise and it will get you noticed, but the # of leads you'll get isn't proportional to your spend. This approach only works well with physical products or unique solutions that can be easily communicated with imagery/text.

Instead, focus more on fostering word-of-mouth and referrals. Doing so does not mean that you lose control of deal flow. You might believe you can't control the volume of referrals you get. That's also not true; there are direct activities you can do that will predictably generate regular referrals.

For instance, if you sell entrepreneurship training courses or programs: events, workshops or webinars, panel discussions, fireside chats, demo day, info sessions, and free consultation or strategy sessions are some of the different ways to expose prospects to what working with you is like, the energy of your community, the strength of your network, the knowledge of your experts. These offer a sample of your experience.

Even though these aren't the paid advertisements or social postings that we're used to, they all still cost time and money and result in predictable sales. It's still a form of marketing/sales.

Here are more ideas and examples:

Proactively solicit reviews/referrals
When was the last time you left a positive review? We're more inclined to leave negative reviews. Instead of waiting for customers to review or refer organically, a sincere, personal, and unpressured solicitation at the right time (see: Positive "Milestones", page 170) will greatly increase the number of reviews and referrals for your organization.

The best advocate you can find is someone who has already experienced your solution.

Share their stories
Instead of tooting your own horn, actively share your customers' stories and their transformations. Better yet, have them do the sharing. Not only speak about their transformation but also what they learned and how your offering helped them in their journey.

Explore ways to integrate referrals directly into your offerings
For a detailed example, you might have heard of personal

development, life-changing, or leadership programs like Landmark or PSI. They are highly experience-driven, as participants walk away with something different depending on their initial circumstances, how they interpret the lessons, how they apply them to their personal situation, and what actions they take. Many of these programs even come across as somewhat "cult-ish" because participants who experience eye-opening transformations are overly enthusiastic about encouraging their friends and family members to go through the same.

I'm not a fan of how they design word-of-mouth, but there are some elements worth learning from and some improvements that could be made to make it less cult-ish.

> *Disclaimer:* Many of the lessons and frameworks they share are truly valuable. Often, the impact is greatest for those who are "broken". Although I use the word broken, it would be incorrect to describe these individuals as flawed or damaged. Many relationship issues or our sense of self-worth stem not from personal flaws but instead from an incorrect mindset or misattributed meaning to events that have occurred to us. The fewer problems, misconceptions, blindspots, incorrect beliefs, etc., you have, the less life-changing such a program will be for you.
>
> *Worth mimicking:* They build open sessions directly into their program. There's an evening where participants can (and are encouraged to) bring guests to join the program. This allows guests to hear what participants have learned and listen to the real life-changing impact that it has had on their friend, his or her family, and other participants. Not only does this provide prospects with a chance to get a taste of the experience, but it's also designed to facilitate and encourage word-of-mouth.
>
> Another thing done well here is how they manage expectations and build trust. It's made clear for program participants to maintain confidentiality regarding the sensitive and very personal things that others share. The organizers also make it clear that participants should only share what they're comfortable with in this open session, as they're exposing

themselves to outsiders who have not committed to the same oath of confidentiality.

What they could change: They do a lot to encourage participants to invite and share the value with others; however, they don't provide much guidance on how to properly share without coming across as overbearing.

Another idea that I've yet to have the opportunity to implement is to do something similar for mastermind groups. In groups that I facilitate, we have hotseats for each session. These hotseats are 30-minute presentations designed to give a single company room for a deep dive into their problem and to receive detailed feedback. To encourage word-of-mouth and to expose outsiders to the experience, we could run occasional open sessions whereby existing members could invite a friend whom they believe might benefit from being on the hotseat. This also gives members of the group an opportunity to be creative and work on solving new problems. By looking at someone else's problem, it helps them put their own in perspective and come up with new ideas.

Community Events

A rising tide lifts all boats. Instead of promoting your events solely for your own agenda, explore collaborative events that aim to collectively excite and educate the greater community.

Vancouver Startup Week is one such example. It's a week-long event with workshops, startup open offices, competitions, and even parties. It exposes and elevates the entire sector whilst promoting collaboration and referrals between the various organizations that serve similar customers.

Enable your offerings to sell themselves

Ultimately, if you have something amazing, there's no substitute for letting prospects experience it first-hand.

- We don't need to look far to see how Apple has reengineered their retail space to prioritize the prospect's shopping experience.
- The Jet Business is another great example. Instead of relying on selling directly to CEOs or wealthy decision-makers, they've found success by designing an immersive retail experience that welcomes both influencers (not social media influencers, but individuals who sway a prospect's decision) and decision-makers to experience first-hand what's special about the planes they sell.

(Life-size fuselage mockup in their retail showroom. Photo credit: Oliver Pohlmann)

- BabyLand General Hospital for the Cabbage Patch Kids dolls leveraged retail to create an immersive storytelling experience for their toys.

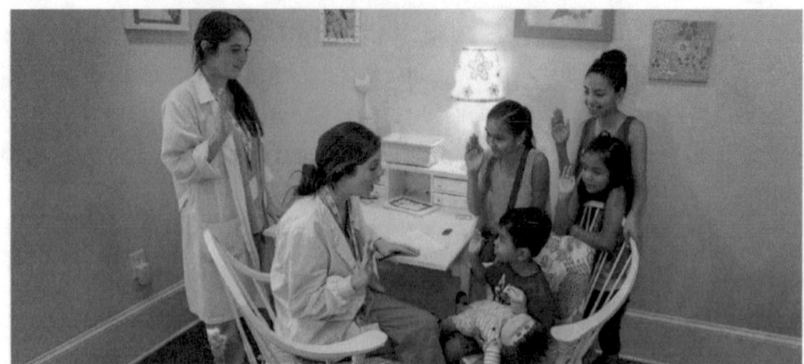

(Children taking an oath of adoption at the BabyLand General Hospital adoption office).

Build strategic partnerships

Look for other organizations that also serve your prospects. Find ways to add value to them, refer to them, or amplify their message. They will gladly reciprocate if your offerings are a fit for their customers. Just like reviews and referrals, it's also a good idea to proactively solicit for them (in moderation, of course).

STICKY ENGINE

Another way to grow is by enhancing the quality of your offering and improving the customer experience. Satisfied customers are more loyal (improved retention) and it also increases organic word-of-mouth (WoM) referrals.

WoM is about encouraging customers to actively and intentionally (unlike VIRAL which happens as an involuntary byproduct of usage) share or refer. All elements of STEPPS can be applied here as well. Eric distinguishes the two as distinct but considers WoM a form of VIRAL. I've intentionally included WoM under STICKY as opposed to VIRAL because I interpret VIRAL primarily as increasing exposure and providing prospects with an experience. However, with WoM, if you don't offer a good solution or a high level of service, people won't make referrals, no matter how much you encourage them to do so.

It's important to remember that WoM and retention are interconnected; focusing on one without the other won't drive substantial growth. Furthermore, WoM isn't constant; it is proportional to the size of your customer base. Therefore, by improving retention, you maintain a larger customer base, which also leads to more WoM. It starts to compound and you experience exponential growth when your WoM growth rate exceeds your churn rate (a.k.a. attrition rate, the rate at which your customers leave. Downgrades are also a form of churn). Notice the use of the word "rate" here, which is expressed as a percentage (%), not as an absolute number. For example:

100 customers and 10 leave this month	Churn rate = 10%
1000 customers and 30 leave	Churn rate = 3%

Churn increases as you scale, which is normal. Having 30 customers leave versus 10 isn't a bad thing as long as your overall churn rate (%) is maintained or lower, as WoM will also grow as you scale.

To learn more, read this post by Lars Lofgren: https://larslofgren.com/engines-of-growth/

Some businesses can't avoid high churn, despite high customer success/experience (e.g., dating sites, job placement agencies, coaches). Their very nature of problem-solving leads to customers leaving once they're satisfied. That's completely normal and you shouldn't attempt to force a subscription model on a business that isn't fundamentally a subscription business with ongoing value. Instead, focus on other metrics like:

- #of qualified leads each month
- Close rate
- Customer success rate
- Referral rate

Besides increasing retention, you can also reduce churn and even achieve a *negative churn rate* through upselling & cross-selling (page 198). A negative churn rate occurs when you generate more revenue from existing customers than the revenue you lose due to cancellations and downgrades.

Here's a visual elaboration of negative churn:

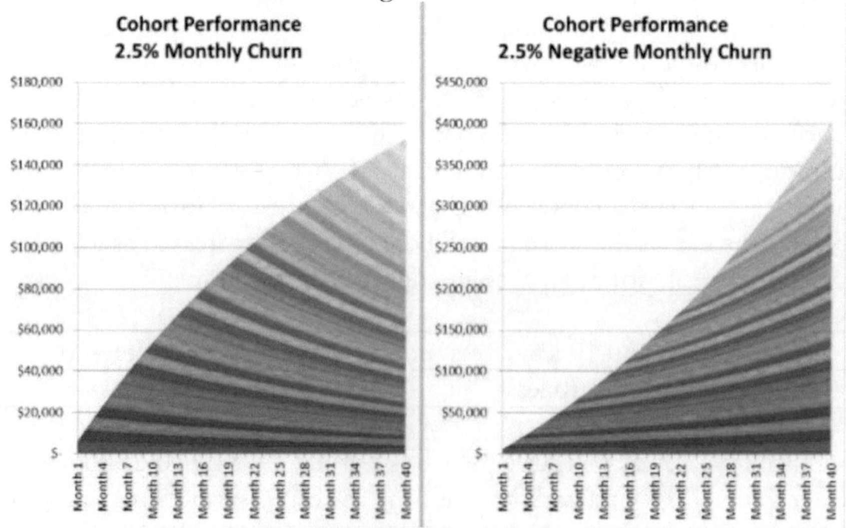

The graph above illustrates the growth rate of a company with a constant acquisition rate (lines indicate new customers acquired per cohort, i.e. # of new customers each month):

Left: With positive churn, the graph plateaus, ultimately

creating a growth ceiling. More revenue is lost through cancellations and downgrades than the revenue generated from existing customers.

Right: With negative churn, you observe the characteristic hockey stick trajectory representing exponential growth. The increased revenue generated from existing customers exceeds the revenue lost through cancellations and downgrades.

Although we're examining 'hockey stick' financial projections, it's perfectly fine not to have or aspire to achieve them. Not every business needs to or is equipped to handle such rapid growth. Exponential growth of this magnitude usually necessitates venture capital and frequently disrupts the organization if it hires too rapidly and implements too many new initiatives.

IMPROVE RETENTION/COMPETITIVE DEFENSIBILITY

How can you make your solution more "sticky"?

DON'T use
Manipulative Dark Patterns
The practice where a cancellation process is intentionally made difficult. For example, making it challenging to locate cancellation buttons, requiring customers to call in and cancel, and, even worse, inadequately staffing these cancellation call centers, leading to long wait times for customers on hold."

DO instead:
Develop Feedback Loops for Your Offerings
Never assume you know what customers want; be open to listening and understanding their needs. This is crucial for developing the best possible offerings and user experience. This will also enable you to better integrate your offering into their existing habits and lifestyles.

The variety of tools at your disposal includes, but are not limited to: interviews (page 144), user observations, surveys, ratings, and reviews.

Integrate

Consider how you can better tie your solution into your customer's existing workflows/systems/processes/technologies. The tighter your integration, the harder it is to switch to an alternative because it would require reorientation, training, and reintegration.

For example, if you sell accounting software, consider providing features such as invoicing, payroll management, or POS (Point of Sale) solutions. These can be included or offered as strategic cross-sells (page 199), adding more value to your customers whilst reducing the likelihood of them seeking alternatives.

Eventbrite is another example, they offer not only event publishing but also attendee tracking (custom registration questions, check-in), pre/post-event communication, and event marketing.

HubSpot is yet another example, they are not only a CRM, but also a landing page builder, a social media dashboard, workflow automation, a sales pipeline, and more.

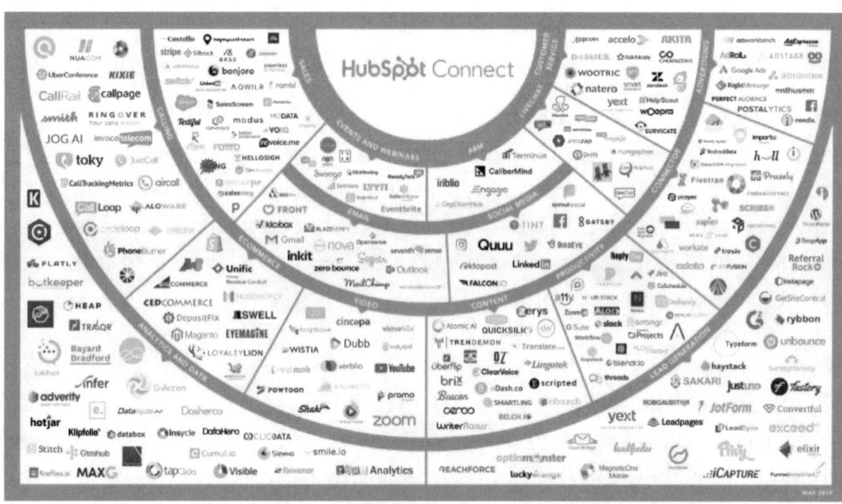

(Network of integrations through HubSpot Connect)

Create Communities or Nurture Existing Ones

Leverage community mechanics whereby you're getting your users/customers to be a part of something bigger than themselves (and even possibly something bigger than your brand). Communities are sticky. It's hard for someone to move into another community (even if it's for a similar cause/topic that they're passionate about) because they've already established relationships and their reputation in their current community. All this needs to be done again from scratch if they migrate to another community.

Patagonia Action Works is a great example of an organization empowering the community to do good while strengthening the brand. It serves as a focal point for content & learning, connecting volunteers, discovering events, and more.

Cultivate a Strong Brand Identity

If you have a good solution, competitors *will* eventually move into your space. Ideas, design, and technology can be replicated. However, a reputation/brand is much harder to mimic. Be intentional and start cultivating your brand angle and identity early. Leverage Trademarks, Copyright, and Industrial Design strategically to strengthen and defend your brand.

Consumers will still prefer to buy from you if you've done a good job establishing trust, built a reputation around quality, and fostered a brand image that consumers resonate with. It's more important to move fast to establish this reputation early rather than being overly stealthy and hung up on patents.

Example: Allbirds isn't the first and certainly not the last sneaker company. However, they've done an excellent job of clearly cementing their brand identity in that space.

Activation & Habit Creation

Activation is slightly different from Acquisition. You could be great at marketing and getting someone to download your widget or buy your product, but if they never actually use it, they haven't truly "Activated".

Basic Activation would be a customer using your product and getting value out of it. For instance, booking a meeting using your software or going skiing with your new product. Take it further by identifying habitual Activation. I'll elaborate with an example:

> Foodee, a Vancouver-based corporate catering company, defined activation as the first time a customer would use their platform to make a catering order. They analyzed their long-term customers vs. customers that tried but discontinued shortly after, and discovered a key behavioral factor that separated the two. Those who had made at least 3 orders on their platform were much more likely to stay on as long-term customers. Learning about this enabled them to implement initiatives that better encouraged new users to get to that 3-order mark and become more loyal customers.

What's going on here? If you have a great solution that isn't used frequently, customers may still forget about it. Identifying your Habitual Activation point enables you to implement initiatives that will help keep your solution top-of-mind for your customers and create a habit around using your product every time they face the need for your solution in their daily lives.

What could this look like in implementation? Say you have a healthy breakfast cereal product. To encourage repeat purchases of your cereal, you could include a collectible giveaway with the purchase of each box. This would encourage customers to buy more often to collect them and, while doing so, entrench your brand as a staple product to get every time they're at the grocery store. That's just one idea. Of course, success depends heavily on understanding your target users and what they would value as a collectible in this giveaway campaign.

ASSIGNMENT

What specific ideas, initiatives, partnerships, or campaigns do you want to explore to improve retention?

Notes:

HOW TO INCREASE WOM REFERRALS?

Solicit testimonials and reviews
Obvious, but if you aren't already doing so, be proactive, intentional, and confident in asking for them. If customers like you, they'll be happy to reciprocate.

The best time to ask for one is after a positive "milestone". You'll need to identify what this looks like for your solution(s). These solicitations can be set up to trigger automatically.

Examples include: after a customer has used your solution to launch their first campaign, or after you've sent a monthly report showing how much time they've saved or the additional revenue you've helped them generate.

Feature *them*, not *you*. Stories > Case Studies
Interview your customers, not with the sole purpose of creating case studies or testimonials, but rather to create a platform or space that will elevate or feature them. Most people will be happy to receive more exposure (**S**OCIAL CURRENCY: Status) and gladly participate.

Of course, during your interviews, it's beneficial to ask them to elaborate on how your solution has aided in their journey.

They'll also often willingly share their interview with their network, so make it as easy as possible for them by providing pre-written blurbs or images they can use.

Be a collaborative partner
Are there other organizations that serve your customers?

For example, if you are a wedding planner, partnering with makeup artists, photo/videographers, and popular wedding rental venues can be highly beneficial. Be generous with referrals to them if you have no intention of providing those services.

If you want to take it a step further, you can also track and follow up (**T**RIGGERS) on the referrals you've made to improve the quality of your referrals. This also helps keep you top-of-mind with them, signals your genuine interest in supporting them, and communicates your value as a partner to them (if they can see you've made lots of good referrals that have converted). They'll gladly reciprocate by sending people who are a fit for your services over to you. Similarly, provide them with feedback on the people they send your way. It demonstrates your responsiveness, that you treat referrals with care, and it also helps them improve the quality of their referrals. The same can be applied to products. If you sell a kayak, consider partnering with a paddle manufacturer for co-referrals.

If possible, explore how you can build referring directly into the experience of your offerings

The previously mentioned buy 1, give 1 (page 155) campaign (**S**OCIAL CURRENCY + **P**RACTICAL VALUE) is one such example for product companies. An example for a group coaching business would be to have an open session where the group can invite an outsider to participate and receive feedback.

In their early days, Gmail employed this strategy by allowing people to create an account only if they received an invitation from an existing Gmail user (**S**OCIAL CURRENCY: Exclusivity). Once they joined, they were given a limit of 5 referral codes that they could use to invite others (**P**RACTICAL VALUE).

Caution! Providing incentives like cash or credits, which are a form of external motivation, decreases referrals. They offset the intrinsic desire (or internal motivation) for someone to make a referral because they genuinely believe it's valuable to the receiver. People want to share on their own accord. For a more detailed explanation and supporting evidence, consider reading Jonah Berger's book.

Should the receiver be aware of the sharer's reward, it also decreases their perception of value for what's being referred, as the act of referral is seen as inauthentic. My personal experience aligns with this. In the early days of Spring Activator, we explored implementing referral credits for our programs, only to see referrals drop to 0.

ASSIGNMENT

What specific ideas, initiatives, partnerships, or campaigns do you want to explore to improve WoM?

Notes:

To summarize, if you're prioritizing STICKY, increase:

- Retention by
    - Improving your solution
    - Enhancing your customer's experience
    - Being strategic and intentional with your brand identity
    - Nurturing community
    - Integrating with their existing workflows, processes, and other solutions.
- Average Revenue Per User (ARPU) or Lifetime Value (LTV) of your customers through upsells and cross-sells.
- WoM (improving your solution and customer experience will also contribute to this): make it easier for customers to share and make referrals (recall STEPPS for some ideas).

ASSIGNMENT

Besides WoM and retention, what improvements would you like to make to your offering or customer experience? What common complaints or requests do your customers have? Use these to identify potential customer experience enhancements and value-added upsell or cross-sell opportunities.

Notes:

Notes:

Growth Engines Summary

It's important to understand the differences between PAID, VIRAL, and STICKY Engines of Growth because when growth stagnates, most companies default to pushing more money into sales and marketing (PAID ENGINE), which isn't effective for every type of solution.

And although VIRAL seems identical to WoM, they are distinct. The former involves passive transmission while the latter encourages active sharing. The metrics you track and campaigns you create for VIRAL vs. WoM are different, utilizing varying resources and approaches. In addition to WoM, the STICKY ENGINE includes other elements such as negative churn and retention strategies, which are relevant primarily to businesses with recurring revenue.

As Eric says in his book, it's possible to implement multiple Engines of Growth simultaneously; however, it's beneficial (especially for newer companies) to focus on the one that best applies to your business.

Here's a quick recap:

If you	Engine of Growth	Initiatives
• Have a product • or unique service that's easily describable/visual.	**PAID**	• Traditional marketing • Visual ads
• Are in a relatively competitive market, • have a unique and hard-to-understand solution, • or require people to experience your offering firsthand before they recognize its value.	**VIRAL**	• Explore **S**OCIAL CURRENCY, **E**MOTION, **P**UBLIC, and **P**RACTICAL VALUE from STEPPS. • Give prospects a sample of the experience. • Can you leverage a network effect? • Can you speak to status or a sense of identity?
Your offering generates recurring revenue	**STICKY**	Improve WoM: • Proactive solicitation • Sharing stories • Partnerships Improve retention: • Brand identity • Community • Integrate Other: • Polish your solution & customer experience. • Explore value-add upsells and cross-sells.

♦♦♦

REVENUE OPTIMIZATION

Having identified your primary engine of growth, let's explore how you can maximize revenue. This will be relevant to you even if you're not generating revenue yet. It should provide you with ideas that might motivate you to change your offerings, pricing, or even your business model, which, in turn, will affect your sales process (page 250).

Eric's Engines of Growth approach focuses on growing your company through *customer acquisition* (even the STICKY Engine, as WoM is a core component of it). It's important for obvious reasons: you can't make more money without first having customers. However, we also need to pay attention to how to structure our unit economics. The days when investors were willing to support a company solely based on impressive acquisition metrics (glances at Snapchat) are long gone. Today's (and tomorrow's) investors want to see some evidence of a viable business model before they're willing to invest. If you're bootstrapping (building and growing your company without external funding from investors or loans), it's even more crucial to ensure you optimize revenue sooner rather than later.

Per Josh Kaufman's bestselling book, The Personal MBA, there are ONLY 4 ways of increasing revenue.

1. Increase the # of customers.
2. Increase average transaction size.
3. Increase the frequency of transactions.
4. Raise prices.

Sounds oversimplified but it's true, I've attempted to challenge the simplicity of this but every campaign or initiative I've been exposed to thus far can indeed be explained in these 4 ways. They are pretty straightforward so I'll jump right into specific initiatives and example campaigns that might help spark ideas for you.

INCREASING CUSTOMERS

Beyond your Engine of Growth, the following are some specific initiatives to explore:

TARGET MARKET

Expand to a new region: Are there any other areas that are easy to serve because they share the same time zone? Have opposing seasons that can offset your slow seasons? Or share similar culture or market characteristics?

or

Service a different customer type: For instance, if you have scheduling software for doctors, consider expanding to serve dentists as well.

ASSIGNMENT

What are some strategic regions worth exploring? Are there other customer archetypes you could also serve?

Notes:

CHANNELS
Are where you find your customers. Here's a sample of examples, grouped by type:

Physical Presence:	Retail, Wholesale, Trade shows, Magazines
Online Platforms:	E-commerce, Facebook, LinkedIn, Google
Direct Outreach:	Cold calling, Email drip campaigns
Educational Platforms:	Webinars, Workshops, Info sessions
Digital Content:	Landing pages, Podcasts, Video series, Blogs
Public Engagements:	Speaking engagements

Perhaps you're not reaching your customers in the right places. Test new/different channels for better *quality* leads. Some channels might:

1. Serve different purposes more effectively
Prospects at different stages of their decision-making process (page 235) prefer various mediums for getting their questions answered. For example, a blog or YouTube is excellent for basic education, while workshops or customized consultation calls are more effective for capturing prospects who are intent and ready to take action.

2. Have better conversion
You might find that only 2 of 10 people who viewed your ad on one channel visit your website, yet on another, 4 of 10 do.

3. Cost less
Advertising on LinkedIn is more expensive relative to Facebook (but it might be worth it IF the quality of leads justifies the cost).

4. Require less effort
A lead at the right stage of their decision-making process will require less convincing.

5. Lead to faster sales
Related to better conversion and less effort, but different. Prospects may be more active on certain channels when they're more ready to buy. For example, if you're a restaurant, prospects browsing on Google may only be looking for potential dining ideas vs. prospects browsing on Google Maps are more likely to already be in their car and looking for a place to eat nearby.

6. Be a better fit for your solution
Certain customer personas or communities are more active on specific channels.

7. Lead to more loyal customers
For example, customers who convert from a forum are often more analytical. They may also exhibit higher loyalty because they have already evaluated alternative options. As a result, they are less likely to experience buyer remorse or consider switching in the future, as they are already aware of the limitations of other alternatives.

You don't have to be on every channel. Instead, focus on the ones most effective for reaching *your* customers and meeting *your* objectives. Different channels serve different purposes; for instance, LinkedIn is great for thought leadership, while Google Pay-Per-Click (PPC) ads excel at attracting prospects actively searching for a solution. Not every business needs to be on social media, and some get by fine even without a website. The most important point is to be where your prospects are looking.

Related side note: Be cautious of marketing agencies that propose applying a generic setup framework, such as creating all your social accounts and websites. Of course, they'll want to do it all; they have a monetary interest in more work.

Focus on your primary channel while you experiment with other channels. To simplify how to identify the efficacy of a channel, you can focus on Customer Acquisition Cost (CAC) as a metric. Measure CAC separately for your different channels and find the lowest one.

The formula for calculating CAC is as follows:

$$\text{CAC} = \frac{\text{Total Marketing and Sales Expenses}}{\text{Number of New Customers Acquired}}$$

An oversimplified example, but assuming all other factors are equal: If you spend $50 on Facebook and the same amount on LinkedIn simultaneously, and Facebook yields you 2 customers while LinkedIn yields you 10, the CAC calculations would be as follows:

FB CAC = $25
LI CAC = $5 (WINNER!)

ASSIGNMENT

1. What channels are you currently utilizing?
2. If you aren't already, how can you measure the effectiveness of your channels?
3. What other channels are worth exploring?

Notes:

REFERRALS

Refer to page 170 for tips to improve WoM and STEPPS (page 148) for more ideas.

THOUGHT LEADERSHIP

If you're not already doing so, increase inbound leads by establishing yourself as a leader in your industry. Explore potential topics to address and mediums to use, such as podcasting, webinars, videos, blogging, or even writing a book. Additionally, explore guest speaking opportunities or consider participating as a subject matter expert at conferences. Exploring the above may also open up new acquisition channels for your business. Besides sharing your knowledge on the topic, are there any frameworks, models, templates, or guidelines you can pioneer?

FACILITATE REGULATORY COMPLIANCE

Not possible for everyone, but if you have an offering that benefits from specific regulatory changes or policies, consider how you can encourage or play a role in accelerating it, as it will lead to greater market penetration and expedite adoption. Here are a few real-world examples:

- Priopta, a consultancy specializing in Life Cycle Assessment (LCA) for green buildings, offers a unique perspective. While current industry standards only account for operational carbon (carbon emissions during a building's use), Priopta advocates accounting for "embodied carbon" in local regulations. This concept factors in the environmental footprint associated with the production and procurement of materials like concrete, steel, wood, glass, and insulation used in construction before a building's completion. Anthony, the founder of Priopta is also the founder of the Carbon Leadership Forum (CLF) British Columbia, a collaborative community and resource hub focused on addressing embodied carbon emissions in the construction and building industry. Anthony's significant contributions to this field have established him as one of the foremost experts on the subject, leading to frequent invitations to speak at universities and conferences, which, in turn, contribute to client acquisition as they naturally look to him as a trusted provider for a solution.

- A mentor I know of (who sold call recording hardware) shared how his business exploded after the government mandated that bank call centers record their customer service calls. I don't recall if he was directly involved in advocating for that mandate, but the point is to proactively create the right opportunities instead of passively hoping for the right timing.
- During my work visit to Vietnam in 2019, the Vietnamese government was implementing a ban on plastic take-out packaging in restaurants. Concurrently, AC-COOL, a company nurtured within the Foreign Trade University Innovation and Incubation Space (FIIS), was pioneering the development of bioplastics derived from agricultural waste. Positioned as one of the few bioplastics companies in Vietnam, they were primed to cater to the market once the regulations were enforced. Unfortunately, AC-COOL has since discontinued operations due to operational challenges brought about by COVID-19.

SHORTER SALES CYCLE(S)

Increases # of customers by speeding up the rate at which you close them. This is worthy of a subsection of its own because there's a lot to explore on this topic.

Conversion Rate Optimization (CRO) is the practice of improving the conversion rate of a particular step or Call to Action (CTA) in your sales process. Doing so not only helps capture more customers but also potentially speeds up their conversion process. I won't delve into CRO and optimizing CTAs in this section but will instead share ways to shorten the time it takes to convert a lead.

In my humble opinion, a sales cycle lasting more than three months is too long, even if you're dealing with traditional, highly regulated, or bureaucratic organizations. So, how can you address this?

Reduce # Of Steps In Your Sales Process.
The more steps or handoffs there are in your sales process, the longer it takes to convert a prospect. Consider which steps could be eliminated or shortened to reduce the time a prospect spends in each stage.

Also, remember that not every prospect needs to go through the same hoops before converting. Evaluate what's truly necessary and design a sales process that adapts to your prospect.

Budgeting Cycle/Purchasing Periods
When does their fiscal year end? Some organizations rush to deplete their budget at the end of their fiscal year.

When does their new budget get approved? At the start of a new budget cycle, they may also more readily spend or put out Requests For Proposals (RFPs).

If they're not at the right stage in their buying process, or if their purchasing schedule doesn't align, move them to "parking" as leads to be followed up with at a later time or move them back into the marketing funnel to be nurtured. Don't forget to set up automation that will remind you to follow up with them when the time is right.

Lead Scoring
The best response is a "Yes", the next best is "No". "Maybe" is a waste of time. Don't waste time and attention nurturing leads that are still on the fence. Engaging with unqualified leads unnecessarily lengthens your sales cycle because it inaccurately defines its starting point. If your prospect isn't ready to buy yet, leave them in the marketing funnel and only pursue them as a sales lead when they're ready.

That said, it's never too early to build relationships. However, prioritize your activities and efforts to match their readiness. Ensure they're only receiving what's relevant to them depending on where they are in their buyer's journey or decision-making process (page 235), and don't pester them to close if they're not ready.

We've already discussed lead qualification and the BANT framework (page 129). Let's now explore lead scoring: the practice of assigning a value (i.e. score) to help identify and prioritize "warmer" vs. "colder" leads that are closer to making a purchase. Here's an example:

Each time a prospect visits our website	+1 point
Prospect unsubscribes from email	-50 points

Prospect attends 3 or more workshops	+30 points
Prospect visits product page	+15 points
Prospect adds product to cart	+40 points

A prospect's overall score is a tally of individual scores associated with their actions and behaviors. Since you can't assign a value to an action or behavior that you're unable to observe or track, the effectiveness of your lead scoring will heavily depend on your data capture practices. The actions you choose to score and the values associated with specific actions vary across industries and solutions. There's no one-size-fits-all approach or best practice for lead scoring; instead, it's an evolving process that you'll refine over time as you gain a better understanding of which actions hold the most significance.

A good lead scoring model should take into consideration:

- Customer profile fit (page 128), accounting for characteristics in the BANT framework – BUDGET, AUTHORITY, NEED, and TIMELINE, that you can identify.
- Engagement behaviors that you can track. such as the # of pages viewed on your website, specific pages visited (e.g., product page, pricing page), the # of emails opened, email open rate, the # of times an email was forwarded, conversions from specific emails, form submissions, and downloads of lead magnets, among others.
- Intent behaviors (page 129), such as searching for solutions, visiting competitor websites, reading reviews, and comparing alternatives. These behaviors are often observed on external websites, not your own. To capture and utilize this valuable data, companies can turn to intent data providers like Bombora, Cognism, and 6sense.
- Recency decay, the assumption that a lead's interest diminishes over time without any additional purchase-signaling behavior.
- Accumulate with repeat visits. For example, if someone visits your pricing page repeatedly, we can readily assume they're extremely interested.
- Negative behaviors like unsubscribing, posting negative reviews, and abusing free trials.

Not applicable to all businesses, but here are some additional considerations you might want to include in your scoring framework:

- Opportunity size or deal value.
- Potential for future business.
- Reputation of the lead and the potential to leverage them to close other prospects.
- Complexity of the potential project

That said, scoring models can become relatively complex. Don't worry about accounting for everything when you begin; it's more important to start small and improve from there. As you grow, or if you're a large organization, you can also consider Artificial Intelligence (AI) or Machine Learning (ML) powered lead scoring tools. They are capable of running much larger comparative models across larger datasets and can self-improve and learn over time with minimal supervision.

With lead scoring in place, you can establish automated workflows or notifications that activate when a prospect's score surpasses a specific threshold, typically designating them as a Sales Qualified Lead (page 241). This designation signifies their status as a high-priority prospect warranting direct engagement in the sales process. Most established CRM tools (page 327) provide the ability to automatically track your customers' behavior and assign lead scores, but you can also do it manually when you're beginning.

ASSIGNMENT

1. What are some positive engagement and intent behaviors that you can capture? Assign values to them along with the customer characteristics you've defined in the previous qualification assignment.
2. What are some negative behaviors? Assign negative scores to them.

Notes:

RISK: REDUCE, ADDRESS, OR REVERSE IT

Most purchases are not made with the intention of selecting the absolute *best* choice. Instead, the *safest, good-enough* choice is what matters more. The safer choice is easier, more familiar, and carries less risk. The better choice is usually more innovative, but anything new is often associated with uncertainty or unfamiliarity (recall: Decision Threshold, page 139).

Consider reducing the anxiety of a purchase by addressing the potential risks associated with it. Common concerns could be:

"Can I afford this?"
"Will it work for me/work as advertised?"
"How quickly will I see results?"
"What if I don't like it?"
"What if it breaks/doesn't work?"
"What if this startup goes out of business?"
"Sounds too good to be true. What's the catch?"

Narrowing the scope of the project is one such way to reduce risk for both your prospect and yourself. Refer back to Thin-Edge-Of-The-Wedge (page 141) for more ideas.

Simpler projects are also easier for your prospects to approve because they are less likely to require escalation to upper management. Once they've begun working with you, they're much more likely to continue if they are satisfied with your solution or service.

Risk Reversal

Bolder yet, if you're confident about your offering, it's worth exploring risk reversal. Free returns with postage paid is one such example. You're right to be concerned about people abusing it; there will be a select few who will. Even so, many companies still embrace risk reversal because it helps them capture many more customers than they would not have otherwise been able to. The benefit outweighs the cost.

Here's what addressing and reversing risk could look like for a buyer/seller marketplace:

- We are the largest marketplace for X.
- List your offering, and we'll guarantee it will sell, or we will buy it from you if it expires (perhaps at a reduced rate).
- It's free to create a listing; you only pay us a % of the transaction when it's sold.

A way to frame risk reversal is with IF, THEN statements: IF we don't deliver on our promises, THEN we'll compensate you by assuming X risk.

The crucial aspect of risk reversal is your THEN proposition must outweigh the original risk that deterred action. If your compensation is of equal or lesser value, prospects would prefer to avoid taking any action altogether. Prospects want to perceive a win-win outcome in either scenario before they are willing to take the leap.

Not everyone will value a money-back guarantee. Compensation is subjective and varies from person to person. To address this, connect the compensation to your original promise or tie it back to your company values to emphasize your genuine commitment to serving customers with integrity.

Let's examine a real example of such a risk reversal initiative and its impact on the business:

> Temu is an online general goods marketplace, similar to Amazon, but with numerous knockoff and low-quality products manufactured and imported from China. They're not my preferred company to use as a case study because there's no indication that they're purpose-driven (the design of their app suggests their sole purpose is profit, at all costs). Nevertheless, there are some interesting insights from how they've implemented their price adjustment guarantee.
>
> Customers are guaranteed to receive a credit or refund if the price of the product they purchased has dropped within 30 days of placing an order. This guarantee will also be honored if they find another vendor offering an identical product at a lower price.

> They even take it a step further and make the process as painless as possible. When you log in to view your orders, if there has been a price change in any of the items within your order, the option is automatically displayed. You don't need to check each item and reference the current price versus the price when you ordered. The difference is automatically displayed (if the same item from the same vendor has changed in pricing) and totaled across however many items you purchased in that order.

What does this do for them?

- You'll worry and hesitate less when shopping. With less concern that you might be missing out on a more opportune time to buy.
- If you decide to receive a credit (page 209), it is applied to your account instantaneously. Applying a credit instead of a cashback also guarantees you'll come back to spend that money on their platform, even if you end up buying the item you originally intended to purchase somewhere else.
- As easy as they make it, the price adjustment request isn't automated and still requires the user to initiate. This encourages people to use their app more often to check if prices have dropped. It creates a habit, and while they're in the app, they're also more likely to browse for other items.
- And of course, it decreases returns initiated due to price differences. This saves them a lot of logistical costs (shipping, restocking, payment processing), and as a side effect, is also better for the environment.

This specific initiative, though obviously strategic and intentional, doesn't come across as manipulative, as it ultimately serves their customers' best interest. It turns a potentially negative experience (discovering you've spent more money than necessary and needing to navigate a refund process) into a positive one that exceeds the customer's expectations and further builds loyalty.

Reduce Formalities

Contracts typically involve a lawyer and require more time for approval. I'm not suggesting you shouldn't protect yourself, but consider exploring alternative approaches if possible. For instance, consider using proposals and memorandum of understandings (MOUs) instead of contracts. Proposals frame the interaction as a partnership: You're proposing something, to which the other party may suggest amendments. This less prescriptive and more collaborative approach helps build a stronger relationship with your client.

Paul Brassard, a mentor of mine from Volition Advisors, employs a variation of this in what he calls "whiteboard sessions" with his prospects. During these sessions, he gathers decision-makers in a room, ideally with a large whiteboard, where they will outline the challenges, opportunities, and plan for moving forward. He then captures a picture of the whiteboard and uses it as a basis for drafting an MOU. Nothing in this MOU should come as a surprise as it's already been thoroughly discussed, and all concerns and objections should have been addressed. In most cases, a formal contract isn't necessary. However, when it is, if they've had a positive experience working with him, they'll readily commit to signing one for a larger project.

Disclaimer: Contracts are still necessary; they're important for aligning expectations and ensuring there's something to fall back on in the event of disagreements. They help clarify goals, outcomes, and initiatives, thereby minimizing ambiguity to mitigate dissatisfaction. They're important for larger projects and usually necessary for working with the government or larger organizations. The point here is to explore alternatives or smaller ways to work together in advance, if at all possible.

In another real-world example, I had the opportunity to work with a company that offered software designed to assist doctors in managing their student interns during residency training. Their target customers were hospitals and universities, both known for their complex regulatory requirements, bureaucratic decision-making processes, and stringent technical standards. Selling to these institutions was notoriously slow, resulting in an average sales cycle of about one year.

To explore what we could do about this, I suggested "mystery shopping". We assumed the role of a hospital to investigate how our competitors finalized deals and onboarded their customers This undercover research revealed a significant difference: our competitors didn't rely on contracts. Instead, they allowed hospitals and universities to test their platform for free and later upgraded them on a subscription model to access premium features. They safeguarded against liabilities through the platform's Terms & Conditions, requiring only a simple proposal for hospitals to initiate a small pilot within a department. By adopting a similar approach, they managed to dramatically reduce their sales cycle to about a month.

Set Clear Next Steps

Prospects don't want to feel manipulated during the sales interaction, but this doesn't mean you should relinquish the responsibility of guiding the interaction. You still need to lead them through to the next stage of their decision-making process.

Ensure you book follow-up meetings during a call or meeting instead of going back and forth via email to arrange a time afterward. Identify who needs to be present in the room and ideally have them all in the same meeting, rather than going from person to person to schedule individual meetings. Walk them through the transition and onboarding process. Being clear and removing ambiguity eliminates risks and uncertainties that might be holding them back.

Avoid Time-based Trials and Freemium

Offer a 14-day free trial? Congratulations, your sales cycle is now a minimum of 14 days. Avoid needlessly extending your sales cycle, as most prospects tend to use the entire trial period and often only convert after it concludes.

What about the popular Free vs. Pro or Tiered approach where users pay to unlock more features? I don't encourage it for two main reasons. Firstly, it assumes you know what users are willing to pay for. Secondly, your power users may differ from your free users.

Consider a photo editing service. Your free users, typically average individuals, may need occasional touch-ups, while power users, like professional photographers, have different needs. These diverse user groups demand distinct marketing approaches. Professional photographers may also need unique features that the average individual wouldn't consider. For instance, individuals might be willing to pay for printing and framing, whereas professional photographers may be more interested in bulk editing.

Even if you decide to focus solely on individuals and consider them your power users (i.e. power users being the same as free users, not a separate and different persona), you're still assuming they're willing to upgrade for features like prints and framing. However, this assumption may not align with their priorities, and they may settle for the free tier.

The freemium approach often results in feature bloat as you add various features to cater to different power users. Some of your added features may not align with your customer's true needs. Each new feature is a test of a new value proposition, demanding trial and error to confirm the right power users and if those features are indeed what they're willing to upgrade and pay for.

Instead, adopt Usage-Based Pricing (UBP)
Both free trials and freemium models aim to provide prospects with a glimpse of the experience before committing. However, there's a growingly popular approach known as UBP (also called volume-tiered pricing). In this approach, customers upgrade not to unlock new features but to get more of what they already find valuable. With UBP, there's no need to test additional features. Users of the base version of your offering already see value in it and are willing to upgrade to access more of what they're already using. For example, you might offer all features for free initially, then charge $10/month for 10GB of storage, or $18/month for 20GB, and so on.

The crucial element in creating an effective UBP (Usage-Based Pricing) model is to tier it based on the appropriate usage metric. This metric should reflect the value users derive from your solution, their growth potential, and their ability and willingness to invest more in your offering. If you choose the right metric, you can encourage users to convert from free to paid even on the same day. However, placing the paywall behind the wrong metric can backfire and discourage users from using your solution.

Mailchimp is one of the most recognizable pioneers in exploring UBP.

In September 2009, they made an outrageous decision to move from freemium to Forever Free. Under this new policy, any user, whether new or existing, with fewer than 500 subscribers, gained free access to all of Mailchimp's features. Here's what their announcement looked like:

Sep 1, 2009

Freemium Email Marketing from MailChimp

I just read about this "freemium" approach to web startups. Basically, you build a cool app, make it free, build up a bunch of users, then find a way to "monetize" later. D'oh! Why didn't anyone tell us about this when we started in 2001? We wasted all this time building a strong, profitable company with an awesome product and over 100,000 users, when we coulda been just giving it all away? We've got to make up for lost time, people!

We're proud to announce our "**Forever Free**" plan, where customers can signup with 500 subscribers and send up to 3,000 emails a month. Noooo, this is not a watered-down, 30-day "free trial" plan. This is a "*forever* free" plan, where you get ***full*** access to our amazing, head-sploding features (and even our world-famous power features) list, so long as your list is under 500 subscribers.

This is perfect for small businesses and e-retailers, artists, bands, bloggers, non-profits, churches, and anyone just getting started in email marketing.

If you know someone out there who could use a powerful email marketing tool, help spread the monkey love, will ya?

What happened next? Small businesses leaped at this opportunity. In a year, their user base surged from 85,000 to 450,000 (+500%). They were consistently adding more than 30,000 new free users and acquiring 4,000 new paying customers each month. Most importantly, their profit (not only revenue) skyrocketed by an astounding 650%.

Under their new Forever Free approach, pricing would adjust as a user's subscriber list expanded (this allowed them to share in their customer's success). For instance, it would be $50 for 1,501-2,500 subscribers, $90 for 2,501-5,000 subscribers, and so on. This pricing strategy also contributed to decreased churn because users were less inclined to explore other platforms once they had imported or grown their subscriber base and became reliant on Mailchimp's interface and integrations.

HubSpot adopts a similar approach, they offer their CRM tool for free. Once you've imported your contacts and started relying on their CRM, it makes it all the more difficult to migrate to an alternative CRM. They blend freemium with UBP by monetizing through sales and marketing add-ons which are priced according to the number of contacts you have in your CRM. They can charge their clients more as their clients grow and make more profit.

YAMM (Yet Another Mail Merge) is yet another example. It's a Google Sheets plugin that enables you to send personalized emails in bulk via your Gmail account. If you install the plugin, it allows you to send up to 50 free emails a day, requiring an upgrade to send more. I've personally used this tool and found myself upgrading almost instantly after sending a few emails to test it. Upon realizing it provides excellent email tracking reports and better deliverability rates compared to other similar mail merge tools, I readily upgraded to continue sending more emails for my outreach campaign.

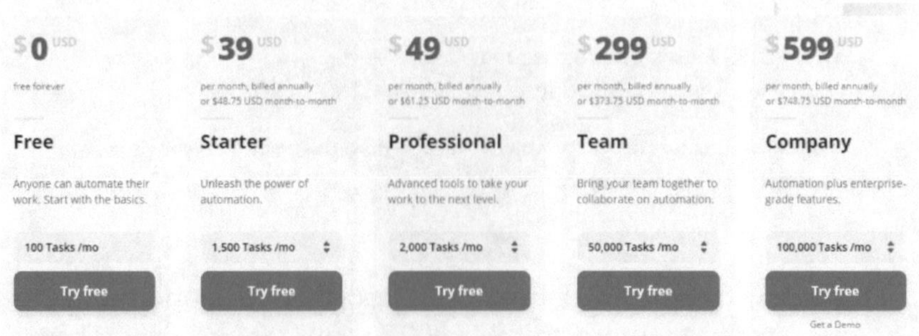

(Usage-based Pricing for Zapier)

ASSIGNMENT

Are there any ideas from the above that you can apply to shorten your sales cycle?

Notes:

INCREASING TRANSACTION SIZE

Besides getting more people to buy (Increasing Customers), you can also encourage customers to buy more when they make a purchase. Here are a few ways:

Increase Minimum Spend

Free shipping thresholds	:	Free shipping for orders over $50
Minimum purchase discount	:	20% off purchases over $75
Volume discounts	:	$20 off if you buy 5 or more

Incentivizing a minimum spend encourages consumers to make larger purchases, ultimately boosting revenue. However, implementing such incentives solely for profit-driven purposes may be perceived as manipulative. Instead, consider how encouraging this type of customer behavior can also have a positive impact, and communicate this clearly:

- Shipping thresholds reduce carbon emissions because customers consolidate their orders into a single shipment.
- Encouraging minimum purchase/volume discounts enables you to negotiate with suppliers more effectively by achieving higher minimum order quantities (MOQ) and benefiting from improved economies of scale. This, in turn, can reduce manufacturing waste. Cost savings from bulk orders can then be reinvested in your business or directed toward supporting a cause you're passionate about.

Subscribe and Save

Is another form of a volume discount, but spread out over time. Not all subscriptions encourage wastage. By giving customers the flexibility to choose how often they'd like deliveries, you can offer convenience and value to them while simultaneously increasing revenue and establishing predictable cash flow for your business.

Soylent is one such example. They provide upfront information on the percentage of savings and also present the cost of each meal with various purchasing options. With their subscription service, they offer the flexibility to customize the delivery frequency, rather than locking customers into a standard monthly period.

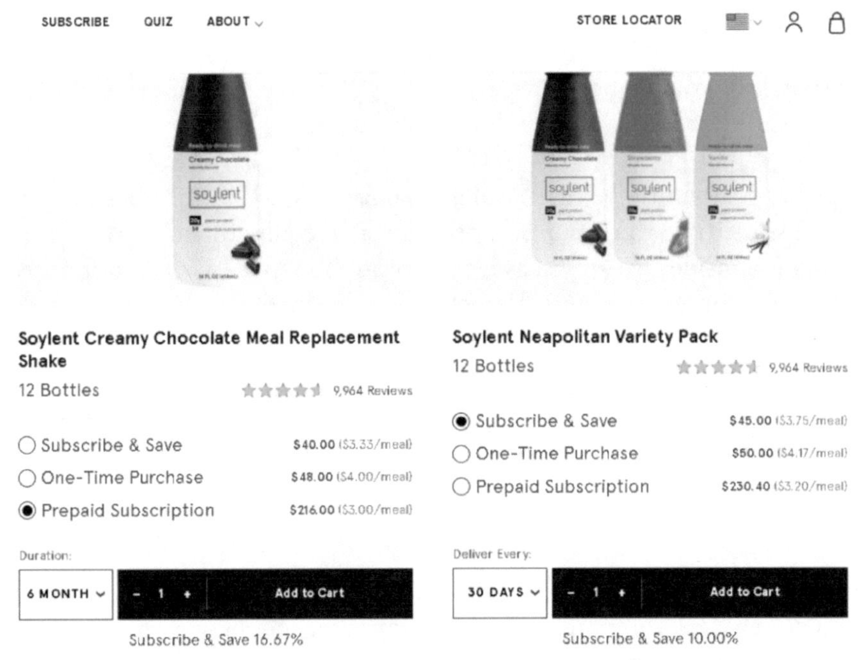

(Screenshot of Soylent's shop page)

Increase the Time Spent in Your Store or On Your Website
Solely for the purpose of maximizing revenue, is manipulative. Casinos employ this by creating intentionally disorienting layouts that make it difficult to find the exit. They may also offer free drinks or bonus credits to encourage patrons to stay longer and continue spending.

Ethically, you can create high-quality long-form content that engages readers and provides valuable, actionable information. This is more meaningful than using click-bait style snippets like "Top 3 ways to do XYZ," which are often overgeneralized and lack depth.

Another ethical approach is to design your retail space to be not only visually appealing but also immersive and experiential. This encourages customers to spend more time in your store because they enjoy the experience, not because you're trying to manipulate them.

UPSELL

Is offering a pricier version of the same product or service. For example, upgrading from an 8-megapixel camera to a 12-megapixel one or switching to a higher-tier subscription plan to access additional features or process a larger volume of transactions.

Upselling shouldn't be unethical or manipulative. It's crucial not to upsell something that your prospect doesn't require or can't afford. Instead, consider the upsell as a way to provide them with an improved experience or greater value. Perhaps your prospect hasn't yet considered the benefits of a waterproof phone, but you've recognized that it aligns with their lifestyle and hobbies. Or your prospect may be interested in your standard SEO package but hasn't fully grasped the added value and impact of ongoing content creation, which is a key feature of your comprehensive SEO package offered at a slightly higher price.

Using Mailchimp again as an example, they offer a pay-as-you-go credit "plan" (e.g. 1 credit per email sent) and various credit top-up options ($100 for 100 credits, $200 for 220 credits, and so on). They also provide tiered options permitting unlimited sends based on the number of recipients.

A prospect might initially opt for the credit option, believing they send a low volume of emails, despite the occasional mass email campaigns. In this scenario, upselling them into a tiered plan would not be unethical; in fact, it would benefit them more. Although the tiered plan may have a higher monthly cost, the savings from sending those occasional mass emails are substantial when considered over a year.

An ethical approach to upselling is about providing prospects with the freedom to choose based on their needs and preferences. Focus on building trust and being transparent. It's never wrong to present better options for your prospect, as they may not have considered it or know as much as you do about your market.

CROSS-SELL

A cross-sell is when you offer a complementary product or service that is different from your primary offering. It's often designed to enhance or complete the prospect's experience or provide additional value. Unlike an upsell, which encourages the prospect to buy a more expensive or upgraded version of the same product or service, a cross-sell introduces something new to the prospect.

Here's an example:

- Upsell: When you're buying a smartphone, the salesperson encourages you to choose the higher storage capacity model of the same phone you intended to buy.
- Cross-sell: While you're buying a smartphone, the salesperson suggests purchasing a high-quality phone case or screen protector to protect your new device. The case and screen protector are different products that complement the smartphone purchase.

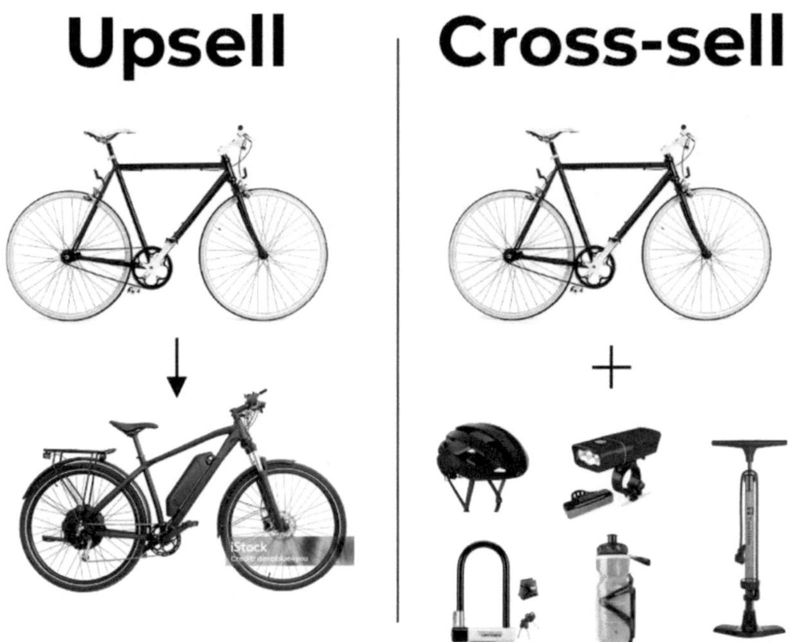

(Upsell vs. Cross-sell: Bicycle Example)

Bundling

Grouping items as a package is another way to cross-sell. Like all techniques, it's not inherently unethical and depends on how you use it. Fast-food meal combos (including a drink and fries) are one example of bundling. Another example would be if you bought a bicycle, and the SDR offered you a starter package that includes a helmet ($30), a water bottle ($10), and a bicycle lock ($70) together for $90 (saving you $20).

Amazon is arguably not the best ethical example. However, you can learn from what works because you'll probably most readily recognize this. Their digital "items often purchased together" and "similar products" sections, which appear on every product page, expose users to other complementary products they may not have considered. This contributes to increased cross-sales.

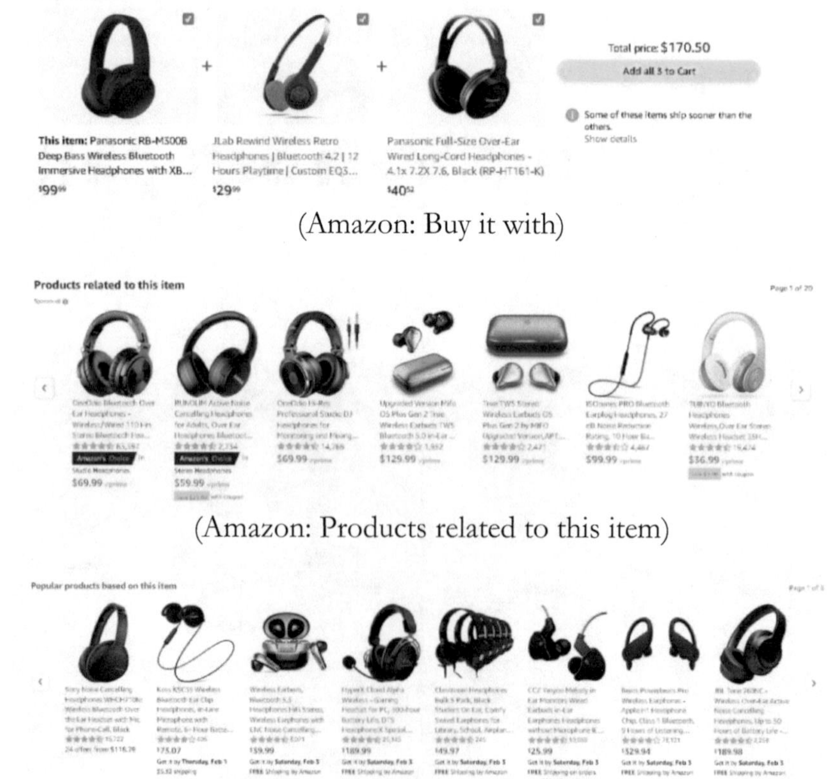

(Amazon: Buy it with)

(Amazon: Products related to this item)

(Amazon: Popular products based on this item)

When it comes to cross-selling, the most common objection from SDRs is that they feel uncomfortable pushing more offerings right after closing a sale. This discomfort stems from approaching cross-selling with the wrong mindset. Cross-selling, like upselling, should not be seen as unethical or manipulative. It involves presenting related offerings that enhance the prospect's overall experience, meet their needs, or fulfill additional requirements. If you properly (A)SSESS your prospect's needs, you shouldn't find yourself pushing additional offerings that your prospects don't require. Your complimentary offerings *should* add value and support your primary offering. For example:

> *"Would you like to add breakfast for 2, normally $49, to your room for just $29?"*

Is more affordable, convenient, better value, and enhances their experience. Profit should never be your *objective.* Aim to help your customers succeed. By focusing on providing convenience and helping them save more money, you will naturally maximize the transaction's value. Profit is the *result* that follows.

Timing is crucial when attempting to cross-sell
If you do it too early or too late in the interaction, your prospect might misunderstand and perceive it as a desperate attempt to earn more commission. Like when asking for a review or testimonial, the best time to position a cross-sell is after reaching a *positive milestone* in your customer's journey. Common positive milestones include:

- Right after they've agreed to buy your main offering: They see clear value and are ready and excited to move to the next step.
- After they've begun using your solution and see its value (set up automatically triggered email campaigns).
- If a customer has left a positive review or made a referral: You might want to follow up right after to reward their compliment by offering them something that complements their original purchase or fits well with how they use your solution.

By choosing the right timing, you're more likely to engage your customers in a way that feels helpful and valuable, rather than pushy.

Here are some different ways to frame the upsell or cross-sell:

Offline (In-person)	Online
"You may also like…" *"This is a more fully featured item than the one you're looking at"* *"I think this would be a better fit for you because…"*	Explaining your different offerings, what they're suitable for, or showcasing other products that complement and augment the main offering. Done via: Newsletters, Tutorials, Blog posts Recommendations on your product page: Customers also liked/Similar items/Often purchased together

---

ASSIGNMENT

What could you explore to increase your customer's average purchase size? Minimum order thresholds? Subscriptions? Upsells? Cross-sells? Improving the experience to make it more engaging?

Notes:

Notes:

INCREASING FREQUENCY

You can also increase revenue by getting your customers to purchase more often. Consider how you might build recurrency into your revenue.

REFILL MODEL

The printer vs. cartridge or razor vs. blade are examples of the refill model. Printers, once expensive, have become more affordable, and profits are now driven primarily through cartridge refills. Some companies enhance this strategy by making it extremely convenient for customers to refill their cartridges. This includes providing low-ink notifications, offering online ordering, and even implementing refill subscription services to ensure customers won't run out of essential supplies.

If you wish to take this approach to encourage more frequent purchases, do not deliberately short-change your customer to encourage spending. For instance, requiring replacements before they are genuinely necessary can harm your brand and erode trust. Instead, focus on transparent and ethical practices where you're prioritizing the customer experience (low-ink notifications, ease of online ordering), value (lower upfront cost to purchase a printer makes it more accessible), or convenience (subscription). Moreover, consider incorporating circular design principles to reduce waste, such as offering options to reuse or recycle old cartridges. Profit doesn't have to come at the expense of our planet, and responsible business practices can lead to both financial success and sustainability.

ADJUSTING PACKAGING

If your product has a short shelf life, it might be worth considering reducing the quantity packaged or purchased in a single transaction. For instance,

500g of cookies for $10 ($0.02 per g)
Vs.
20g of cookies for $1 ($0.05 per g)

This not only helps reduce waste from products expiring before consumption but also lowers the purchase price (despite the higher cost per volume) and makes it easier for people to buy and try (reducing CAC). Additionally, this approach could potentially lead to a higher profit margin. However, it may not be a suitable option if it results in significantly more packaging waste and cost.

STAYING TOP-OF-MIND

The more they remember you, the more often they will come back to buy from you (vs. a competitor). Achieving memorability is intrinsically tied to the clarity and positioning of your brand. If you aren't already, consider how you can align your brand with a distinct lifestyle, activity, habit, or behavior. It's advantageous if this area of focus pertains to something that happens regularly, as opposed to infrequently (e.g., travel).

While in Vietnam during my recent engagement with BizCare, I had the opportunity to work with Bh. Nong, a female-founded company that employed ethnic minorities to ethically source sustainable ingredients in the mountainous region of Quang Nam province for the production of healthy and delicious snacks.

(Taking a break with the Bh.Nong team at a red rice paddy)

(Bh.Nong products)

In my consultation with them, I observed that their product line encompasses a variety of items, including rice tea, starch tablets, rice crackers, rice flour, germ powder, forest flower honey, and more. While they have a strong commitment to promoting healthy food products and ingredients, their product lineup appeared somewhat fragmented. Although diversification is valuable, it's essential to establish distinct brands or product lines for clarity.

One possible strategic shift could involve targeting corporate offices and supplying them with healthy snacks. Their tea, forest flower honey, wild rice crackers, and nuts all fall into the category of complementary products for this purpose. Adopting such a focus would provide the brand with a clear and defined position in the market. Moreover, it would lead to more consistent revenue generation, as these snacks could be repurchased when supplies run low or even through a subscription service.

Without such strategic focus, customers might purchase various products for trial purposes, but repurchasing them would be less frequent.

To give a contrasting example, let's look at Traveller Collective, a social venture on a mission to reduce the negative impact of tourism by promoting sustainable travel and eliminating single-use plastic in the travel industry. Most individuals typically travel only a few times a year on average, their brand was naturally linked to an infrequent activity. Since they couldn't select the frequency of the activity they were associated with, they adopted a strategic product approach. Traveller Collective started with a simple keychain:

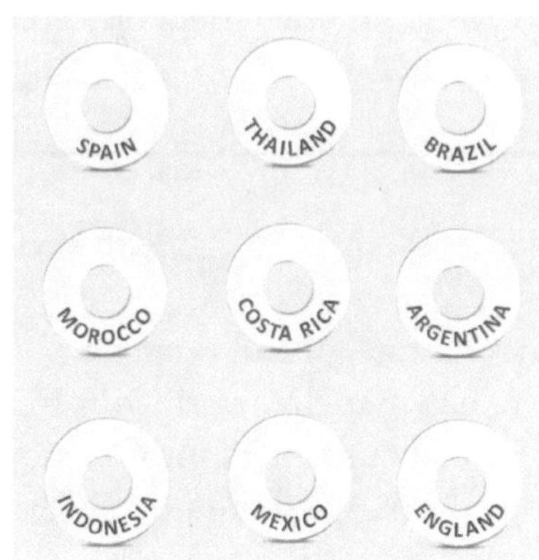

Simultaneously, they introduced a range of custom-stamped rings that customers could add to their keychain to record the countries they had visited. This not only increased their average initial order size but also facilitated the creation of a loyal customer base. These customers would add new rings whenever they visited a new country, making it an effective strategy for both profit and their social mission. By retaining customers, they could progressively build a community around their brand and further advocate for sustainable travel while sharing their initiatives and donation campaigns with their audience.

As of my last conversation with Darryl, around 2019, they were generating approximately $60,000 in monthly revenue, with 5% of their earnings donated to Plastic Change, a Danish non-profit.

ENCOURAGE BEHAVIORS THAT FACILITATE PURCHASING YOUR SOLUTION

Ever wondered why the Michelin (a tire company) Awards are associated with restaurant prestige? It was a clever content marketing campaign to encourage people to drive more (ergo buy more tires). Their rating system:

- *: A very good restaurant in its category

✻✻: Excellent cooking, worth a **detour**
✻✻✻: Exceptional cuisine, worth **a special journey**

Awards are one such way to reward and encourage behaviours, the effectiveness of which depends greatly on how coveted you can make those awards.

ASSIGNMENT

Are there strategic and recurring behaviors, activities, hobbies, or habits that you can associate with your brand? If not, how can you transform transactional customers into relational customers? What ongoing value can you offer? Are there new offerings you can integrate to keep them returning for more?

Notes:

LOYALTY PROGRAMS

It's easier to sell to an existing customer who is already familiar with and likes your brand than to a completely new prospect who hasn't yet experienced the value of your solution. Don't underestimate the importance of creating a positive customer experience and providing excellent customer service. Invest in the relationship; happy customers keep coming back for more and remain with you for much longer.

Two common loyalty initiatives are credit or points programs and stamp cards.

1. Credit/Points Programs

Customers accumulate credits or points (usually not cash) as they make purchases or through referrals. This typically involves creating customer accounts, which, in turn, allows you to gather valuable data on customer behavior. With customer accounts, you can track metrics like purchase frequency, average order size, churn, and preferred products, giving you a more accurate view of customer lifetime value (LTV). Instead of offering cash rewards, you provide credits customers can redeem for your offerings, or use them as discounts on future purchases. This approach is more cash flow-friendly and ensures that customers return to spend with you.

2. Stamp Cards

Like those you find at restaurants (buy 10 get 1 free), are another loyalty initiative, and they can also be implemented digitally. These cards can be applied to businesses beyond traditional product-based ones.

Both credit programs and stamp cards incentivize customers to make more purchases to reach the reward threshold.

Myst Asian Fusion restaurant has effectively implemented loyalty programs to enhance customer engagement. They offer a membership card that provides a 10% discount on every meal. To obtain this card, patrons need to provide their email address, enabling the restaurant to send marketing and promotional emails that help them stay top-of-mind with customers. The membership card also requires annual renewal, which comes at a nominal fee of $10. This annual renewal not only keeps customers engaged but also assists in tracking inactive customers. The fee motivates patrons to dine at the restaurant frequently, ensuring they get the full value of their investment.

In addition to the membership card, Myst Asian Fusion introduced a digital stamp card program. This program works both independently and in conjunction with the membership card, making it accessible to non-cardholders. Customers earn 1 point for every $10 spent, and these points can be exchanged for various appetizers and drinks, each requiring a different number of points for redemption.

Not directly related to our current topic on Loyalty Programs, but the well-established, family-friendly Myst also intentionally added neon signage, a massive TV wall, and expanded their drink menu. This move allowed them to capture the younger late-night crowd by presenting themselves as a hip hangout or pub-style establishment.

PIVOT TO SOLVE A MORE FREQUENT PROBLEM

By no means an easy option. But are there other problems your customers more frequently struggle with?

Let's illustrate this concept with the story of Push Operations, a Vancouver-based company that initially offered accounting services to the restaurant and hospitality industry. They quickly realized accounting services were primarily used once a year, mainly for tax season. To maintain a consistent presence in the minds of their customers, they decided to expand their services to include payroll management, a necessity for most companies on a monthly or even bi-weekly basis.

This strategic shift significantly enhanced customer retention. Why? People tend to closely evaluate their options and consider alternatives for solutions they use infrequently. By *integrating* payroll services with their accounting offerings, Push Operations further minimized customer churn. Customers became less inclined to switch to another provider that didn't offer both services seamlessly. The result? Not only did they reduce customer turnover, but they also increased their revenue since customers were now paying more frequently for the combined services.

MEMBERSHIP

Consider repositioning or bundling some of your offerings or activities into memberships. For instance, if you conduct paid workshops, don't view them as standalone; offer a membership where members enjoy unlimited access to all your workshops.

Engage in customer discovery (page 144) to gain insights into what your customers truly value. Are there extra benefits you can provide to your members? How can you structure your memberships with different tiers based on these varying benefits?

SUBSCRIPTIONS/AUTOMATE RECURRING PAYMENTS

Subscriptions are appealing to customers due to their convenience. Offering a discounted price for subscriptions compared to single purchases further motivates them. This not only leads to a higher initial purchase value (if they pay for the subscription upfront) but also encourages *increased* usage of your offering as customers develop a habit around repeat usage. When a customer subscribes to your solution, it reduces the likelihood that they will switch to an alternative brand, ultimately improving retention and increasing customer lifetime value (LTV).

Soylent (page 196) is an example of this.

GAMIFICATION/COMPETITION

Can you incorporate gamification elements? These can include leaderboards (provide visibility on how users compare to others), checklists, progress bars/trackers, contests, achievement streaks, badges, adding friends (social accountability), and more.

Gamification should not be seen as manipulative or as a means to encourage addiction. When used appropriately, it can be a powerful tool for fostering healthy habits. For example, the meditation app Headspace encourages users to complete their first meditation session within three minutes of opening it. They celebrate this accomplishment. They also track meditation sessions and highlight users' streaks to encourage consistency and the development of a meditation habit.

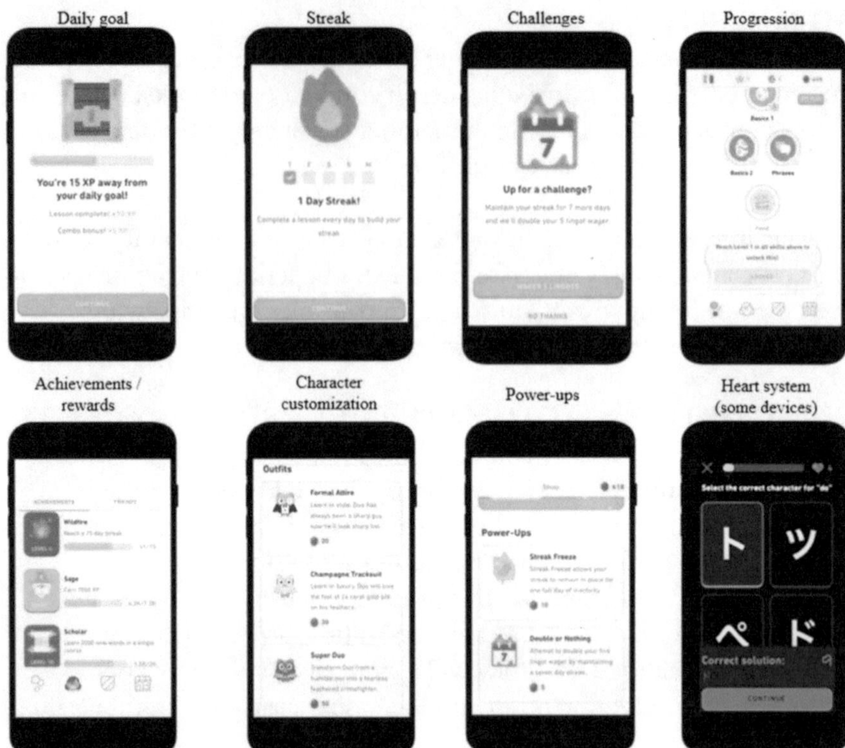

(Duolingo's gamification elements. Compiled by Shantanu Tilak)

Here's a great article on How Duolingo uses gamification to improve user retention: https://strivecloud.io/blog/gamification-examples-boost-user-retention-duolingo/

ASSIGNMENT

Can you apply any of the above to create recurring revenue or increase how often your customer uses your solution? Remember, it should be about adding value, convenience, or building a better experience for your customers. Profit is the *result*, not the *objective*.

Notes:

Notes:

INCREASING PRICES (OR FINDING THE RIGHT PRICE)

Over 90% of businesses underprice when they start. While there has been a lot of attention on guiding startups toward finding product-market fit, the emphasis on business model fit has been lacking. Yes, it is much more important to achieve product-market fit before even worrying about pricing; however, the disproportionate attention on this has led to many companies applying a lackadaisical approach to pricing. Poor pricing has as much power to destroy your business as does a terrible product. BOTH need to be in alignment.

The good news is that pricing isn't as mystical or complicated as you might think. There are proven business models and frameworks that have been vigorously and scientifically tested. Your goal should be to identify and iterate on the one that works best for you.

I won't dive into the intricacies of various business models, but I do want to dedicate some time to discuss commonly overlooked factors that affect pricing and provide specific frameworks to assist you in establishing (or revising) your initial pricing.

BRAND VALUES & PRICING

While it's not catastrophic to set pricing based on what other competitors are doing in the market, doing so without thoughtful intention can lead to attracting the wrong customers or creating mismatched expectations, resulting in unnecessary friction.

Have you ever found yourself in a situation where you're consistently trying to pull on a door that only opens when pushed? These are referred to as 'Norman Doors', a term coined by design expert Donald Norman. Norman argues that people instinctively respond to the design of objects. Thus, when the design doesn't align with the expected function, confusion ensues.

This mismatched expectation is what leads to a poor user experience. It applies not only to product design but also to all forms of communication: sales, marketing, and even something as simple as the pricing of your offering. For instance:

Should you charge $299 or $300?

This seemingly trivial decision, barely noticeable on your balance sheet, highlights the importance of beginning your pricing journey with a clear understanding of your company's or brand's value. Common knowledge suggests $299, despite the mere $1 difference (even if we acknowledge the psychological fallacy we fall victim to), creates the impression of a lower price compared to $300. However, understanding the psychological rationale behind this tactic alone is insufficient without awareness of the contexts in which it is effective.

If quality is one of your company's core values and you provide premium solutions, you might benefit more from charging $300. Affordability and value-for-money aren't always the messages that will resonate with your customers. Sending the wrong signal or even leaning into discount-oriented campaigns will only lead to attracting transactional customers when you should instead be targeting relational customers. This may result in poor conversion, or worse, negative reviews and complaints about your solution being overpriced.

There is no right or wrong approach. If your business is designed to cater to bargain seekers, you might want to send the right signals to communicate that your offerings provide good value for money. Your task is to be mindful and not blindly execute ideas or campaigns. Begin your pricing journey (and, in fact, every company decision) by understanding the values that will guide your evaluation of the pros and cons of your choices. Values are the HOW to your WHY (your company mission, page 264).

INITIAL PRICING

With your brand values and objectives in mind, you'll now understand your goals and have the foundation to determine how to proceed with pricing:

- If growth is a priority, you may be more comfortable with a lower starting price to reduce friction.
- If profitability or quality is a priority, you may opt for a different approach.

Quick reminder, there's no need to reinvent the wheel every time. Many founders have a natural inclination for innovation. If you've already crafted a groundbreaking and novel solution, you don't have to recreate every aspect around it. Certainly, customization is required as different situations, solutions, and markets demand a unique approach. However, begin with what's tried and true, then experiment and adapt as needed. Here are 4 key activities that will give you a frame of reference for your pricing:

1. Mystery Shop
Use mystery shopping to better understand and emulate your competitors (direct or indirect).

SkiClaws, a company in Whitehorse, Canada, has designed an innovative attachment that interfaces between your bindings and ski. It enables skiers to ascend slopes without needing to remove their skis or use the tiring herringbone technique (which doesn't work well for steep, icy, or narrow slopes).

As an innovative solution, they don't have any direct competitors. However, there are alternative indirect competitors like ski skins, crampons, or even snowshoes. They all compete similarly for a skier's accessory budget. While working with Doug, I recommended he use these products as benchmarks for pricing. If he priced SkiClaws too low, even if production costs were significantly lower, it might be perceived as an inferior or low-quality product. On the other hand, pricing it too high could create adoption barriers.

If the idea of increasing pricing despite low costs, just for the sake of increasing adoption, makes you uncomfortable, consider the following:

- The additional revenue could be reinvested to further improve your offerings, scale your organization, or even provide you with an opportunity to give back or amplify your impact if you're already doing so.
- You might be underpricing to begin with. Yes, if you sell more, economies of scale will bring down production costs. However, this might not be the same for operational costs at scale, which you might not have accounted for when coming up with your original pricing.

For another example, listen to Episode 122 of the Masters of Scale podcast with Reid Hoffman, the founder of LinkedIn, to hear Warby Parker, the online eyewear retailer, discussing their need to adjust their pricing to meet market expectations set by industry incumbents.

2. Learn From Your Customers

Customer Discovery (page 144) never ends; it's not only something you do for product design and market validation. Now is a good time to revisit customers or approach prospects to gauge their sentiment on different price points.

What is acceptable?
What is expensive?
What is outrageous?

Again, keep your brand values in mind, e.g. if your solution is designed for a premium or exclusive market, you may *want* to start with an outrageous price point, even if it would alienate general consumers. They're not your early adopters or target market anyway, so it's fine!

3. Understand Their Default Expectation

Not only the price point, but you'll also want to understand their preferred payment method. Do they typically pay by the hour, a percentage of the transaction, a flat fee, in installments, or only upon receiving the product or project completion? To reduce friction, start with what they're familiar with.

4. Cost-based vs. Value-based Pricing.
Many companies follow this practice, but it's important not to base your pricing solely on your Cost of Goods Sold (COGS). This also applies to service providers (hourly rate is a common cost-based approach). Costs may not always align proportionally with volume. Instead, consider how you can quantify the value you provide and price accordingly.

How then, do we quantify value? First, you need to understand the impact of your solution:

> *How much money are you saving them?*
> You can likely charge 10% – 15% of their annual savings.
>
> *How much money are you helping them make?*
> You can likely charge 10% – 25% of the expected additional monthly income you're helping them make.
>
> *How much time are you saving them by solving their problem?*
> A little more complicated, start by identifying how much time you're saving them, then estimate what their time is worth or the opportunity cost associated with what they could be doing instead. You can charge around 10% of their missed opportunity cost per month.

To illustrate this point, let's look at Green Chair Recycling, a social enterprise that provides recycling bins and volunteers for events like music festivals and large conferences. When I had the opportunity to work with them, they were generating quotes based on their costs for servicing an event.

For example, if they were asked to cover a 3-hour with 100 attendees, it would require them to have 3 employees present for 3 hours, and they would charge $540 (3 x $60/hr x 3hrs). If they were requested for a 3-

hour event with 500 attendees (five times more), they would need 6 employees for the same duration (only twice as many), and they would charge $1080 (6 x $60/hr x 3hrs). Their rate is made up here, but it illustrates the point.

The number of staff required was not proportionate to the scale of the event and was primarily dependent on the size of the venue and the duration of it. Instead of pricing based on the cost of operations, I encouraged Liliana to adjust their pricing to align with the "volume" of attendees. This approach would enable them to charge more, as organizers were willing to pay higher rates due to increased revenue from more ticket sales. This change enabled them to increase their margins and become more financially sustainable. The additional profit would allow them to amplify their impact through their recycling training programs and initiatives.

Another similar example is Integrate Play Solutions, which serves companies by offering experiential workshops that promote team communication, collaboration, and innovation through play, using Lego! Kirsten considered various factors such as the number of participants, the complexity of the workshops, duration, and even the potential for future work when designing quotes for clients. However, these were all primarily cost-oriented considerations. One day, she received an inquiry from a multinational video game company to run a workshop for them. A large company like them can and is willing to pay a lot more than the smaller clients she was used to working with.

What would you do in her situation?
Would you continue to charge the same rate based on costs?
If not, how else might you justify pricing for a premium client?

You could decide to keep pricing as-is to secure a reputable client to help build your reputation and attract more prospects. However, recognize it'll be difficult to increase pricing with them in the future if you've underpriced to begin with. Alternatively, you could decide to increase pricing to reflect the value and impact you're able to create in a larger organization. There is no right or wrong answer, but your choices should be made with strategic intent.

In any case, I'm not advocating for price gouging. Instead, I'm suggesting pricing that will grow in proportion to the success of your customers. This will allow you to better scale your impact without feeling like you're constantly scraping the bottom of the barrel. A higher price also doesn't equate to making your offering less accessible. The extra profit from more successful clients could be applied toward subsidizing the cost of working with earlier-stage, less profitable, or underserved prospects that you want to support but otherwise find difficult to justify financially.

Identity as a form of Value

There is one category where I can't imagine value-based pricing being possible: offerings that satisfy a desire instead of solving a problem. Games, entertainment, fashion, and snacks are some examples. If your offering falls under this category, activities 1, 2, and 3 above should still help. The closest comparison to "value" for these offerings would be the sense of identity people seek to associate themselves with through the proxy of your brand. Pricing is simply one of the many components that reflect and inform that identity.

To elaborate, let's look at VGreen, a company in Vietnam that brews and sells various kombucha products in a wide variety of flavors. They've priced competitively in the market to match coffee shops, teahouses, and bubble tea stores. Effectively (though perhaps unwillingly) positioning themselves as a casual beverage option. They struggled with low margins due to the higher production costs associated with kombucha fermentation, and the local market was unfamiliar with the product and its health benefits.

(VGreen Kombucha Products)

I encouraged them to consider pricing for a more specific target market to strengthen their brand positioning. For example, targeting yoginis and professional women, or positioning themselves as a non-alcoholic alternative for social events. This approach would align their pricing and branding more closely with beer: not about letting loose or socializing, but rather as a carefully crafted and fermented product.

Even if their goal is to popularize kombucha as an everyday drink, beginning with a higher-end market isn't restrictive. Apple provides a parallel example. They defined a clear target customer: the creatives, the visionaries, and those unwilling to settle for the status quo. In doing so, they didn't alienate those who don't fit that mold; instead, they offered a clear persona to aspire to.

Selling diamonds is another example. It's just a piece of rock; where's the value in that? Yet we purchase them at a high price because:

1. It's become a love symbol, communicating our commitment to another (no thanks to some clever marketing by De Beers. Tune in to Episode 30 of the Empire Builders Podcast to hear about this in detail).
2. It's a status symbol, communicating our identity as someone who is well-off. Though men say it's for their women, men are the ones who buy and are willing to spend on it because it speaks to their identity as someone wealthy enough to splurge on such luxurious items and who values their partner enough to do so.

Is your solution an Investment or a Cost?

To take it a step further, consider pricing not only from the perspective of *your* cost (operational) vs. the value you create for your customers'. But also explore ways you can tie your solution to increasing your customers' value (revenue) instead of cost (being an expense for improvement). In Episode 10 of The Empire Builders Podcast, Steve and Dave discuss JD Power's transformation. JD Power started as a company that provided customer survey data to automakers. However, they pivoted into positioning their surveys as rankings which assisted automakers in increasing sales. By doing so, their surveys shifted from being *costs* for data collection to a marketing investment which would generate more *revenue* for automakers.

OPTIMIZING PRICING

Now that you have a foundation, here's a quick and scientific way to pinpoint your optimal price. But before we delve into that, here are some quick reminders:

- Begin with your objective in mind. If your priority is growth, you may be willing to sacrifice profit to reduce CAC (I'll explain how pricing affects it below).
- Conduct cohort analysis in controlled groups to ensure that pricing is the sole variable affecting changes in your customer acquisition and churn rates.
- Test rigorously and make it a data-driven process.

Step 1: Gradually increase prices. If you suspect you've underpriced initially, double your price, assess, and then double it again…

e.g. $50 → $100 → $200 → $400 → $800 → $1,600 → $3,200

Depending on your initial price point and the extent to which you've underpriced your offering, the difference between $50 and $100 may not be significant if your prospects are accustomed to paying around $1,000 for this solution. The doubling method will help you rapidly identify the range between what's considered expensive and what's seen as exorbitant. Within that range, you can refine your pricing with smaller, gradual adjustments.

Step 2: Measure and track CAC, Churn, and LTV. When increasing prices, you should generally expect to observe:

Higher CAC: the more expensive something is, the more challenging it is to convert prospects into customers. Why? Because

- Fewer prospects can afford or are willing to make a purchase.
- It might require more marketing dollars to convince them of your solution's value.
- Prospects take more time to make a decision, and time translates to money.
- They may even need to consult with an SDR before

committing. For instance, solutions priced over $300 usually necessitate at least one in-person interaction, which is more expensive than a solution sold entirely through marketing automation.

- There are complex formulas for calculating CAC. You don't need to account for everything, but more details improve accuracy. At a minimum, advertising expense provides a simplified measure of CAC. For instance:

Ad 1	Spent $10, acquired 10 customers	CAC = $1
Ad 2	Spent $10, acquired 5 customers	CAC = $2

See page 180 for another example.

- Extended costs should also include the salaries of employees involved in all activities leading up to acquisition.

Higher Churn: Expensive prices may lead customers to seek cheaper alternatives, causing them to leave or discontinue your offering sooner.

While higher CAC and Churn may seem like negatives, they don't always result in lower LTV. Let's examine a hypothetical example for context:

Imagine, you've created an Uber-like platform that connects nannies/babysitters with parents who are looking for trusted temporary caregivers. Your business model is having babysitters pay $10/mo to use the platform to find childcare gigs. These babysitters stay on the platform for an average of 6 months. Average LTV = $10 X 6 months = $60.

As you gradually increase your price, churn will also increase proportionally. For example, now that you're charging $80 a month, customers might only stay on your platform for an average of 3 months before leaving. This seems concerning at first, but consider this: the average Lifetime Value (LTV) is now $80 X 3 months = $240. A 4X increase! However, it's also essential to consider how pricing affects customer acquisition. This price increase is justifiable if it doesn't significantly impact our ability to acquire new users.

Maintaining this new pricing is logical if caregivers typically do not engage with the platform for more than six months. This could be attributed to the nature of temporary caregiving roles, which are often viewed as short-term transitional opportunities. That said, consider your context. Despite higher LTV, high Churn could disproportionately harm your business if you rely heavily on word-of-mouth or network dynamics (whereby when the more people use the platform, the more beneficial it is to everyone else) for growth.

To help visualize this pricing "sweet spot", track both the LTV and CAC associated with each price point on a spreadsheet. Here is an example of this in another hypothetical scenario:

Price	Lifecycle (in months)	LTV	CAC	LTV/CAC Ratio (higher value = better)
$50	6	$300	$20	15
$100	6	$600	$60	10
$200	5	$1,000	$60	16.67
$400	5	$2,000	$80	25
$800	4	$3,200	$100	32
$1,600	4	$6,400	$400	16
$3,200	3	$9,600	$1000	9.6

Here's a graph of the above table for better visualization:

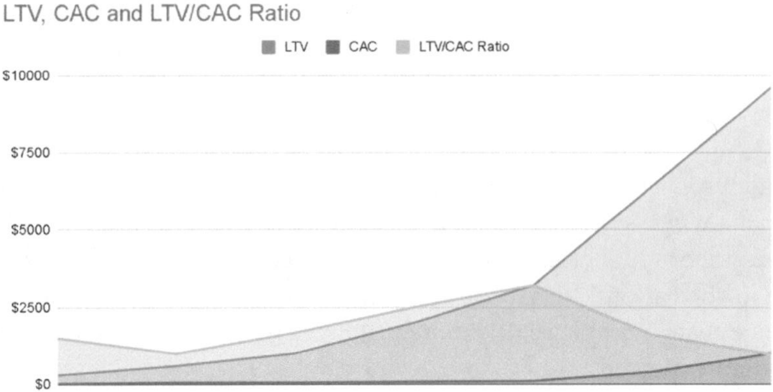

**Your graph may not reflect a similar pattern and may be more complicated if you have upsells/cross-sells.*

Your goal is to find the price where you have the highest **LTV to CAC ratio** – this is where it is most profitable. You're getting the most from them whilst CAC is minimal in comparison.

Yes, it's scary. Increasing prices will make it harder to attract new customers and might even alienate existing ones. However, it's important to remember that those customers who leave may not have been your ideal customers from the start. Additionally, you can consider segmenting and testing new pricing strategies within a smaller market, specific location, or through a particular sales channel before implementing a major change.

Increasing pricing might enable you to add more value to improve your offering, thereby better serving your customers. This could also potentially attract new prospects who previously overlooked your solution because it didn't meet their needs or wasn't sufficiently distinguishable from competitors.

DISPLAYING PRICING

If you sell a high-ticket solution or if pricing depends heavily on complex quotations based on many variables, you might notice that it's common in your industry to either display a lower price (out of concern that prospects might be scared away due to sticker shock) or not to display pricing at all.

Recall what we discussed in (E)XPECTATIONS. What do you think happens when someone expects a lower price but then finds out the actual price is higher after going through a consultation? It leaves a sour taste in their mouth! Instead, it's better to overestimate (but not outrageously) and pleasantly delight them when they find out it costs less than expected.

What about hiding pricing entirely and asking customers to reach out for a quote? Tune in to Episode 62 of the Empire Builders podcast to hear Matthew Burns from Armadura Metal Roof talk about why you *should* transparently display pricing on your website.

As a closing thought, it's crucial to understand that price is a reflection of value. Don't be afraid to charge what you're worth! Many founders, especially those who are self-employed or in service-based businesses (e.g. consultants, artists, and even dentists who own their practice), face imposter syndrome and end up underpricing not due to a lack of value but because they lack confidence.

If you're running a social venture and do not want to monetize directly from your beneficiaries (e.g., students or homeless individuals), you'll need to identify stakeholders who are willing to pay and ensure your offerings also create value for them. The price you charge should be proportional to the value you provide to them, not to your beneficiaries.

DISCOUNTING

Since we touched on pricing, I want to briefly discuss discounts here. I generally discourage discounting as it devalues your offering. Here are some other creative ways to approach it:

Giveaway

Instead of reducing price (which reduces perceived value), consider offering a giveaway (which adds perceived value). For example:

	Option 1: Discount	Option 2: Giveaway
10hrs of service	$100 (at $10/hr)	$100
20 hrs of service	$180 (at $9/hr)	$200 + 3 free hrs
40 hrs of service	$300 (at $7.5/hr)	$400 + 13 free hrs

Besides offering more of your primary offering, you could also create low-cost secondary offerings you can give away, further enhancing your customer's experience.

Flexible payment

During COVID-19, many businesses and individuals reduced spending due to decreased demand caused by lockdowns. Layoffs and increased costs due to inflation only exacerbated the situation. If you're a seller, instead of lowering pricing to incentivize purchases, consider offering flexibility in payment terms (how vs. when they can pay). This might include allowing prospects to buy-now-pay-later (BNPL) by financing their purchase in installments or sharing in the risk and reward (if appropriate), such as accepting shares or revenue sharing in lieu of upfront cash.

Guarantees

During the 2008 recession, Hyundai introduced a job-loss guarantee: if you lost your job within a year, you could return your car and walk away from your loan obligation, with Hyundai covering most, if not all, of the difference. This addressed prospects' fears and concerns during that period of economic uncertainty, enabling them to continue selling cars without the need for discounts. This move gave Hyundai a significant advantage over many other automakers.

Hyundai reintroduced a similar program during the COVID-19 pandemic. Their Job Loss Protection Program offered a 90-day payment deferral on new purchases and provided up to 6 months of payments for new buyers in the event of job loss.

Focusing on retention during downturns
If all else fails and additional concessions fail to aid with acquisition. Your remaining option is to slow down and take the time to improve your customer's experience. Consider providing white-glove service to existing or new customers during this period, a more hands-on, personalized, and customized level of care. This ensures you make up for higher Customer Acquisition Cost (CAC) with higher Lifetime Value (LTV).

EXERCISE

STOP: Don't do this without first reviewing the 4 ways above! Why does IKEA have a restaurant when they sell furniture?

(Ikea Restaurant Meatballs)

Answer on the next page

Increase # Of Customers?
Not really.

Raise Prices?
No.

Increase Average Transaction Size? Yes!
Not because of food profits, they barely break even on it. But because longer time in store = More items purchased.

Increase Frequency Of Transactions? Yes, as well!
Some, like myself, visit IKEA for the food and often end up purchasing something while we're there.

ASSIGNMENT

Pause and consider what adjustments can be made in your offering, pricing, business model, or sales/marketing strategy to optimize growth and revenue.

Notes:

SALES STRATEGY

Now that we've covered the basics, we're finally ready to begin developing our Sales Strategy! I only use the word Sales Strategy here because this is a book about sales. However, at the strategic level, sales + marketing strategy are and should be one and the same.

A better way to put it = Acquisition Strategy.

If you're a startup, you can also use what you build from this module as your go-to-market (GTM) strategy. Sales vs. Marketing are merely the different activities that influence acquisition. Whether you're doing Sales vs. Marketing depends on the prospect's readiness and entry point into your funnel.

What is a funnel you ask? The funnel represents the step-by-step process prospects go through, from the initial awareness of their problem to making a purchase decision. It's a structured framework that guides the journey from lead generation to conversion. We will explore the intricacies of constructing a funnel when we discuss the Sales Process (page 250).

Let's begin with the first step in creating your acquisition strategy:

MAPPING THE BUYER'S JOURNEY WITH GRADUALIZATION

Gradualization is a copywriting term from marketing. In sales, it's also known as "advancement" or "escalation": How can you advance your prospect to the next stage in their decision-making process?

Would you propose to someone you just met on a first date? Probably not a good idea. The same applies to sales. We don't purchase in a single interaction; there's usually a series of steps we need to go through. For example:

- See an ad

- Visit your website
- Read a review
- Add an item to their shopping cart
- Enter payment information
- Enter shipping information
- Reading about returns & guarantees
- Checkout
- … (continue planning beyond the purchase if you're interested in developing a comprehensive customer experience.)

Realize that not every prospect needs to go through the same series of steps. Some prospects enter your funnel (page 250) with more knowledge and experience, while others enter at different points. I don't use the term "Advancement" because it suggests a specific and unidirectional escalation.

Rather than viewing your buyer's journey as a linear or process-oriented funnel, envision it as a map. It has a clear end goal, checkpoints that help us understand if we're trending in the right direction, but many possible paths to get there, some of which might even take us backward a few steps.

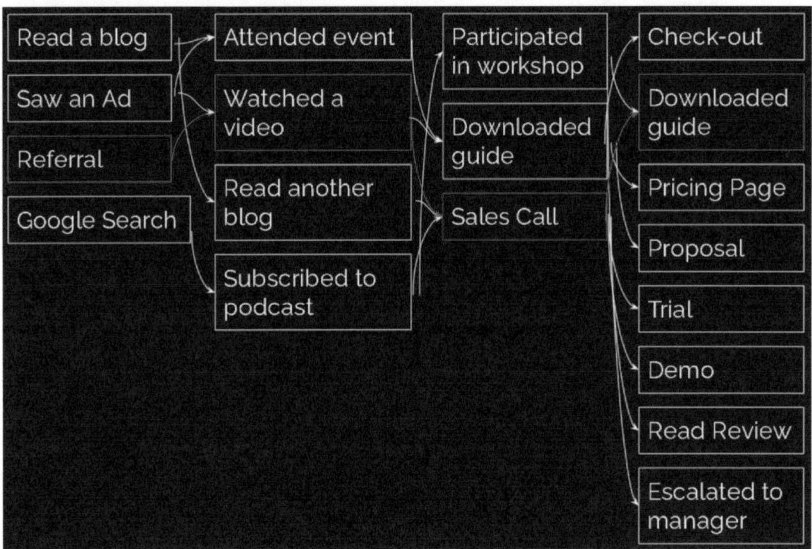

(Example Buyer's Journey Map)

To map the buyer's journey (their actions), we first need to understand their underlying intent and motivations (*why* are they taking those actions?). This is where gradualization comes into play, it represents the sequence of realizations a prospect must experience before they're ready to make a purchase.

If you run a social media training program, here's a series of realizations your prospect might go through:

- I need to realize what I'm doing right now isn't working.
- I need to believe there is a more effective way to generate leads and close sales.
- I need to believe it's possible to make 6-7 figures a year without outbound prospecting.
- I need to believe building a strong brand is the path to achieving this.
- I need to believe social media is the optimal choice for brand building.
- I need to believe THIS social media training program will yield faster and easier results than any other alternative.
- I need to believe I need to take action NOW.

It usually follows a pattern like this and often culminates in the prospect recognizing the value of your solution and realizing they should *give you their money* to get this solution *now*. However, the specific journey may vary depending on your target customers, organization, or offerings.

It's also helpful to not only define it for one customer persona but define multiple to address all your different target customers. Gradualization could look significantly different for them even if you're selling the same solution, this will reflect differently in the messaging you use to appeal to them.

This marketing matrix illustrates the point:

	Marketing Manager	Small Business Owner
Problem:	Under pressure to get more leads from your boss?	Looking to generate more leads for your business?
Messaging:	Too busy managing all your marketing campaigns? We help marketing managers to...	We've worked with many plumbing contractors like you to grow their businesses. Contact us today for a free no-obligation consultation

If you need help defining customer personas, check out this comprehensive guide: https://bit.ly/customer-personas-guide

Gradualization doesn't only help us with mapping the customer's journey; it also assists in fine-tuning the granular steps within it. For instance, if a landing page is one of the steps in your bigger picture, the landing page itself needs to guide prospects through a micro-journey. Prospects don't want to see "register now" right away; they might want to learn more about who your event is for, what they will learn from it, who else might be attending, the credibility or credentials of the speaker, etc.

From the term gradualization, you might also assume "gradual" equates to "slow"" However, gradual primarily refers to the progression in a prospect's mental awareness. As I've mentioned earlier under Shorter Sales Cycles (page 182), it doesn't have to be slow. In some cases, the entire conversion can occur within a single interaction or conversation. However, this isn't always the case, and if you push a prospect to buy prematurely, not only in terms of timing but more importantly, if they aren't mentally prepared for the transition, you'll come across as pushy.

ASSIGNMENT

What realizations (what do they need to believe?) must your prospects develop before they're prepared to use or purchase your solution?

List distinct series of realizations if you have multiple target customers or offerings.

Notes:

SALES + MARKETING MAP

Now that we understand gradualization, we can begin to map out the different channels, messaging, call to action, and lead magnets that will help us guide our prospects from point A to B. By understanding that it isn't linear, we open ourselves up to the different possibilities and combinations we can use.

Although every prospect goes through a different series of realizations, there are common checkpoints. A customer's journey, like any journey, has a beginning, a middle, and an end. Specific realizations commonly occur at certain stages, some markers help you identify if someone is ready to move to the next stage, and there are activities you can use to guide someone from one stage to the next. We'll begin the creation of our map with the inbound ACDC framework popularized by HubSpot. It will help us categorize our prospect's realizations and our activities into 4 main buckets: AWARENESS, CONSIDERATION, DECISION, and CLOSE.

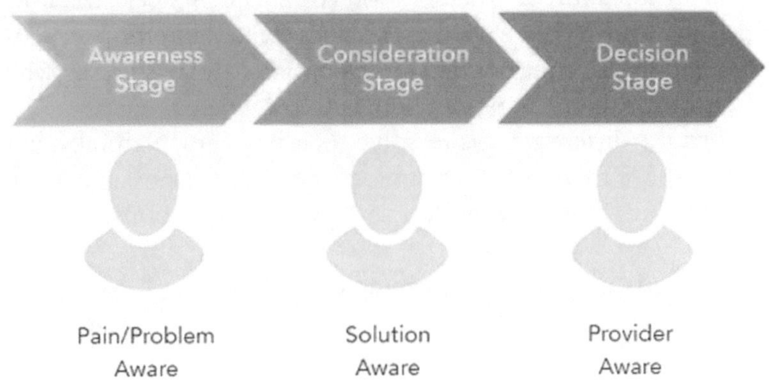

(HubSpot's Buyer's Journey Framework)

AWARENESS
Not in reference to awareness of your solution or even of your company, it refers to the prospect's awareness of a problem or a need.

The prospect has to first realize what they're currently doing isn't effective. They start to look for information to better understand their situation. Your aim here is to create brand awareness and thought leadership on the topic by providing educational content to attract prospects. Avoid addressing high-level problems and instead focus on addressing a specific need for your prospect. These needs typically manifest as *"What is"* questions.

Let's consider FoodMesh, a Vancouver-based company with a B2B marketplace that connects surplus food to a verified network of businesses and charities. We'll use a hypothetical example of the ACDC framework with them as a case study.

> High level = Food is being wasted
>
> Specific need = I have food that I've spent money on that's going bad
>
> *AWARENESS question = What can I do to reduce my food waste?*

CONSIDERATION

Not in consideration of your solution (yet). The prospect has now defined their problem or need and is actively looking for potential solutions. They're considering various options and evaluating which is the best fit for them. Your aim here is to provide content that highlights the different ways to solve their problem. Naturally, you'll want to expose them to your solution as one of the possible ways. These inquiries typically manifest as *"How do I"* questions.

To follow up on the previous example (FoodMesh)

> *CONSIDERATION question: How can I get rid of bulk food?*
>
> Throw it away? Compost it? Donate it? Run a flash sale to clear inventory? List it on Craigslist? Or try to sell it to another business that might need it (and this is where their solution comes in)?

DECISION
Here's where the prospects start to actively consider you as the best solution. They're narrowing down their choices and comparing you with competitors, trying to understand how you work, pricing, reading your reviews and testimonials, and comparing features. Your aim here is to provide information that helps prospects see you as the best vendor amongst others. This typically manifests as *"Who is the best* questions.

> With the previous example, a prospect might then start to search for excess food marketplaces, Bulk food suppliers, or Food buyers

CLOSE
This is the stage where the prospect becomes a customer by making a purchase. It involves the actual transaction and closing the sale. How do you get them to commit and go with your solution? What are clear next steps? How do you eliminate risks (guarantees/refund policies)? How do you onboard your customer? What drives urgency to do it now? Typically *"Why should I"* questions.

After this stage, the focus shifts to delivering on promises, ensuring customer satisfaction, and building a long-term relationship.
Here's an example of the Buyer's Journey Map against the ACDC Framework:

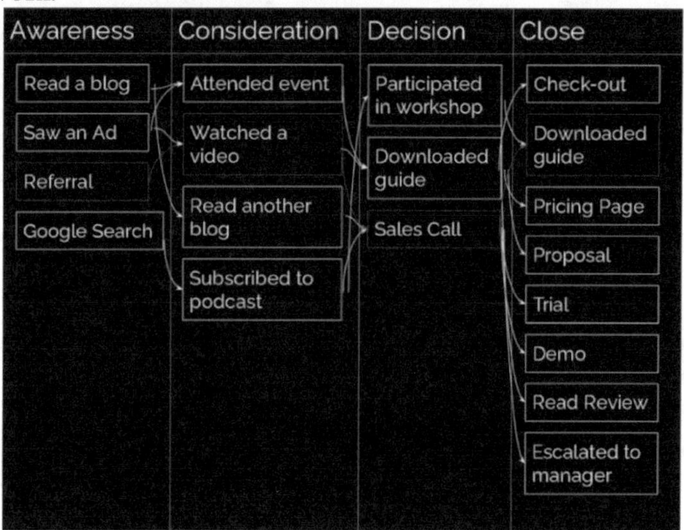

The ACDC framework emphasizes the importance of guiding prospects through their journey, providing them with the right information at the right time, and ultimately closing the sale. It's a more prospect-centric approach that aligns with the idea that buyers are already actively researching and evaluating options before making a purchase.

Here's a visualization of our previous example:

Stage	**AWARENESS**	**CONSIDERATION**	**DECISION**	**CLOSE**
Pain/ Need/ Motivations	-Reduce food waste. -Recoup expenses.	-Meaningful & convenient way to get rid of food surplus.	Find the most efficient vendor to work with.	-Seamless integration with current inventory management systems. -Ease of use to ensure this initiative doesn't create an additional burden on our business.
Questions	*What* -Can I do to reduce my food waste? -Should I do with food that is expiring soon?	*How* -Can I get rid of food in bulk? -Can I find suitable buyers and coordinate multiple different purchases?	*Who* -Are the trusted local bulk distribution platforms?	*Why* -Is it beneficial to use FoodMesh's platform? -FoodMesh's platform makes it easy and helps you liquidate faster.

This Buyer's Journey Map is only part of a bigger picture. To build a comprehensive Sales + Marketing Map, we need a few more things:

Channels

Different questions are best addressed through different channels. For instance, having a booth at a conference or scheduling a consultation call would be ideal for prospects interested in delving deeper into potential solutions. However, these channels might be unsuitable and premature for prospects who are still in the phase of seeking information to diagnose their problem. Different channels also vary in effectiveness for different businesses (page 178).

Continuing the previous example:

Stage	AWARENESS	CONSIDERATION	DECISION	CLOSE
Channels	-Blogs -Ads -Guest speaking	Blogs, Videos, Workshops, and Paid promotions on software suggestion platforms like Capterra (or other similar, relevant aggregators).	-Infographics -Demo -Case Studies.	Trial, Pilot, Reviews, Testimonials.

Call-to-Actions (CTAs)

Similar to above, "Buy Now" or "Create an account" may not be the ideal CTA if your prospect is still in the Awareness or Consideration stage and learning about how to be a greener organization. When choosing a CTA, consider the questions and concerns going through your prospect's mind at each stage. Which CTA would best resonate with what they're trying to accomplish?

Stage	AWARENESS	CONSIDERATION	DECISION	CLOSE
CTAs	-Read more -Learn more -Take the quiz	-Sign up for the Newsletter -Download the guide -View the buyer database	-Book a demo -See what our customers have to say about us	Create an account

Lead Magnets

These are giveaways you can offer to your prospects in exchange for their contact information. Quality and alignment are crucial. Prospects will gladly disclose their information if they believe what you have to offer will genuinely benefit them. Lead magnets also help you identify where the prospect is in their journey and make it easier for you to position your solution as a tool to better solve their problem.

For example, you might ask prospects to provide their email address in return for a media kit template. Their act of downloading suggests that they aren't merely learning (Awareness) but may be ready to take action (Consideration). This enables you to reach out and inform them about your marketing agency's relationships with media outlets and how you might assist them with their press release.

Back to our example:

Stage	AWARENESS	CONSIDERATION	DECISION	CLOSE
Lead Magnets	-Quiz whereby they could input type of food and volume to determine the best option for food disposal or redistribution. -Event registration	List of potential local buyers (if they wish to manage the transaction manually on their own).	-Free consultation session -Download our case studies -Waste reduction reports	-Request a quote -Sign up for a free trial

Lastly, specify **Requirements to advance** and **Targets** for each stage.

"Requirements to advance" ensures that you collect the right information at each stage. This helps not only to progress leads but also to qualify or disqualify them and tailor follow-up messaging.

"Targets" you set are arbitrary. They serve as a benchmark for measuring and adjusting progress. The two important characteristics of the buyer's journey for which you should define targets are:

MQL: Marketing Qualified Lead
An internal term we use to describe someone exhibiting behavior that indicates their interest in learning more and suggests that we can provide them with further details for education and advancement.

For example:

- Visiting your blog over 10 times in the last week.
- Staying on the same article for over 30 minutes.
- Clicking a CTA, downloading a guide, or signing up for a webinar.

SQL: Sales Qualified Lead
Behaviors that justify transitioning your lead from the marketing process to an active sales conversation, as they are likely ready to make a purchase

For example:

- Visiting your pricing page more than 5 times.
- Filling out an application.
- Emailing you with a product-centric inquiry.
- Resetting on their budget cycle, especially if you target companies that depend on a regular funding schedule.

MQL and SQL markers can be used to trigger workflows or assign scores within your Lead Scoring framework (page 183) to aid with prospect prioritization. In the Sales and Marketing Map, defining monthly or quarterly targets are adequate.

Stage	AWARENESS	CONSIDERATION	DECISION	CLOSE
Requirements to advance	Email	Email	Schedule date & time, Identify decision-makers, Phone #	Banking or credit card information
Targets per month	1000 new contacts captured	200 Marketing Qualified Leads (MQLs)	50 SQLs	5 Closed

As every business is unique, here are 4 more examples of the Sales + Marketing Map for various business types (product, services, or software):

Product: Health supplement to combat the flu

Stage	AWARENESS	CONSIDERATION	DECISION	CLOSE
Pain/Need/ Motivations	-Fever, sore throat, ache all over. -Pain, discomfort, frustrated, worried, tired.	-Find a cure that works best for me. -Driven to take action, uncertain about treatment options.	-Find the most effective supplement. - Frustrated & overwhelmed with options.	-Start treatment immediately. - Concerned it might not be effective.
Questions	-What causes fever, sore throat, and body aches? -What are the symptoms of the flu? of a cold? of food poisoning? -What is the flu?	-How can I treat the flu? -How can I boost my immune system? -How can I treat it without using unnatural medications?	-What do I need to know when considering nutritional supplements? -How do I select the supplement that is right for me? -How do different supplements compare?	-How much does it cost? -Are there any guarantees? -How soon can I see the results?
Channels	Blogs -5 signs you're coming down with the flu. -Cold vs. Flu: What are the symptoms? What is the difference? -What is the flu? -How long does the flu last?	Videos, Blogs -Ways to treat the flu without medication. -What is the best medicine for the flu? -How do you cure the flu quickly? -What could happen if you don't treat the flu?	Infographic, Workshop, Videos -Comparison chart of different supplements & their effectiveness. -How to make your own immune	Landing page or website -Pre-authorized payment with automatic renewal for subscriptions.

			booster supplement.	-30-day money-back or satisfaction guarantee.
CTAs	Read more, Learn more, Take the quiz	Download this recipe or guide	-Book a consultation session. -Read our reviews	-Subscribe for monthly deliveries -Order a sample -Discount code for referrals
Lead Magnets	Self-diagnosis tool -Fill out this quiz with your symptoms to determine if you have a flu or a cold.	Downloadable recipes -Natural home remedies for the flu. -5-day smoothie recipe to boost your immune system.	Free health consultation session with a licensed medical professional.	-
Requirements to advance	Email	Email	Schedule date & time, Phone #	Credit Card/Bank info
Targets per month	2000 new contacts captured	200 MQLs	100 SQLs	20 Closed

Service: Startup Support Organization

Stage	AWARENESS	CONSIDERATION	DECISION	CLOSE
Pain/ Need/ Motivations	-Have an exciting idea. -I don't know what I don't know.	Reduce risk & likelihood of failure.	To get the right support from the right organization.	-Time vs. Monetary commitment. -Convinced of value.
Questions	-How do I start my business? -Will someone steal my idea? Is it even a good idea?	-How to find a mentor or advisor? -How do I find a co-founder?	-Is this type of support right for me?	-Should I join now? -Is it worth my investment? -Will it really help my business?
Channels	*Presentation, Webinar, Blogs* -Startup 101 - Basics before you start a company. -What and where to find help or support. -Business planning or critique sessions.	*Workshops, Webinar, Blogs* -When are you ready and how do you raise capital from investors? -How to find your ideal co-founder? -Differences between an Incubator, Accelerator, MBA.	-Mock mastermind sessions. -Demo Day.	-Applications to join an upcoming cohort. -Interviews.
CTAs	-Learn more -Sign up for our next event	Download the guide	-Invite a friend -Testimonials from entrepreneurs we've supported	-Apply now -Join the waitlist
Lead Magnets	*Checklists, Quizzes* -What to have in place before you incorporate? -Checklist to	*Checklists, Templates* -Ideal investor checklist -Sample Sales Script -Sample Marketing Strategy	Strategy session with a business advisor	Money-back & performance guarantees

	review before you quit your job and become an entrepreneur. - Entrepreneurship grit test: Do I have what it takes to start a company?	-Sample Sales Strategy		
Requirements to advance	Email	Email	Schedule date & time, Phone #, Business plan	Credit Card/Bank info
Targets per month	300 new contacts captured	80 MQLs	20 SQLs	2 Closed

Service: Sales Consultancy

Stage	AWARENESS	CONSIDERATION	DECISION	CLOSE
Pain/Need/ Motivations	-I want to launch my business, product, or service. -No idea how to get customers. -New users, customers, sales.	-To find a process proven to generate results. -Overwhelmed.	To find the right person to work with.	-To see results soon. -Justify ROI.
Questions	-What is a launch plan? -What do I need to know to launch successfully? -What is Go-to-market? -How do I create a sales & marketing strategy?	-How do I get customers? -How do I price my offerings? -How do I convert customers? -How do I build a sales process? -What tools and processes should I put in place? -How do I do email outreach? -How do I build a prospect list?	-How do I select the right marketing or sales consultant? -Do I need a marketing/sales consultant?	-How much does it cost? -Are there any guarantees? -How soon can I see the results?
Channels	Blogs, Videos, Workshops	Videos, Blogs, Workshops	Strategy Call	-MOU -Pilot
CTAs	-Read More -Learn More	-Download this guide -Sign up for the newsletter	-Book a consultation -Read our customer testimonials	Satisfaction guarantee
Lead Magnets	Product launch checklist	Sales + Marketing Map template	Case studies	-
Requirements to advance	Email	Email	Schedule date & time, Phone #	Credit Card/Bank info
Targets per month	500 new contacts captured	100 MQLs	50 SQLs	2 Closed

Software: Customer Relationship Management Tool

Stage	AWARENESS	CONSIDERATION	DECISION	CLOSE
Pain/ Need/ Motivations	-Get more customers. -Grow my business.	-Manage and improve customer relationships. -Convert more leads.	-Makes my job easier.	-Meets the needs of my business as it grows. -Integrates with existing tools and automates processes.
Questions	-What is inbound marketing? (e.g. landing pages, email drip campaign, social media). -How do I scale my business?	-How can a CRM tool help me manage my customers & leads? -How do I create good email marketing campaigns?	-What is the best CRM tool with email marketing features? -What is the difference between HubSpot, MailChimp, and Active Campaign?	-How much do I have to pay monthly? -How long is the contract for? -Will it integrate with my existing tools?
Channels	-Blog post -Tutorial videos -Workshops	-Webinars -Mini-courses	-Blogs comparing different marketing software -Demo	-Proposal -Onboarding training
CTAs	-Read more -Download a guide	-Download templates -Register for webinar	Schedule a Demo	Create a free account
Lead Magnets	Guides	-Templates -Courses	Tailored demo + setup	Freemium
Requirements to advance	Email	MQL Behaviour	SQL behavior -Phone number. -Calendar availability	Credit Card info
Targets per month	2000 emails captured	1000 MQLs that go into specific drip campaigns	200 Demos	50 customers closed

Your Sales + Marketing Map isn't a static document. As Mike Tyson famously said, *"Everyone has a plan until they get punched in the mouth"*. This doesn't mean that planning isn't important; instead, it emphasizes that plans need to account for uncertainty. The market can react differently, and it's continuously evolving, with buyer demographics and behaviors constantly changing as different generations mature into various market segments. Additionally, unforeseen variables, like COVID-19, can emerge. Let this map serve as your framework for experimentation and improvement.

Since there's no such thing as a perfect plan, this should also relieve you from the pressure to get everything perfect before launching. Avoid overanalyzing and overbuilding; it's more important to start with something basic and refine it from there.

It's still worth doing this exercise even if you've already launched your business or have an effective sales and marketing strategy in place. This Sales + Marketing Map will help ensure that everything serves a valuable purpose, is intentional, and aligns with each other. Often, existing businesses have a wealth of disjointed content, resources, and tools. Don't simply create content for the sake of it; ensure everything works cohesively to support the prospect in their purchasing journey.

Revisit it yearly to make the necessary adjustments to respond to the changing market or better capture predicted opportunities. More importantly, this Sales + Marketing Map is reusable and can be used for every new product, update you release, or target market you're expanding into.

ASSIGNMENT

1. Create your Sales + Marketing Map using this template: https://bit.ly/sales-marketing-map. Pay attention to stages in the buyer's journey that you're not currently or poorly addressing. Start to fill in those gaps.
2. Now that you have your Sales + Marketing Map, draft an actionable launch plan to create your missing pieces. Below is an example for a group coaching program:

To-do (Channels & Lead Magnets)	CTA	Follow-up
6 long-form blog posts	-Subscribe -Download this free tool -Read this other post	Email to welcome them as a subscriber.
4 landing pages with downloadable tools or checklist	Download for Free	Drip email to check out more articles and learn more about our program.
2 events and webinars in August	Book a free strategy session	Summary email with feedback from strategy session and invitation to be a member and receive more support.
-Program info session. -Mock group coaching session.	Book a qualification interview	Deposit to hold a spot.
Landing page with program details	Apply now	-If the lowest tier is chosen → to the payment page. -If group coaching is chosen → Book a qualification interview.
Payment page	-Collect payment depending on the membership chosen. -Register pre-authorize payment.	-Add to member portal. -Send a welcome email. -Invitation to create their member profiles.

SALES PROCESS

Your Sales Strategy consists of a variety of interlinked Sales Processes that feed into and interact with each other. Each process is a specific step-by-step procedure to acquire and convert customers. Continuing the map analogy, there are specific paths prospects follow to reach their destination, and there can be multiple possible paths that lead them there.

Sales Funnels

The Sales Funnel is a visual representation of the Sales Process. It's called a "funnel" because more people will come in at the top, and as they go through the series of actions or processes, fewer of them convert out the bottom. For instance:

See Ad → Visit Landing Page → Sign up for Webinar → Attend Webinar → Receive post webinar Drip → Sign up for free strategy session → Strategy session → Qualified → Instructed to apply for program → Application received → Payment set up → Onboarding

Ad → Landing Page → Order a sample → Subscribe for monthly deliveries

Walk by your store → Notice it → Stop to look → Come in → View a product → Pick it up → Checkout

Here are some visual examples:

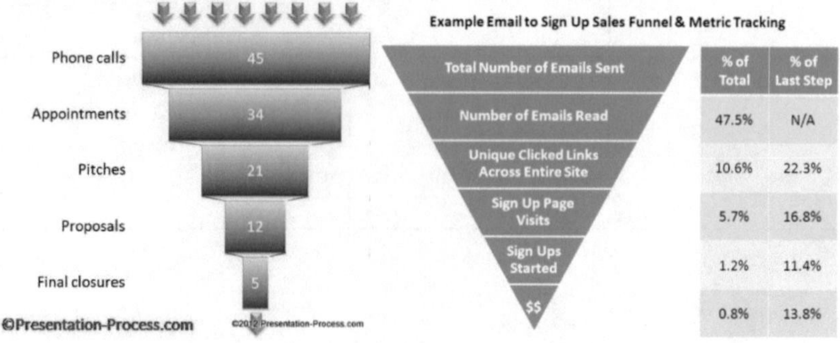

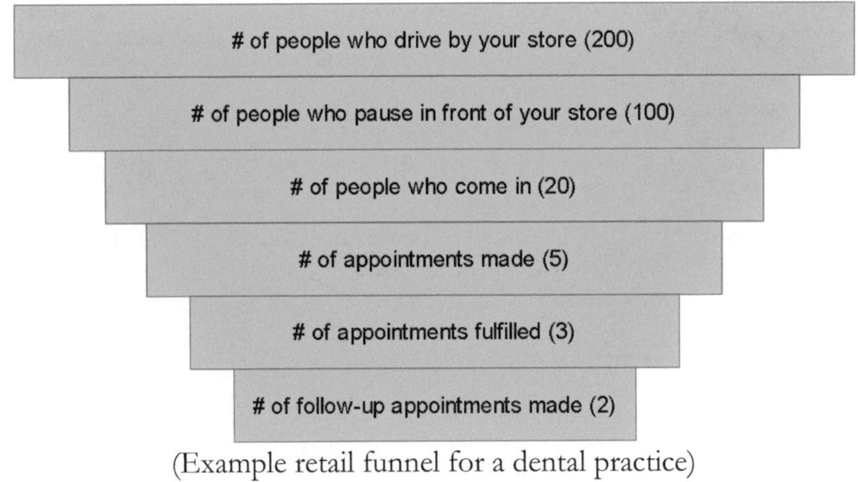

(Example retail funnel for a dental practice)

It's valuable to map and track specific funnels because it provides us with granular insights into how our prospects progress and the effectiveness of our tools. With conversion data, we can take tangible actions to reduce funnel leakage (page 259), optimize conversion rates, or expedite our sales cycle (page 182).

PROCESS-ORIENTED FUNNEL

If you run a copy-paste business, this is where you'll want to begin. A copy-paste business is one that may not be particularly innovative, but there's nothing wrong with that. There is ample room for more of the same, especially in underserved markets. Examples include dental clinics, marketing agencies, accounting firms, and restaurants.

Step 1: Mystery shop
Emulate what your competitors are doing. They have already developed an effective process for finding and closing leads. Despite the education system's negative view of copying or plagiarizing, there's nothing unethical about learning from others. It only becomes problematic if you're infringing on trademarks or copyrights, but that's not what I'm suggesting here.

Recall the software startup that helped hospitals manage their student interns shared on page 190. Find a successful funnel that resonates with you. If possible, go through their process and purchase their product. Pay close attention to how they convert you, the persuasive language they use in their copy, their CTAs, and their onboarding process.

If you're not impressed with what your direct competitors in the industry are doing, consider expanding your options by looking at indirect competitors. Indirect competitors are offerings that also vie for your prospects' attention, interest, and budget within the same lifestyle or activity category.

For instance, if you run a restaurant:

Direct competitors =	other restaurants
Indirect competitors =	food preparation, meal kit, or food delivery companies like Methodology, Nutrition for Longevity, or Sunbasket

If you run a movie theater:

Direct competitors =	other theaters
Indirect competitors =	bowling alleys, arcades, or even escape rooms

Step 2: Mimic it

What elements do you like? What would you like to change? This may include descriptive text, imagery, layout, and CTAs. Don't copy and paste, take the time to customize these elements to resonate with your specific audience and offerings.

You can explore Facebook's Ad Library to view their ads if they are currently advertising on that platform.

Step 3: Be seen in the same places

Use a competitor analysis tool like similarweb, Semrush, Moz, or Serpstat to analyze their sources of website traffic. Keep in mind that traffic volume data provided by these platforms is often estimated and may not be entirely accurate.

If they are achieving success with advertising on specific websites, social channels, or through referring partners, you should be able to as well, even if your budget is more limited. By reaching your audience in the same places with similar and proven-to-convert ads or landing pages, you can attract potential customers who might otherwise go to them.

If you happen to run a dental or healthcare practice, you may also be interested in this article I wrote for a client in Australia: https://classynarwhal.com/how-dental-or-gp-clinics-can-apply-modern-business-practices-to-increase-profit/

USER JOURNEY FUNNEL

The process-oriented funnel works well only if there is a proven and linear process that your customers follow to purchase a similar offering. If you have an innovative solution or are targeting prospects who have not encountered this solution before, you should not limit yourself to it. Instead, consider building what I call a User Journey Funnel.

This funnel should reflect the key decision-making stages, as outlined by the previously mentioned ACDC framework (page 235). Although it looks similar, it's used in a completely different way. The Sales + Marketing Map helps us understand the various potential paths a prospect might take to convert. It allows us to meet them where they're at through the right channels, with the right resources, and the appropriate CTAs. On the other hand, the User Journey Funnel is a live tool for tracking and visualizing your various prospects, allowing you to determine where each one is in the journey.

This approach better encourages SDRs to use different tools and actions instead of persistently trying to push a prospect to take the prescribed "next step" in their outlined process. For instance, not requiring prospects to jump on a demo call, but instead offering a trial to prospects who want to experience something first-hand.

Here's what it might look like:

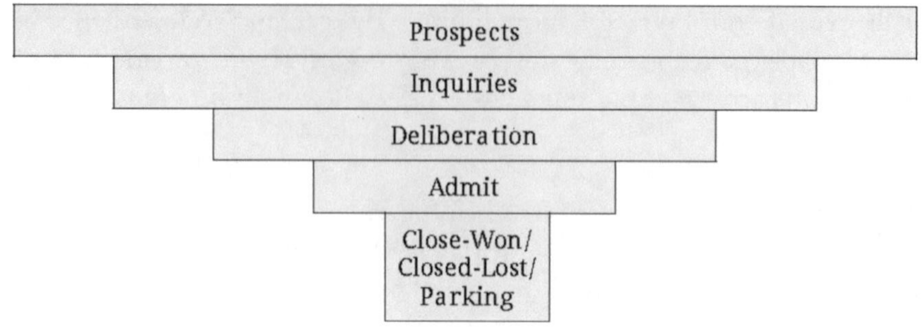

(Example User Journey Funnel stages)

The terms you use to define the stages are up to you, the important thing is ensuring your team is aligned in their understanding of these definitions. Below is how I've defined this example:

Prospects: People whom I've identified as potentially a good fit for my program but haven't yet displayed active interest (outbound, I typically need to guide them through the entire gradualization process).

Inquires (Awareness/Consideration): People who might be slightly interested and are trying to learn more. Might be an inbound lead or an outbound lead that has been converted to this stage.

Deliberation (Decision/Close): Expressing strong interest. High likelihood of converting these leads into a sale.

Admit: Verbally committed to signing up, but have yet to pay.

Close-Won: Cash in bank/Contract signed.

Close-Lost: Not interested.

Parking: Interested, but circle back later (e.g. Going away on vacation, no budget now, etc.

Here's a real albeit simplified example of gradualization applied to creating a User Journey Funnel for a program that helps entrepreneurs learn how to raise capital from investors.

Top of Funnel (ToFu)

Realization #1: I need to scale. Goal: Make them realize that if they're not growing, they're dying.
Options: Ads, Meetups, Email Drips Potential Topics: • Analysis/reports showing growth trends for startups. • How to launch into new markets. • Navigating the recession. • How to go beyond early adopters and reach the mass market. • Metrics and signs to check to know if you're ready to scale your business.
Capture email addresses to track intent, via: • Event registration page • Subscribe to newsletter • Download guide Track: Email responses/open rates/click-throughs

Middle of Funnel (MoFu)

Realizations #2: Funding will help me scale. #3: I don't know anything about fundraising. #4: Your company is the expert in fundraising. #5: I need to start the process early to succeed. Goals: Show them the merits of raising capital vs. bootstrapping and build our credibility.

Options: Webinar, Workshop, Discovery call Potential Topics: • How to find your ideal investor. • Bootstrapping vs. Raising from investors. • Pitch workshop. • Valuation and dilution. • How to negotiate with investors.

Bottom of Funnel (Bofu)

Realization # 6: This program will save me time and money in raising my round. Goals: Familiarize them with the fundraising process and our program. Generate a sense of urgency (not a false one, but because fundraising takes a while, and most entrepreneurs have incorrect expectations about the timeline)
Options: Course Page, Interview, Demo Potential Topics: • Walk them through the fundraising process and timeline. • Review program curriculum and what's expected of them vs. from us. • Discuss program pricing and emphasize that we do not collect commission on investor referrals nor do we seek equity for their participation.

FUNNEL OPTIMIZATION

With your funnel created, the next step is to use it to start tracking leads. This will allow us to identify bottlenecks and areas for improvement.

CONSISTENT TOP-OF-FUNNEL

A funnel isn't of much use if you don't have people to put through it. Start by addressing and prioritizing sales issues from the top and work your way down. Here are a few factors to explore:

1. Test different Copy

You might not be using the right language or messaging that resonates with your customers, gets them interested, and motivates them to take action.

2. Explore different Channels (page 178)

Trying to find your clients on Instagram? Perhaps they're more active on another platform. Not every organization needs to be on every social media platform. Are you meeting your prospects where they are?

3. Target different Customers

Are you defining them correctly? Are there different target markets to branch into? Perhaps there is another segment that is less resistant or more eager to adopt your offerings.

4. Develop Evergreen Content and Consistently Promote it

Don't limit yourself to posting only when inspiration strikes and create content that can be reused. Given the vast amount of content online, repetition is necessary for visibility, rarely will your post be seen by the same person over and over again.

5. Failure to Capture Leads

Many organizations are overwhelmed with doing a lot, but are you ensuring your activities are serving their purpose? Publishing a blog or organizing an event without a clear CTA means missing out on the opportunity to identify those interested in more. Every piece of content you put out or activity you do should tie back to your funnel and help you move (and track) prospects from one stage to the next.

6. Not Prioritizing Sales

This is often an issue for smaller organizations and founding teams that are not comfortable with sales. Although they know it's important, their activities don't reflect it. Selling becomes a byproduct squeezed into their day whenever possible (which they'll often find excuses not to do) instead of something they build a routine and rhythm around. If this is you, instead of trying to fit it into your day, structure your day around it to avoid procrastination.

7. Make it a Habit

Service-based businesses often experience cyclical revenue due to fluctuations in project loads. They become engrossed in ongoing projects, neglecting sales efforts, and then scramble for new sales when projects conclude. Establish a routine for prospecting even during busy project phases to maintain a steady flow of opportunities.

8. Explore a different Growth Engine (page 146)

We've been taught and trained on the most common – Paid, but it may not be the most effective for every offering or organization.

CONVERSION RATE BETWEEN STAGES

Identify stages with poor conversion or high drop-off rates. For example, if you're noticing that people get stuck at the demo stage with a low conversion rate from demo to proposal, investigate what might be causing this issue.

1. Right Target Audience but Wrong Messaging?

2. Wrong Audience?

Even within your target audience, there may be non-ideal customers. Define red flags to help you more easily identify habitual procrastinators, allowing you to prioritize your efforts accordingly.

3. Wrong Timing?

You might get both the above right but still end up targeting them at the wrong stage of their decision-making process and communicate the *right* messages to them at the *wrong* time (recall gradualization). For instance, you may be advancing too quickly and trying to close them too soon when, in fact, they aren't ready. They need to spend more time in your marketing funnel to be nurtured or have their concerns properly addressed first. This could be either because you aren't properly identifying and qualifying (page 128) them or lack proper sales/marketing processes to nurture them.

4. Underperforming SDRs?
Is it possible that a particular inexperienced SDR is negatively impacting the conversion numbers?

5. Bad Techniques or Poor Resources?
This is the sales version of wrong messaging and stems from a lack of or poor techniques. Perhaps they lack experience or confidence, are afraid to ask for a sale, have the wrong mindset and approach, aren't setting clear next steps, are disorganized and poor at following up, or are weak at handling objections. Your sales team might need better training or resources to deliver a more effective demo.

6. Wrong Process?
Or, should you consider revising the stage itself? Could a demo be unnecessary, and prospects might benefit from experiencing a free trial to test the product themselves? This is why I advocate for a User Journey Funnel rather than a Process-oriented Funnel.

TIME TO CONVERT BETWEEN STAGES

You might have an excellent conversion rate from workshop attendees to consultation requests. However, this step might take a long time, thus extending your overall sales cycle. Explore the potential reasons for this. One solution could be to speed up the process by sending a follow-up email to workshop attendees with a link to schedule a consultation.

Refer back to Shorter Sales Cycles (page 182) for more ideas.

FUNNEL LEAK

Occurs when someone exits your funnel. For instance, if someone adds an item to their e-commerce shopping cart but doesn't complete the purchase. It's important to address those who don't convert and find ways to guide them back into the funnel.

1. Retargeting
Have you ever noticed that after visiting a company's website, their ads seem to follow you everywhere on Facebook, Google, and more? This is possible through the use of "cookies", which capture data from website visitors. These cookies, stored on your computer, allow advertisers to remarket to you, encouraging you to revisit their site. Moreover, it enables them to customize the content displayed to you. For example, on your return visit, they might skip the introductory video and show you the full website since you've already gone through the tutorial.

2. Follow-up on Action Abandonment
If you've captured their email, consider sending a reminder about the items left in their cart. You can also include them in an email drip campaign to further nurture their interest in your solution. Additionally, circle back in the future to schedule a demo. If they were seeking a quote, you might even want to follow up with a call. Don't assume you're being pushy; they might have accidentally closed the window or hesitated due to an unaddressed uncertainty.

COLLECTIONS

Closing a sale is one thing; however, receiving payment and securing cash in the bank can pose an entirely different challenge.

In an ideal world, we would set up pre-authorized debit with our customers to automatically withdraw payment from their accounts when due. However, it's not uncommon for many businesses to operate on models where products or services are delivered prior to payment. Even if you strive to enforce upfront payment, you may need to make concessions to secure larger clients who have the leverage to negotiate more flexible payment terms. For instance, large retailers like Walmart typically require suppliers to ship inventory, only releasing payment 30-90 days later. This practice is also common in project-based work, such as consulting or construction, where a smaller deposit might be cleared upfront, but the bulk of the payment often won't be released until the work is completed and deemed satisfactory.

For obvious reasons, this can pose a significant risk to a business, and good cash flow planning is essential for sustaining operations or preparing those orders before receiving payment. If this applies to you and you haven't explored financing, consider looking into factoring, purchase order financing, or supplier financing for some non-dilutive options.

However, if you're experiencing issues with delinquent accounts, here are some tips:

Maintain open and transparent communication with customers
Clearly outline payment terms and expectations from the beginning. Send timely and polite reminders before payments are due, and follow up promptly if a payment is missed. Communicating that you expect on-time payments will help prevent recurring tardy behavior. If you set the precedent that you're lax with enforcement, it will only lead to poor discipline, and clients may delay payments more often because they know it's easy to get away with.

Automate Reminders
Automating payment reminders is a good idea because it helps maintain

consistency in communication to reduce missed payments. While it may make communication less personal, this can also work in your favor. By eliminating the necessity for SDRs or account managers to repeatedly remind customers about payments, you avoid putting at risk the relationships they have cultivated with their clients.

Offer Flexible Payment Options

Try to uncover the reason for their lapsed payment. If it's unintentional and they are facing unforeseen constraints, make it clear you're open and flexible to work out an agreeable solution for all parties. This could include installment plans or temporarily adjusting the payment schedule to accommodate your customer's financial situation.

Escalate Gradually

Have a systematic approach for escalating collection efforts. Start with gentle reminders and progress to more assertive communication if necessary.

Offer Incentives

Consider offering incentives for early or on-time payments. This could be in the form of discounts or other benefits that encourage customers to meet their payment obligations on time.

Document Everything

Obvious, yet still often overlooked: keep detailed records of all communication and agreements with customers regarding payments. This documentation can be valuable in case of disputes or legal actions.

Escalating to a collection agency or pursuing litigation is a last resort and should only be considered once all other options are exhausted. The bridge is burned once you've crossed this point. They will likely discontinue working with you. Even if they don't, you should consider terminating them as a customer, as past behavior is a good predictor of future behavior.

SALES LEADERSHIP

Here are some strategic advice and lessons I've learned from fellow business owners who have made mistakes or received poor HR guidance from professional recruiters or managers.

CULTURE

Culture solidifies and becomes much harder to shape once you've grown past approximately 25 employees. If you don't take the time to proactively define your organization's culture, screen candidates for it, and intentionally cultivate and encourage it, it will be defined for you by the people you inadvertently add to your team. Like Newton's first law of inertia: *an object in motion stays in motion unless acted upon by a force.* Negative culture is harder to weed out once it has begun to take root.

Culture entails much more than having a foosball table, beer nights, and flexible work hours. It encompasses but is not limited to:

- Your organizational chart or chain of command (e.g. hierarchical, flat/horizontal, etc.).

  On this note, especially if you're a startup, my advice is not to try to reinvent every wheel. You're probably already taking on risk by creating a novel solution, addressing an underserved market, or doing business in some other unique way. Try to keep your org chart simple by starting with what already works. You can test and improve from there.

- Your organization's Mission, Vision, and Values
- Work Ethic (e.g. 9-5 vs. hustle culture, organized and detailed vs. quick and scrappy).

Culture is a long-term play. If your goal is to make a quick profit and sell your company, this isn't the approach for you. Opting to be intentional with culture will, in the short-term, slow down decision-making, as more time is required for deliberation and debate, and to create a space where individuals are encouraged to challenge decisions that may not align with the organization's values. A culture-conscious approach also lengthens your hiring process, as it takes more time to screen for mission and value fit. But in the long run, fostering the right culture leads to a healthier and more enduring organization.

MISSION, VISION, & VALUES

Are all taught as important pillars for a business. But how do you get it right?

Using Tesla, here's an example to help you better understand the differences between each of them:

Mission: the purpose of your organization.	The WHY: Your motivation	To accelerate the expansion of sustainable and renewable energy.
Vision: the tangible or measurable outcome that allows you to "see" if it's been achieved.	The WHAT: Your destination	Become the leading automobile company of the 21st century by spearheading the world's shift to electric vehicles.
Values: your ethos.	The HOW: Your mode of transportation (how you'll get there)	Doing the best, taking risks, respect, constant learning, and environmental consciousness.

There's understandably a lot of emphasis on the importance of having a clear mission for your organization. I won't argue. It IS important! Because I won't go into this topic, if you haven't already seen Simon Sinek's TED Talk – How Great Leaders Inspire Action (or read his book Start with Why), I recommend starting there.

Not enough attention has been given to the HOW: your values, which are equally important. Clarity on values enables us to achieve our objectives without selling our soul. The journey is as important as the destination; it's not about getting there at all costs.

VALUES

If you have a list of 10 core values plastered on your company's wall, you're probably off to the wrong start. Why? 10 is too many. At any given time, an individual (or an organization) only has the capacity to prioritize and focus on no more than 3 core values.

Focus on your top 3, at this moment. Values will shift and should change as an organization grows and evolves, and that's normal. For instance, a startup may prioritize *innovation*, but as it scales, it may start to place a heavier emphasis on *security* or *integrity*. This is purely an example; there's no right or wrong approach to defining what matters most to you and your organization.

GET SPECIFIC

Security could be defined as stability to one person, a bulletproof data and privacy approach to another, and safety to yet another. Be clear about how you define your values and what they mean to your organization. For instance,

> *Security:* Ensuring the safety and protection of our employees, customers, and sensitive information. We prioritize creating a secure environment where everyone feels safe and confident in their interactions with our company.

Values in Decision-making

Take it further by defining manifestations of them in employee behaviors and giving examples of how they inform and influence decisions. With the previous example:

> Manifestation of *Security* in a Decision: When considering a new software vendor for handling customer data, our company prioritizes security as a core value. Instead of solely focusing on cost or features, we carefully evaluate the vendor's data encryption protocols, compliance with industry regulations, and track record of security incidents. This decision-making process ensures we uphold our commitment to security and mitigate potential risks to our customers' data.

The decisions we should make become a lot clearer once we understand our values. For instance: The government is approaching you with an interest in licensing your software for surveillance.

If one of your core values is:

Growth	This could be a great opportunity to build credibility and secure a stable anchor client.
Privacy	You might opt to pass on this in favour of fostering long-term trust with your existing users.

INTERNAL VS. EXTERNAL

Not all values need to be customer-facing (external); some values are inherently skewed towards how your organization operates (internal). Neither is better, but understanding the difference can help with how you communicate it with your employees, use it in recruitment (page 276), or leverage it for marketing to attract prospects that resonate with your approach. For example,

> *Fail forward:* Could be a valuable internal value intended to encourage employees to experiment or signal it's okay to make mistakes as long as they're learning from them. However, this may not be appropriate for external communication. It may inadvertently create concerns or doubts among customers or stakeholders about the reliability or competence of the company. Customers might prefer to see a polished image of success and expertise rather than being reminded of the possibility of failure.

PUSH VS. PULL VALUES

This is another important distinction to understand when applying values in the workplace.

Many organizations make the mistake of solely pushing values in an effort to encourage employees to adopt them. *Push*-related initiatives aren't inherently negative; however, an excessive reliance on them can lead to a sense of inauthenticity. Values are integral to an individual's sense of self, and while a person's set of core values can change over time, they are relatively entrenched. If an employee does not already align with one of your organization's core values, pushing it on them will only further alienate them.

Example *Push* Initiatives:

- Framing your values on your wall.
- Celebrating people who exhibit behaviors indicative of those values.
- Creating an "innovation" department or organizing internal hackathons to encourage innovation.

Instead of only using *Push*, also consider *Pull*-oriented approaches that foster the growth of desired values. What does this look like? Instead of getting people to do more of X, enable people who already WANT to do X to do it more easily. This can be achieved by thoughtfully designing your workplace environment and policies to naturally invite, encourage, and signal that certain values and behaviors are welcomed.

Example *Pull* Initiatives:

- Google's 80/20 policy, also known as "20% time" or "Innovation Time Off," is a famous approach to employee productivity and innovation. The policy allows Google employees to dedicate 20% of their work time (one day per week) to pursue projects that are not necessarily part of their primary job responsibilities. This time is intended for employees to explore their passions, work on pet projects, or experiment with new ideas that could potentially benefit the company.

  The 80/20 policy has led to the creation of many successful Google products and features, including Gmail, Google News, and AdSense. By giving employees the freedom to pursue their interests, Google fosters a culture of innovation, creativity, and entrepreneurship within the company. This policy encourages employees to think outside the box, collaborate across teams, and drive forward-thinking initiatives that can have a significant impact on the company's growth and success.

  It's not about forcing employees to be more entrepreneurial.

Instead, it's about making their company a place where entrepreneurial-minded people want to come and work.

- Netflix's unlimited vacation policy, often referred to as "unlimited time off," gives employees the freedom to take as much vacation time as they need without strict limitations on the number of days off they can take each year. Instead of tracking vacation days, Netflix focuses on achieving results and trusts its employees to manage their time responsibly.

  This policy reflects Netflix's culture of freedom and responsibility. It empowers employees to take ownership of their work-life balance and encourages them to prioritize personal well-being alongside professional commitments. By offering unlimited vacation, Netflix demonstrates trust in its employees' judgment and dedication to delivering high-quality work.

  Furthermore, the policy aligns with Netflix's emphasis on outcomes over processes. Instead of micromanaging employees' time off, Netflix focuses on the results they achieve. This fosters a culture of accountability and encourages employees to manage their time efficiently to meet their goals and deadlines.

Netflix's unlimited vacation policy is not without criticism, primarily raising concerns about employees paradoxically taking less time off for fear of appearing less dedicated than their peers or leaving a bad impression on their managers. The success of policies like these depends highly on how they are implemented and communicated to ensure all employees share the right expectations of what is reasonable and appropriate. Regularly reflect on how your initiatives are playing out to assess whether they are encouraging the intended behaviors or causing unwanted side effects.

Pull initiatives are not only good for cultivating those values in existing employees but also for attracting talent that already resonates with those values. If you are someone who cares about sustainability, you would be more attracted to work with a company that also cares about it. Here are some other example initiatives designed for popular organizational values:

Integrity

Push

- Creating a Slack channel to celebrate instances of integrity.
- Annual awards to celebrate the employee who best manifested integrity in the workplace.

Pull

- Leading by example: following through on promises.
- Turning away prospects that lack integrity: refusing to work with a shady client despite being offered a large sum of money.
- Freedom to work policies:
    - Ability to work remotely
    - Open vacation policies
    - Highlight you are result/outcome-driven and trust your employees to act with integrity.

If you focus on *pull*, you send the signal that this is a place where people who have integrity work; this organization has integrity. You trust your employees to make decisions with high standards in mind because you believe they will act with integrity.

Boldness/Courage

Push

- Screening for boldness/courage in the interview process:
    - Excluding meek or timid candidates.
    - Asking candidates about a previous instance where they demonstrated boldness/courage.

Pull

- Creating an environment where it's OK to be bold:
    - Creating space and opportunities to invite others to comfortably voice their opinions and ideas (anonymous if necessary).
    - Empowering employees to make certain decisions with autonomy.

If you only *push*, people feel pressured to be someone they're not, whether it's for the sake of getting hired, keeping their job, or pleasing others. Instead, by also *pulling*, you signal that you aren't forcing them to be someone they aren't comfortable with. On the other hand, if they have a natural inclination towards boldness, they'll enjoy your company because it embraces boldness. Your organization won't dismiss or chastise bold suggestions, and you welcome new ideas or candid discussions on new possibilities.

MERCENARY VS. MISSIONARY

Why am I discussing culture so extensively in a book about sales? Because I often find sales teams are the breeding ground for toxic cultures. If culture is not approached intentionally and if incentives are applied toward rewarding the wrong metrics, it can unintentionally encourage the wrong behaviors.

If short-term outcomes are all you care about, you can get away with recruiting skillful mercenaries. However, it is critical to proactively seek and filter for mission and value alignment in the people you add to your team if you wish to create a healthy long-term environment. I've witnessed this firsthand in the workplace:

During my time at WIND Mobile (now Freedom Mobile), I had the opportunity to work closely with the company's top salesperson nationwide, whom I'll refer to as Adam for anonymity.

I first met Adam during a visit to our flagship store at Metrotown Mall while exchanging inventory with the manager. Even then, Adam's aggressive sales tactics and reputation for "stealing" sales from colleagues had already made him unpopular among coworkers. Despite this, his sales performance didn't warrant termination, leaving his manager in a dilemma.

Although Adam's sales performance contributed significantly to company objectives, it was overshadowed by the negative impact on team morale and our brand's reputation. Customers would often return to complain about false promises and misinformation he provided.

Recognizing the need for intervention, I proposed transferring Adam to one of my stores to coach and address his behavior. However, despite my efforts, Adam persisted in his conduct, creating a toxic atmosphere among my employees. Eventually, I initiated the termination process, meticulously documenting his behavioral issues, coaching efforts, and issuing formal warnings.

Also check out: https://classynarwhal.com/5-mistakes-organizations-make-when-implementing-values-in-the-workplace/

ASSIGNMENT

This exercise comes from Tony Robbins' book: Awaken the Giant Within.

For founders/business owners: this exercise can be done with your team to surface organizational values from the bottom up. It's worth doing this even if you've already defined your company values, as values can and should change over time.

For individuals: Although you may lack the ability to influence your organization's values, this will still help you better understand yourself, especially if you haven't already defined your values. Clarity of self enables you to better identify your authentic style and determine which sales techniques or methodologies best suit you.

1. Come up with a list of 10 values important to you or your company.
    a. E.g. integrity, adventure, humor, sustainability, innovation, trust, transparency, etc.
2. Rank them from 1-10.
    a. If you find it challenging, isolate and compare two values against each other; the more important one is ranked higher. Repeat this process by comparing either of those values with a new one.
3. Focus on your Top 3 values. We engage in this roundabout process because it's challenging to be decisive and limit yourself to only 3 core values right from the start.

Notes:

DIVERSITY & INCLUSION

You might argue overemphasizing organizational values promotes groupthink. However, it does the opposite. It enables the right kind of organizational diversity and improves creativity without slowing down decision-making. This is possible because clarity on values eliminates ambiguity regarding what is right vs. wrong and encourages diverse ideas that are still grounded in the same mission and ethos.

Since we're discussing organizational diversity, a topic gaining in popularity, allow me to share some personal insights. This isn't about hopping on the trendy bandwagon; correctly approaching D&I brings clear benefits for any organization.

Inclusion before Diversity

To look good, some organizations emphasize diversity for diversity's sake (e.g. % of women or visible minorities on your company's board of directors); instead, it's more important to create a culture of inclusion. Diversity metrics will naturally follow when you have a welcoming and inclusive environment.

For instance, if LGBTQ+ employees are recruited without first establishing an inclusive environment, they may feel marginalized. Creating such an environment is not a simple task and requires ongoing effort. An example of an inclusion-oriented initiative could be implementing a 'no judgment' policy, allowing employees to ask questions and learn about their LGBTQ+ colleagues without fear of prejudice or mislabeling.

Cognitive Diversity leads to measured Diversity

Focus instead on improving cognitive diversity within your organization. When you put together people who think differently, their different perspectives allow you to come up with more unique solutions to problems. Scott Page, Professor of Complex Systems at the University of Michigan uses the ketchup example to illustrate this point.

> *"In North America, ketchup is typically stored in the fridge. When running out of ketchup, Americans often default to alternatives like*

> *mustard and mayonnaise, which are commonly stored nearby.*
>
> *In Europe, ketchup is typically stored in the cabinet. Consequently, when it runs out, the popular alternatives are vinegar or Tabasco."*

Without a diverse team, your reflexive response will be mayonnaise every time.

I paraphrase an important insight shared with me by Caitlin Webster, Director of Talent Development at AbCellera, a biotech company in Vancouver specializing in cutting-edge antibody medication. Although my data may be outdated, last I spoke to Caitlin in 2019, AbCellera boasted a 67% female team despite having a male CEO. They achieved this without explicit diversity initiatives by prioritizing cognitive diversity.

> *"When seeking individuals with different opinions, skills, experiences, ideas, and perspectives, they often originate from diverse backgrounds. Consequently, it's natural for them to have varying appearances (your diversity metrics).*
>
> *Recruiting for diversity shouldn't necessitate compromise. If you genuinely seek the best talent, diversity will naturally emerge within your team."*

So, what type of diversity should you be looking for? Winning teams are:

> *Moderate in diversity of opinion*: Too much and you won't agree on anything, too little and you risk groupthink.
>
> *High in diversity of expertise*: The less they overlap, the better. This fosters a wider range of perspectives and encourages the development of more creative solutions.
>
> *Low in diversity of power*: Don't let ego get in the way, no one should feel like they're above or below others. This encourages people to voice their opinions.

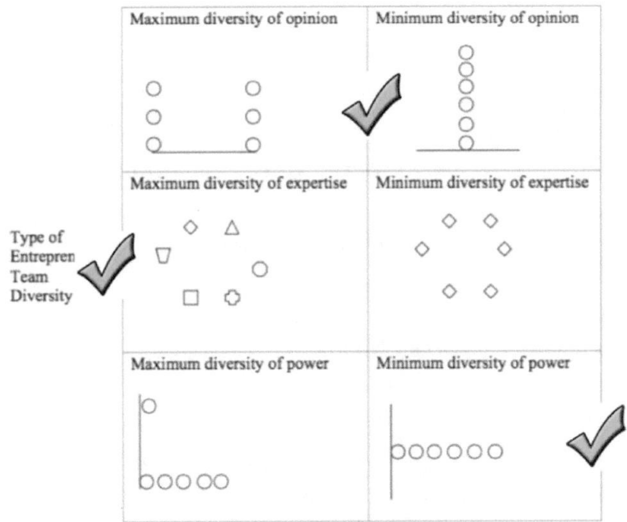

(Source: https://bit.ly/entrepreneurial-team-diversity)

But if your team is too diverse, won't everyone have different opinions? Won't this slow down the decision-making process in your organization?

Yes, it will, but it won't lead to the paralyzing debates you imagine. Hire for diversity in experience and cognition, but ensure you filter for alignment on values and mission. Done correctly, these differences in opinions are healthy disagreements that will help encourage experimentation and innovation within an organization. If your employees align with your organization's values, you won't have to micromanage them. You can empower them and trust they will make decisions that not only help you achieve your company's mission but, more importantly, won't compromise on HOW you'll achieve it.

Diversity in Sales

If you're a sales manager, it's beneficial to embrace and apply D&I initiatives as well. Your team should reflect your customer base. This not only makes it easier for those customers to relate to your organization but also ensures that you better understand them. A diverse sales team is also often more adaptable and creative in problem-solving, benefiting both your customers and your sales processes.

RECRUITMENT

Ready to hire? If you're a startup, a quick word of caution from my friend John Chan, CEO at 2x, a growth agency specializing in sustainable growth for e-commerce and SaaS companies.

"Be a cockroach, not a unicorn"

I don't know which came first, John's quote or Paul Graham's popular reference to Airbnb as a cockroach that won't die, but it's great for illustrating this point: Hiring comes at a high cost. Once you add someone to the payroll, you're increasing your monthly burn rate. Aggressive growth is necessary if you need to corner the market before competitors, but it's only appropriate once you've achieved problem-solution fit + some sense of product-market and business model fit. If you haven't done that and are still experimenting, it's more important to minimize cost and weather the storm.

The cost of a bad hire is also high. Besides an increased burn rate, hiring the wrong person could greatly slow decision-making, create unwelcomed dynamics or politics within your team, negatively impact morale, and ultimately, the process of rehiring and retraining will cost more than if you had done it right the first time around. Never hire merely to fill a gap; take the time to ensure you're conducting proper due diligence to determine if they are the right fit before committing to them.

Once you decide to hire, start by filling sales or marketing roles. Employing individuals whose main role is to boost revenue is always a smart move.

Experience vs. Passion
I favor the latter for SDRs. Skill can be trained, but authentic passion, on the other hand, is nearly impossible to instill. Experience usually becomes more necessary for management and strategic input. In those situations, my suggestion is to avoid hiring salespeople based solely on their experience and familiarity with selling your type of solution; instead, seek out experience with a similar sales process.

It's hard to change habits, especially bad ones built up with experience. If someone is unfamiliar with selling your solution, they get to start with a clean slate. While it may seem like a big benefit to hire someone with a large network of potential customers they've built up with their previous employer, there is no guarantee that network will favor your solution. If they know the process, such as how to sell HR solutions in Fortune 500 companies, they can easily build a new network from scratch.

SDRs who are familiar with your sales process but not your specific offering are often more open to experimentation in finding the most effective way to sell to your prospects. This is particularly beneficial for startups that are still exploring the optimal sales approach.

Compensation

In his book "To Sell Is Human", Daniel Pink discusses the concept of compensation and its role in motivating salespeople. He argues that while traditional, commission-based incentives have long been the norm in sales, they may not be the most effective motivators.

He argues that commission-based incentives are effective only when the task has been optimized and requires increased output at a faster pace. However, in tasks involving problem-solving, such as sales, commission can inadvertently hinder performance because it restricts creativity by limiting perspectives. Individuals are less inclined to experiment and instead focus on replicating existing methods, even if they are not the most effective means of achieving desired outcomes.

(Commissions are just like horse blinkers that narrow your field of vision. Image generated using Bing Image Creator)

Pink suggests in today's world, where salespeople are increasingly tasked with problem-solving and relationship-building rather than transactional selling, intrinsic motivators such as autonomy, mastery, and purpose are more powerful drivers of performance.

Salary-based compensation models have been shown to effectively improve sales performance by enabling salespeople to focus more on serving others rather than closing transactions. I can't speak on behalf of everyone, but as someone who has worked in sales roles, I find this resonates with my compensation preferences. Commission also promotes individualism and runs counter to the spirit of fostering teamwork and collaboration within your organization.

That said, there's a rainbow of options when it comes to how you can compensate your SDRs. This applies to any other employee as well and is especially valuable for startups lacking the resources to offer competitive salaries.

Compensation encompasses and isn't limited to:

- Monetary (salary)
- Commission/Revenue share/Royalties
- Equity/Stock Options
- Strategic Partnerships (e.g. you help me with sales, I'll help you with marketing).
- Work flexibility (hours/location)
- Employee benefits (pension, vacation policy, medical/dental/vision, etc.)
- Perks (daycare, gym, office snacks, etc.)

Be creative and flexible with how you approach compensation!

Ironically, although employers are offering more perks and benefits than ever; employees are still constantly claiming companies are not doing enough for them. The disconnect occurs because employers are shoving bloated one-size-fits-all compensation packages in front of employees without properly understanding what each individual values. It's no surprise that many company perks and benefits are often underutilized.

Suicidal as it may sound, I've personally declined more lucrative contracts in favor of lower-paying projects that give me the flexibility I seek as a new father to spend more time with both my boys. If you truly wish to woo and retain the best talent, it pays to understand and involve them in negotiating compensation that's both reasonable for you and desirable for them. This leads us smoothly to our next topic:

Motivation

It's important to understand this not only for recruitment but also because it plays a key role in employee retention (page 312). I like to think of it this way: there are 4 main dials (I call them the 4Cs), each of which is weighted differently in importance by different individuals. Everyone has an ideal level for each of those factors, and if one is strongly out of balance, or if two or more are subpar, that person is highly likely to leave. The 4 Cs are:

CAUSE

Does your company's mission still align with their personal mission?

This is the reason why pivots are associated with high turnover, especially if the pivot changes who you're serving or what you're providing as a solution. The new direction may not be what your other team members originally signed up for.

It's easy for salespeople to feel disconnected from the bigger picture and perceive themselves as another cog in the wheel, especially if they don't directly influence product design or service their customers. To address this, involve them not only in daily reporting and metrics but also expose them to how the business is growing and changing because of their efforts. Help them understand how their work contributes meaningfully to the larger cause. Celebrate the stories of your customers and growth of your impact metrics.

CAREER PATH

Do they perceive a trajectory for growth? Or do they feel stagnant?

Encourage and support their personal and professional development. Consider implementing an internal mentorship initiative or tailor feedback and performance improvement plans to each individual based on their personal goals.

CULTURE
Is your ethos of doing business aligned with their values?

COMPENSATION
Are you providing a sufficient living wage: a safety net allowing them to bring their best selves to work every day?

I won't delve into further detail as we've already discussed points 3 and 4. Also, note these 4Cs are comparable to Daniel Pink's Autonomy (Culture), Mastery (Career), and Purpose (Cause).

Recruitment Sources
I'm a big advocate of recruiting from your community: your customers or volunteers. What better place to start than with people whose problems you directly solve or who are already inherently passionate about what you do?

Another great option is recruiting from external groups or communities (e.g. LinkedIn, Meetup groups, etc.). If taking this approach, I recommend interest-aligned rather than skill-centric groups. For example:

Interest-Aligned	:	AI Stable Diffusion Group, Embodied Carbon in Construction Group
Skill-Centric	:	Product Managers Group, Game Developers Group

The latter is good for finding skill-specific team members to fill in your gaps; however, it's much harder to filter them for mission and value alignment. On the other hand, if you have already found someone passionate about your cause, it is much easier to screen for skills and experience.

SCREENING

A big mistake many founders, recruiters, or managers make when it comes to fit is they hire people they "like", people who they can get along with, incorrectly attributing this fit as an indicator that the candidate is a good fit for their culture.

Fit isn't about chemistry, personal similarities, shared interests, or even the same background or experiences (recall the benefits of building a diverse team). Instead, a good fit is about alignment with the organization's goals (page 301), mission, and values (page 264). Because we tend to overrate our ability to judge others, it's important to approach interviewing with some form of structure and intention.

Culture > Mindset > Skill

What is "mindset"? I interpret it as the way individuals operate beyond their values. This would include aspects such as how they approach problem-solving, their perspectives on the world (including their opinions and predictions), whether they are self-starters, if they are inherently organized, or if they are resilient. I also consider soft skills like communication, persuasion, charisma, leadership, or creative thinking as part of "mindset".

I believe these qualities are more important than hard skills because they're a lot more transferable and valuable. Roles evolve, companies pivot, markets change, and technology is ever-advancing. Regardless of one's skills, joining a new company often requires a significant amount of retraining. Moreover, with the advent of artificial intelligence, hard skills are overrated as we need to constantly re-skill ourselves to stay relevant.

I recommend prioritizing candidates based on Culture > Mindset > Skill, in that order of importance.

Many organizations approach recruitment and screening the other way around: hiring for a role (e.g., project manager, designer, office assistant, etc.), and then attempting to screen for good mission and value alignment in the interview. I believe this is an inefficient approach because candidates will often tell you exactly what you want to hear, motivated by the desire to land the job. Salespeople, in particular, are particularly difficult to assess because most of them have learned to be charismatic and, if they've done their proper research, will know all the right points to say to sell themselves.

I'm not suggesting you should create your job descriptions without a job title or without specifying the role you're recruiting for. Skills are still important. Instead, I recommend promoting your roles with a mission and value-first approach. What might this look like?

Instead of	:	*"Hiring: Senior Programmer with Python and C++ experience"*
Try	:	*"Interested in advancing the field of quantum computing (mission)? Join our growth-oriented, innovative, and diverse (values) team! We're hiring! Learn more: [link]"*

What if you encounter someone who is an excellent culture fit, fully aligned with your values, passionate about your mission, and possesses a commendable attitude and mindset, but lacks the specific skills you currently seek?

In such a scenario, I would recommend making every effort to involve them in some capacity, even if you are unable to hire them immediately. They still have the potential to provide significant value and discover alternative ways to contribute, especially in a rapidly growing or scaling organization.

If they express keen interest in a role for which they lack skills, they can usually acquire the necessary expertise over time. Alternatively, you might consider allowing them to carve out a role for themselves based on how they can contribute, their desired responsibilities, and the tangible outcomes they believe they can deliver.

If there's absolutely no reasonable way to involve them, keep them on a waitlist, and reach out to them if something suitable becomes available eventually.

Situational vs. Behavioral Questions
This should be familiar to you if you have HR experience, but for those who don't, these are the two main types of questions you can ask to evaluate a candidate.

Situational questions help you assess their approach to problem-solving and decision-making. Here are some examples:

- If you could open your own business, what would it be and why?
- If you won a million dollars in the lottery, what would you do with the money?
- Challenge them with a problem your company is facing: How would you solve this?
- Is it better to be perfect and late, or good and on time? Why?
- What is your ideal management style?
- Tell me about what motivates you.
- What frustrates you?
- What are three positive character traits you have?

Ensure you're not only asking situational questions but also behavioral questions when screening candidates. Responses to situational questions are entirely theoretical; their ability to give the right answer might not reflect how they would actually behave in that situation.

Behavioral questions, on the other hand, are important because the best predictor of future behavior is past behavior. Examples:

- Tell me about a time you set difficult goals. What did you do to achieve them? Walk me through the process and purpose.
- Tell me about a time you screwed up. What did you learn from it? How would you avoid the same mistake from happening again?
- Describe the best boss you've ever reported to.
- What are the top things you are working on right now? How are you working on them?

Some sales professionals might boast about superficial

accomplishments in which they may not have played a significant role. You can uncover this by delving deep with behavioral questioning and applying the STAR(T) interview method when assessing their responses. It's a red flag if they continually dodge a detailed response in favor of highlighting performance metrics, results, awards, or achievements.

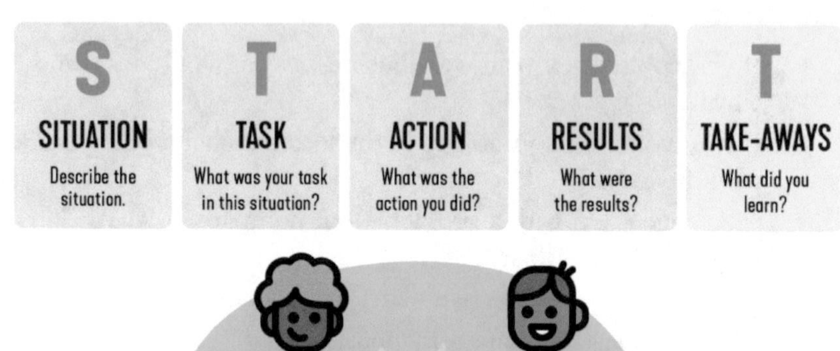

(Source: https://management30.com/practice/star-behavioral-interview-questions/)

Good vs. Great Responses

Define what a great response looks like and train those involved in the screening process to know what to listen for.

During my time as a retail manager, I had an interview guide with a list of questions to ask. However, not much training was provided on evaluating responses and we had to rely on our own judgment to ultimately decide whether to hire a candidate. Among those questions were some related to the company's values. For example, if *Courage* was one of the company values, we had to ask candidates what courage meant to them and for them to give an example of how they behaved courageously.

As you can imagine, it's not difficult to give a nice-sounding answer. As long as it wasn't a terrible answer, I would check off this box to qualify that the candidate "met" that value. Knowing what I know now, I should have been trained to listen for great responses. For example:

Evaluating *Courage*

Good:	*"I'm unafraid of confronting angry customers who are in the wrong"*
Great:	*"I never hesitate to stand up against what I believe is wrong. I've attended the Trans Mountain pipeline and Black Lives Matter protests. I am also one of the co-organizers for Rise Up, a non-profit working to advance gender equity and justice in education, health, and economic opportunity."*

Evaluating *Sustainability*

Good:	*"I recycle"*
Great:	*"I volunteer every year for the local beach cleanup in my neighborhood. I am also a volunteer educator for SeaSmart, a non-profit educating children on the importance of our oceans"*

Are they here for an Experience or to Achieve a Goal

Avoid individuals who are seeking experiences, as they are likely to leave quickly once their experience is fulfilled or if it is not as they expect. Instead, prioritize candidates with clear goals, as they tend to be more ambitious, resilient, and adaptable. For instance, consider the following scenario,

If you ask:

> *"Why are you interested in working for us?"*

An experience seeker might reply:

> *"I want to try working for a startup because I'm sick and tired of the corporate environment where my opinions don't matter."*

Why isn't this a good response? Many individuals are attracted to the idea of working for a startup. They could seek a similar experience at any other startup and may not be genuinely committed to your company's mission. Does your startup align with their idealized perception of startup life? They may be enamored by the idea of working for the next up-and-coming business, but have not considered if the fast-paced, uncertain, low-compensation, or long-hours environment common to most startups is suitable for them.

If you notice frequent job changes on a candidate's resume, it could indicate a propensity for seeking experience. Beware!

Conversely, an individual with a clear goal might reply:

> *"I'm drawn to your company because I believe other telecommunication companies are exploiting us consumers. Your company seems to be doing things differently and prioritizes the best interest of the consumer."*

Their goal doesn't necessarily have to be something that aligns with your organization's mission. Even a career-oriented goal like *"I aim to one day be the VP of sales for an organization"* is still better than an experience seeker. An individual with a career goal seeks experience for learning and growth, not just to try something different, which I believe isn't a bad thing.

Reference checks: DO IT

1 in 3 references are bad! Many individuals provide references who may not have worked closely with them, expecting that they will only provide positive comments about their obvious strengths without mentioning their weaknesses or bad habits in detail. Often, colleagues will assure the candidate of a positive reference but convey their true experiences to recruiters if they did not have a favorable interaction with the candidate.

Instead of inquiring, *"Would you want to hire this person again?"* or *"Was your experience working with them good/bad?"* Ask specific questions about their work experience to determine if the reference has worked closely with the candidate and uncover their genuine opinion of them. Some examples include:

- Is this person among the top 5 individuals you've worked with?
- What contributions have they made that benefited your company?

- Would you rehire them? Why or why not?
- If I were to work with this person, what areas should I focus on to enhance their performance? (Instead of asking for weaknesses)
- What management style is most effective with this person?
- In what areas would you suggest they improve?
- Does this person thrive more independently or as part of a team? Are they more suited to leadership roles or implementing tasks?

Listen to what's not being said. Certain companies may be restricted from providing formal references. While this restriction prevents them from explicitly criticizing the candidate for legal reasons, their lack of commendation can still hint at a negative experience.

ONBOARDING/TRAINING

As with how you should proactively design the experience in your customer's journey (page 96), you should do the same with your employees' journey:

- How do they discover your company?
- What do they learn about you during their research and due diligence?
- The job application process.
- The interview process.
- The post-interview follow-up experience.
- Negotiation and acceptance.
- Onboarding.
- And ongoing engagement.

Unhappy employees have the potential to cause as much, if not more, damage to your external brand than unhappy customers. Ensure you pay equal attention to the experience of your employees' journey, so they may continue to vouch for you even after they've left.

SALES TRAINING

As you implement sales training programs, ensure the following:

1. Customize it for your business

There are many excellent generic sales programs available. While enrolling your new SDRs in these may be more affordable, consider investing in custom-created training for your organization. This is because people retain information better when it's relevant to them. Customization ensures that they are provided with realistic scenarios, prospects, objections, and exercises that will aid them in navigating similar situations when they occur.

2. Practice, practice, practice

We might not have the chance to apply what we learn immediately or do so frequently. Practicing in between by quizzing each other and role-playing helps us retain knowledge. Keep that mental muscle strong using spaced repetition: review the information at increasing intervals over time to improve long-term retention. Adjust spacing intervals based on your performance. If you recall the information correctly, extend the interval until the next review. If you struggle to remember, shorten the interval.

"Knowledge, without action, is just entertainment"
– Original author unknown

3. Phrasing and language matter
Your sales training serves as the foundation of your sales culture. Be mindful of the language used, as phrasing can influence our perception of sales and how we treat others. Avoid phrases like:

"Kill objections", as it frames the interaction as "us" vs. "them", creating a win-lose mindset whereby SDRs strive to win at all costs instead of finding win-win solutions.

or *"it's a numbers game"*, leads to treating customers as a transaction rather than building a relationship.

Check out Anna Taylor's post: https://bit.ly/Anna-Taylor-LinkedIn-Post which proposes shifting away from violent language. Some disagree with her "woke" approach and believe it's excessive. I believe it depends greatly on the specific words used and their context. While I don't think it's necessary to replace all the phrases she suggested, I do support adopting a more mindful approach to our everyday language.

Here's an updated image of her suggestions:

EVOLVING FROM VIOLENT LANGUAGE

Anna Taylor

INSTEAD OF	SAY THIS
We're going to pull the trigger	We're going to launch
I'll take a stab at [it]	I'll take the first pass at [it]
Did we jump the gun?	Did we start too soon?
I'll bite the bullet	I won't avoid it any longer
That'll kill two birds with one stone	That'll feed two birds with one scone
What's the deadline?	What's the due date?
We have to pick our battles	We have to choose our opportunities
Can you shoot me an email?	Can you send me an email?
That was overkill	That was a bit excessive
I bombed the presentation	I didn't do my best
Let's just roll with the punches	Let's just go with the flow
We can soften the blow by...	We can make it a little easier by...
I'm going to take a shot in the dark	I'm going to take a guess
That's not a bad idea	That's a good idea
Let's not beat a dead horse	Let's not focus on that anymore
I was blown away by her presentation	I was impressed by her presentation
I was kicking around an idea	I was thinking through an idea
He's a straight shooter in meetings	He's pretty direct in meetings
You're crushing it/ You're killing it	You're doing extremely well
Let's look at the bullet points	Let's look at the focus or key points
We're under the gun to show results	We're under pressure to show results
Can you send me a headshot?	Can you send me a business photo?
We dodged a bullet	We were lucky
Can you knock this out by Friday?	Can you get this done by Friday?
We need to execute the plan	We need to implement the plan
I'll see you in the "war room"	I'll see you in the "win room"
Can you send me a screen shot?	Can you send me a screen grab?
Who is the target audience?	Who is the priority/primary audience?
Let's divide and conquer the work	Let's split up the work to accomplish the task
There are many ways to skin a cat	There are many ways to approach this task

PERFORMANCE MANAGEMENT

"What gets measured gets managed."
– Peter Drucker, management consultant and author

SALES METRICS

There are 2 main categories of metrics you should pay attention to in sales:

1. Customer Metrics

Conversion rate, sales cycle, customer acquisition cost (CAC), lifetime value (LTV), churn, etc. Clarity on these metrics helps you with further improving your messaging and activities to capture more customers, more quickly, and with fewer resources.

2. SDR Metrics/Key Performance Indicators (KPIs)

Sales target achievement, number of deals closed, an individual's conversion rate, activity metrics (e.g. number of calls made, emails sent, meetings booked, etc.), customer satisfaction, etc. These metrics are necessary to effectively coach and support your SDRs.

I won't go into the details or various formulas you can use for calculating them since there is already an abundance of information available online. I will instead focus more on how to effectively use your data. But before you jump into trying to capture as much data as possible, remember:

"Data is like garbage.
You'd better know what you are going to do with it before you collect it."
– Mark Twain, author

DATA IS ONLY A PART OF THE PICTURE

If you ask, "How did you hear about us?" to try to better understand what led your prospects to you (a.k.a. source), the answer may not paint the full picture.

They may have originally heard your ad on the radio, seen a few Facebook ads, and then searched for a solution to their problem on Google. They happened to select you because they were already familiar with your brand and might answer "Google" due to the recency effect: *the tendency for people to recall items or information they encountered most recently more easily and accurately than information encountered earlier.* Or they might have deflected their response to the most obvious answer because they honestly don't recall where they first heard about you.

Data is important, but make peace knowing it won't be 100% accurate because you're dealing with messy humans. Worst case, with bots, and predictability more so in the coming future, with AI. A lot of what you capture may not even be human, a study found approximately 20% of ad impressions served in the United States alone were fraudulent. It's becoming increasingly difficult to distinguish humans from bots in ad clicks, web traffic, and even social media engagement.

(Click Farmer in China, circa 2015. Now automated at a much larger scale and no longer requiring a human to manually click)

Begin your data strategy with your goal and work back from there:

- What are you trying to improve?
- What do you need to learn to improve it?
- What data can you capture to help you better understand what you're trying to learn or give you an indication if you're trending in the right direction?

SOME THINGS ARE DIFFICULT OR IMPOSSIBLE TO MEASURE ACCURATELY

While transactions are easy to measure, the quality of a relationship is a lot harder to quantify. Even with great referral tracking in place, you might still miss properly attributing a referral if they don't remember who they heard about you from.

Step back to consider the bigger picture and long-term outcomes too.

ACCOUNT FOR INDIRECT EFFECTS

Rarely will data depict a direct correlation between activity and outcomes. Even if it does, it's still important to take a bigger picture perspective and be mindful of other less obvious effects. This story of Kinko's from the Episode 142 of The Empire Builders podcast provides an excellent illustration:

> Many of you may not be familiar with Kinko's. For some context, they were a popular American photocopying and printing retail chain in the 1980s and 1990s. Kinko's was acquired by FedEx in 2003 for $2.4 billion. There was a point in their operations where Paul, the founder, was evaluating with a partner for one of their locations in a convenience store, whether they should keep it open 24 hours.
>
> They would do about $30 worth of business at night and $60,000 during the day. Based on this obvious observation, they decided to close at night; however, as soon as they did, daytime business also dropped by about 50%. This led Paul to get all the other stores to do the same, and it was monumental in helping them grow the business nationwide.

Why in the world would that happen?! They still barely sold anything at night. There are many opinions on possibilities, but here are some potential explanations:

- Perhaps that was when they acquired a new customer because they were the only store open?
- Maybe it made them more noticeable because they were the only store visibly lit up at night?
- Or because it helped anchor an impression of reliability that kept them top-of-mind for their customers?

Whatever the reason, and even if doing the same thing might not create similar results in your context, business, or location, the point here is to be attentive to indirect and less obvious effects that you may not be intentionally measuring or observing.

SOME THINGS TAKE TIME

Data is often captured in short windows. However, some campaigns may take a while to bear fruit. I don't recall the specifics, but I heard an example along the lines of:

> There was a restaurant (in Yukon, if I'm not mistaken) renowned as a high-end establishment, the kind you would take your partner for a fancy date night. In an attempt to grow revenue, they decided to adjust their marketing and branding to better capture casual diners.
>
> In the short term, as they started to pull in both casual diners and fine diners, you could call their campaign a success. However, over time, this shift in positioning ended up sticking more than they anticipated and their establishment became better known as a location for casual dining. This eventually drove down average order value, and they even lost some of their loyal fine dining clientele, ultimately leading to a bigger loss in revenue.

It's hard to predict the long-term outcome of a campaign like this, but before you jump the gun on defining success metrics, ensure

1. Your activities align with your organization's values.

And

2. You not only measure the short-term results but also continue to analyze the long-term trends.

Many of us harbor common misconceptions and unconscious limitations regarding what we choose to measure and set as goals. Most goals, especially business goals, are set on Monthly, Quarterly, and Yearly targets. Paraphrasing Simon Sinek's talk: https://youtu.be/UY-1-9ObaLE

These are unnatural limits because of pre-defined reporting, fiscal, or taxation cycles. We place similar limitations as well when we set personal goals: 30-day diets, resolutions for the new year, etc. While deadlines can be useful for driving urgency and challenging ourselves, we have to also remember life is a continuum, it's not constrained by months or years. Let's look at an example of 2 different sales teams working towards hitting their monthly revenue goals:

Team A:

- Morale is up and down. If the month starts slow and they feel like they won't hit the target, they are not motivated.
- Poor retention, people are quitting all the time.
- There is no trust amongst the team as people compete with each other to steal sales.
- Toxic leadership.

Team B:

- Slow and steady growth, trending towards hitting the goal.
- Good and strong team.
- Good morale, has a capable leader.

We set a monthly revenue target and incentivize both teams to hit that target to obtain their bonus.

Team A aggressively closes customers, scrambles with last-minute discounts, and meets the target.

Team B falls slightly shy of the target but displays all the right behaviors.

If we incentivize Team A with the bonus, this is the message we're sending: *"We don't care how you get there. We don't care if you step on your co-workers. We don't care if you are unethical. If you hit your number, you'll do well in our organization."*

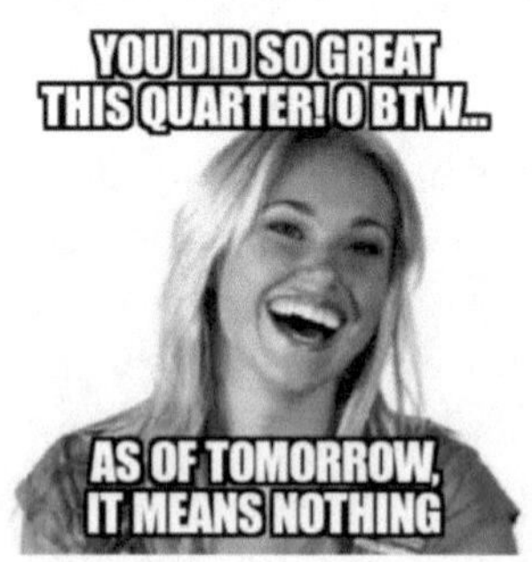

Of course, this is a theoretical example. Team B could also be highly motivated by the bonus and scrambled to meet it. But the point is: **HOW you get there matters as much, if not more, than WHEN you get there**.

As Simon says:

> *"When you have an infinite mindset, absolutely, have the goals, but the trend matters more. How you get there matters as much, if not more, and we pay attention to that. So even if I hit my fitness goal, I'm eating better, I'm sleeping better, my relationships are great, I'm going to the gym. Yes, I miss my goal, but I know if I just keep going, I'll hit it. I'm getting healthier and healthier. I just got the timing wrong.*
>
> *This is what we need to build into business: that infinite mindset. Yes, have the goals; yes, have the ambitions; yes, have the annual targets. If we miss them, as long as we're doing the right things, we have the right lifestyle to take us there. That's a much healthier way to live a life and a much healthier way to build an organization."*

Avoid accidentally encouraging bad behavior by incorrectly incentivizing the achievement of metrics (lagging) without accounting for how we achieve (leading) the desired results and the long-term trends. Recognize and reward the appropriate behaviors that contribute positively to your objectives.

TURN DATA COLLECTION INTO CUSTOMER VALUE

Say you run a restaurant and are trying to learn about your customers: How often does a customer return? How frequently? How much do they typically spend on meals vs. drinks? What's their average order?

You could obtain this data by collecting their phone number or email. Enabling you to associate an individual with their behaviors during each visit and even potentially market promotions or specials to them.

To capture it, you could train your servers to request a customer's contact information before seating them. Don't penalize them for failing to capture this information. Perhaps customers are not willing to readily disclose their contact information without context, as they do not want to receive spam. Instead, create an opportunity to improve the customer experience and add value with this information exchange.

This can be done if you make the benefit of the exchange clear. Perhaps you want their phone number so you can notify them when their table is ready, or they can unlock and track points with their phone number to exchange for discounts or free meals.

LAGGING VS. LEADING METRICS

Lagging Metrics	Leading Metrics
• Outcome/Results • Which you don't control • Usually business-centric	• Output, Behaviors, Activities, or Initiatives • Which you can control • Usually customer-centric
• Monthly revenue • # of conversions • Customers closed	• # of calls or outreach emails sent • # of events organized • # of follow ups

Although the word "lagging" has a negative connotation, BOTH are important. What you choose to display and reward will also greatly affect the culture of your organization. Read this Inc. article: https://bit.ly/dashboards-and-metrics for more detailed insights. To summarize:

Lagging Metrics are easy to define and track. They help assess if your activities are effective and should regularly be reflected upon to determine if your initiatives are yielding the intended results.

Leading Metrics, on the other hand, help you predict where you will go. They're indicators of the *processes* that you predict will produce certain *results*. If you're looking to cultivate and encourage certain behaviors, it's better to focus on leading rather than lagging metrics, since lagging metrics are only indicative of the outcome, regardless of what was done to achieve them.

For instance, if you're trying to improve customer satisfaction:

Lagging Metric	Leading Metrics
Net Promoter Score (NPS)	• How long till calls are answered (wait time)? • % of resolved cases.
If you want to improve it, you need to look upstream to determine what initiatives you can put in place to improve this outcome.	• If it's taking too long to answer calls you may need to hire more Customer Service Representatives (CSRs). • If too many cases are left unresolved, you may need to change something about your offering or possibly empower your CSRs so that they have more options or authority to resolve without needing to escalate.

Related reading: https://wizardofads.org/dont-just-trust-the-numbers/

ASSIGNMENT

Define specific Lagging and Leading Sales metrics. If you need a framework to categorize them to ensure you're accounting for all stages of the customer's journey, the Pirate Metrics framework introduced by Dave McClure, founder of 500 Startups, is a pretty good place to start.

Pirate Metrics = AARRR (like a pirate, get it?)

Stage	Example Metrics	Your metrics (no more than 3 per stage)
Acquisition	Website visits, Ad clicks, Prospects who walk into the store, New leads generated, Downloads	
Activation	Activation rate (% of users completing an essential action - e.g. using a feature, completing their 1st transaction), Onboarding completion rate	
Retention	Churn rate,	

	Customer LTV, Repeat purchase rate, Engagement metrics (e.g. time spent on site/app, frequency of visits)	
Revenue	Average revenue per user (ARPU), Average order value (AOV), Conversion from free to paid, Monthly/annual recurring revenue (M/ARR), Sales cycle	
Referral	Net Promoter Score (NPS), Number of referrals made by customers, Referral conversion rate, Social media shares and mentions	

GOAL SETTING

OKRs: Objectives and Key Results
First introduced by Intel and popularized by Google, OKRs stands for Objectives and Key Results. This widely used goal management framework is designed to better align activities and initiatives with objectives (your goals).

Objectives (Where do I need to go?) • A goal for the future. • Ambitious and inspirational. • Sets a clear direction and provides motivation. • Your company mission/vision is typically an objective. • Qualitative in nature and potentially hard to measure. • Heavily influenced by factors beyond your control.
Examples: • To become the leading X company in X region. • To successfully capture the X market.

Key Results (How do I know if I'm there?) • The metrics that indicate if you have achieved your objective. • Helps measure progress toward your objective. • Quantitative and measurable. • If realistic, mostly under your control.
Examples: • Close 20 new customers each month. • Open/launch in one new location each month.

Initiatives (What will I do to get there?) • The work you will do that might influence your Key Results. • Activities, actions, behaviors, or systems. • Measurable and, if realistic, fully under your control.
Examples: • Call/Email 10 new prospects a day. • Schedule 5 demos a week.

OKRs contain SMART elements (page304). They're not mutually exclusive frameworks. Good OKRs and Initiatives should also be SMART. You can also have multiple OKRs that collaboratively move you closer to an Ultimate Objective (mission/purpose/BHAG: Big Hairy Audacious Goal), example below:

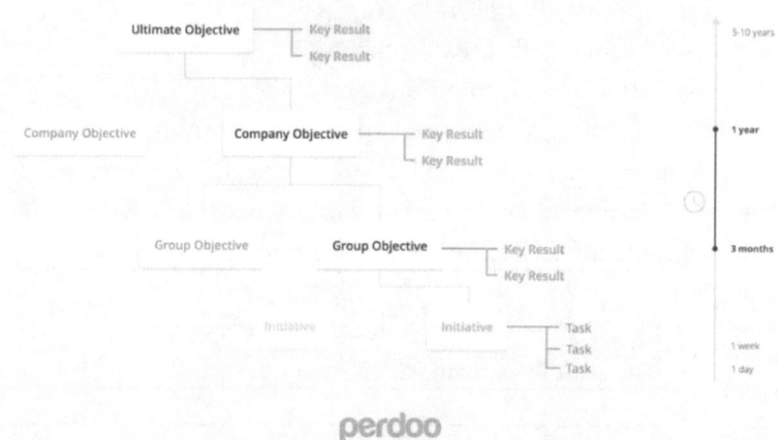

(Hierarchy of OKRs, illustrated by Perdoo)

Initiatives aren't set at every level; they only need to be set at the most basic level. You won't need to define Initiatives to address the "Ultimate Objective" OKR because "Company Objectives" serve as the Initiatives for it.

Using the OKRs framework to map your goals will help you and your team visualize the smaller goals that help move you closer toward a larger and seemingly far-fetched goal.

Here's a detailed example to help you understand OKRs in action:

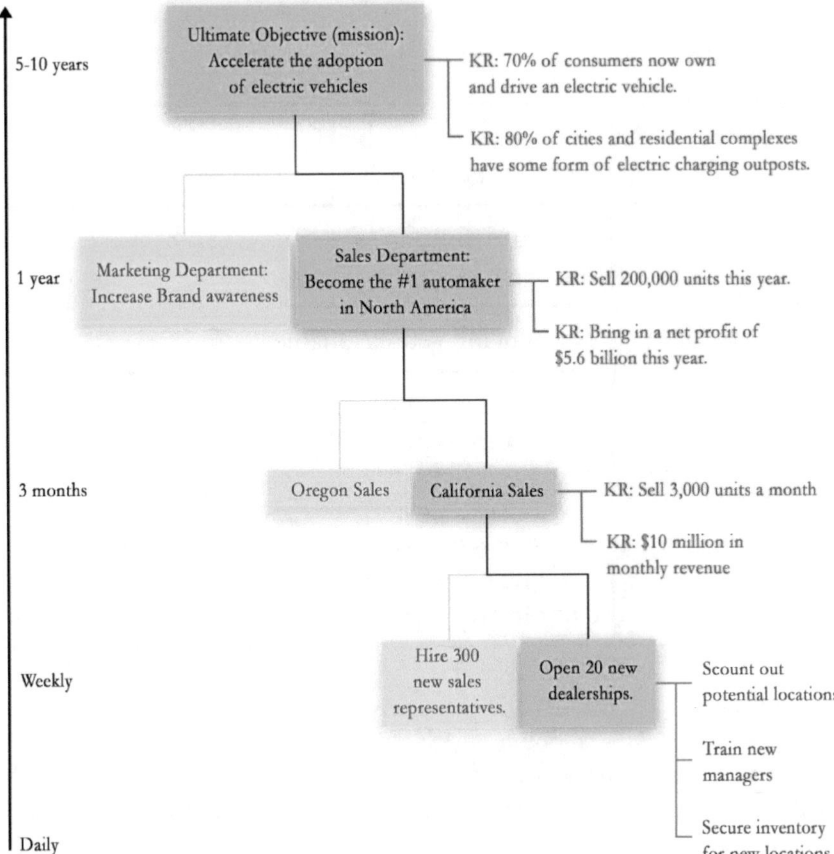

(Hypothetical OKRs using Tesla as an example)

SMART Goals

Use the SMART framework to ensure your OKRs are effective and tangible:

SPECIFIC	Focused and tangible. Otherwise, your goal may be too vague to achieve.
MEASURABLE	A clear definition of success to help you evaluate achievement and progress.
ATTAINABLE	Challenging yet reasonable.
RELEVANT	Does it align with your values? Will it serve you? Is it a current priority?
TIME-BOUND	Parkinson's Law states *"Work expands so as to fill the time available for its completion"*. A specific and challenging deadline will keep you focused and disciplined to get it done.

Examples:

Bad: I want to be more fit.
SMART: I want to reduce my BMI to 20 and achieve a beep test score of 9 by March.

Bad: I want to earn more money.
SMART: I will invest $1,000 a month into my tax-free savings investment account and leverage it with ETFs and stocks that provide a minimum 5% dividend.

Bad: I want to reduce plastic pollution
SMART: I will limit my take-out dining orders to no more than twice a week

Notice in the first example, the specific target date makes it tangible; however, the second and third examples are more effective despite not having a target date. Why? Because they encourage constant improvement while giving you a time window to assess and quantify progress. This is a good example of a system-centric goal encouraging long-term growth. The sense of momentum and progress from achieving these goals will empower you to take further action.

If you choose to set SMART goals with a time window instead of deadlines, don't forget to periodically reflect and evaluate if the habits or behaviors attached to them are positively contributing towards your intended objective.

STOP = STOP, THINK, ORGANIZE, PLAN
Remember! The goals (Key Results) you set for your Objectives are there to serve them. They're the means, not the end; don't overfocus on them.

Google's Chief Decision Scientist, Cassie Kozyrkov, shares a great example of the perils of putting your goals before your objectives in her Advanced Manual of Self-Improvement (https://bit.ly/manual-of-self-improvement). Definitely worth a read, as it discusses goal-setting beyond sales management:

> *"If your goal is to look your best, the point isn't how many ounces of chocolate you do or don't eat each day (process goal/* **Initiative***).*
>
> *The point isn't what the scale says tomorrow morning (performance goal/* **Key Result***).*
>
> *The point is how you look in the long run (outcome goal/* **Objective***)."*

Be mindful of Goodhart's Law: *"When a measure becomes a target, it ceases to be a good measure."* When people or organizations are incentivized to meet certain targets or metrics, they may alter their behavior in ways that distort or manipulate those measures, undermining their usefulness as indicators of success or performance. The Cobra Effect is a real-life anecdote illustrating how metrics used to guide decision-making can lead to unintended consequences if not carefully managed:

> During British colonial rule in India. To control the population of venomous cobras, a bounty was placed on each cobra killed. Initially, this led to a decrease in the cobra population.

> However, people began breeding cobras to collect more bounties, rendering the initiative ineffective. When the government realized this and canceled the bounty program, the breeders released the now-worthless cobras into the wild, resulting in a higher population than before.

A similar situation also occurred in the 1902 Great Rat Massacre of Hanoi, which even led to an outbreak of the bubonic plague, claiming the lives of over 263 people. Never pursue your Key Results for their own sake, continuing Cassie's example:

> *"Imagine that your outcome goal (***Objective***)is better health and your performance goal (***Key Results***) is your weight. At first, you're cutting out junk food, but as the days go by you notice that you're able to get an even better score in the game of Weigh Yourself by drinking less water, taking diuretics, making yourself sweat, and eating all kinds of non-nutritive chemistry experiments. When you see the scale, you're chuffed… but what about that overall outcome goal? Your health will be a wreck if you keep this up. Clearly, the scale has ceased to be a good measure of your health since you've started gaming it in a way that's destructive to your overall goals."*

It's also okay to change your objectives if they are no longer appropriate for serving you and your organization! Doing so doesn't make you a cop-out or someone incapable of seeing your goals through to the end. There's a difference between changing or abandoning a plan as an excuse and recognizing when it's no longer the right plan.

Don't fall prey to sunken cost fallacy: the cognitive bias that occurs when one continues to invest resources (such as time, money, or effort) into a project, endeavor, or decision solely because they have already invested a significant amount, even though the investment is unlikely to yield favorable outcomes in the future. It happens because we often feel emotionally attached to our past investments and are reluctant to abandon them, even when doing so would be the most logical choice. Try not to let past investments influence your decisions about whether to continue investing more resources.

A simple example of this is how many of us are inclined to continue watching a bad movie or TV series because we've already invested money in buying the ticket or time watching a portion of it.

In sales, this could also manifest as an unwillingness to abandon certain prospects or campaigns because of prior investments in them. Worse yet, some organizations abuse this fallacy to manipulate their prospects. They do so through an overly vigorous qualification process, not designed so much to disqualify prospects who aren't interested or a good fit; but instead to deliberately get prospects invested.

What might this look like? Not to encourage you to do so, but rather to raise awareness so you can call it out if you see it.

- Intentionally making prospects jump through hoops to prolong the negotiation process.
- Falsely "allowing" a customer to speak to their manager, even though they may have been able to resolve the inquiry themselves.
- Subjecting a prospect to an "initiation" or ritualistic process before allowing them into a program.

But I digress, let's return to the topic of goal setting!

Set up regular reminders to STOP (**S**TOP, **T**HINK, **O**RGANIZE, **P**LAN) and reflect (monthly, quarterly, yearly). Review results, evaluate if you're measuring the right things, and ensure you are making progress in the right direction. Your goals should always serve your ends, not your means; course correct if your actions or initiatives aren't contributing towards your goals, or if your goals are no longer contributing to your objectives. Don't be overly attached to the resources you've invested in a campaign if it's no longer serving you. Changing your approach does not mean you have failed.

Upon reviewing this section, I realized "goals" might be confused with "objectives". Specific to this section, objectives are used in reference to the OKR framework. Akin to vision/mission. Goals are the measurable key results.

ASSIGNMENT

Using OKRs: Map out organization-wide vs. department Objectives & Key Results and identify potential Initiatives.

Ensure they are **S**PECIFIC, **M**EASURABLE, **A**TTAINABLE, **R**ELEVANT, and **T**IME-BOUND.

Notes:

COACHING

With the wealth of existing literature on this topic, I'll concentrate on the foundational elements I've found to be most valuable:

Speak their Love Language

From a young age, many of us are taught to empathize with others using the Golden Rule: treating others the way we would like to be treated *ourselves*. If we would feel hurt by being made fun of, we shouldn't make fun of others either. This is basic etiquette. If you truly want others to listen and feel valued, apply the Platinum Rule (there's a book about this that goes by the same title as well):

> Do unto others what *they* would like done unto *themselves*.

Just because you value gifts of appreciation for your efforts doesn't mean others value them equally. Someone else might be more strongly motivated by words of praise instead. This necessitates a more thoughtful approach. Learn about the preferences of others and be attentive to them to truly make them shine.

A great book on this topic is "The 5 Love Languages" by Gary Chapman. It primarily focuses on love and relationships but translates well to leadership and management too. The five languages are:

Words of Affirmation:	Praise, Encouragement.
Acts of Service:	Sacrifice, Thoughtful gestures.
Receiving Gifts:	Not dependent on the cost, the thought behind the gift counts too.
Quality Time:	Attention. Could be in the form of direct mentorship or hands-on coaching.
Physical Touch:	The only one inappropriate for the workplace!

Instead of BUT, say AND

When providing feedback, if you follow up a positive sentence with a "BUT...", it discredits everything that came before it. It makes a person feel bad because it insinuates criticism of what they've done.

"AND..." allows us to explore ways to improve without discounting all the positive work done so far.

The Power of Questioning

"Reactance" or "authority resistance" occurs when individuals perceive a threat to their freedom or autonomy, leading them to resist attempts to control or influence their behavior, particularly by authority figures.

Avoid telling people what to do or imposing prescriptions. Instead, even if you know the solution, use questioning to create room for collaboration. People are more willing to buy into an improvement plan if they are involved in coming up with the solution. For example:

> You: *"Why were you late to work today?"*

Questioning instead of stating the obvious also ensures you're not jumping the gun on making assumptions. Yes, they were late, but perhaps you didn't know they had a justifiable reason for being so.

Maybe they stopped to help someone fix their car.
Maybe there was an accident on their way to work.

> Them: *"I missed the bus"*

Even if they were late because of a poor excuse, don't chastise them right away. Proceed with questioning to coach them into independently reasoning out a solution that prevents it from happening again.

> You: *"Why did you miss the bus?"*
> Them: *"The bus I catch to work is supposed to arrive at 6.30am, but it arrived earlier than planned today."*
>
> You: *"What can you do to prevent that from happening in the future?"*
> Them: *"I guess I could wake up a few minutes earlier to be at the bus*

> *stop earlier in case it arrives ahead of schedule or I could catch the bus before that."*

Other ways to question include:

> *"Why did you do it this way?"*
> *"How can we improve this for the future?"*

Or even using a less assumptive like *"Let us suppose…"* This is especially useful for ambiguous "he said, she said" situations where it's unclear which side is telling the truth or in situations caused by misunderstandings among multiple parties.

RETENTION & OFFBOARDING

Good retention is desirable, but aiming for retention at all costs can be harmful. As we've discussed, don't let the measure become the target. Retention is simply an indicator of a good employee experience.

Some degree of churn is natural and should be encouraged. Support employees in their transition and don't be afraid to provide positive referrals to other companies. It will return as good karma when they speak positively about you to others or potentially return to work with you again in the future."

Read Reid Hoffman's Jedi Tours of Duty for a great analogy that helps us frame the roles of different employees in an organization, embrace natural churn, and understand how to best support them in their personal careers: https://www.linkedin.com/pulse/jedi-tours-duty-rebel-alliance-reid-hoffman/

Another great tip comes from Episode 137 of the Empire Builders Podcast: If you find yourself short-staffed and relying on existing employees to shoulder the extra workload, consider compensating them a bit more for their additional efforts. This approach breaks the cycle of employees leaving due to overwork and frustration. They shouldn't have to bear the brunt of your challenges in recruiting and retaining talent.

Lastly, if you have to let someone go because they are causing problems, fire fast; don't drag it out. This is not only for your own sake but also because it will be better for them to move more swiftly to a place that is a better fit for them or their next opportunity.

3: TOOLS & TECHNIQUES

Specific and actionable advice you can implement to see immediate results.

"You do not rise to the level of your goals.
You fall to the level of your systems."
– James Clear in his book "Atomic Habits"

As crucial as this is for individuals, it is even more so for organizations. On an organizational level, systems encompass individual behaviors, group routines, processes, procedures, and technology for automation.

If your goal is to reach 200,000 customers, a supporting system could be your prospecting process and the consistent commitment of at least 2 hours a day to it. Our ability to achieve our goals hinges on our compliance with the systems we establish. It's crucial to ensure we implement correct, effective, and user-friendly systems everyone is willing to adopt.

James even says "True long-term thinking is goal-less thinking. It's not about any single accomplishment. It is about the cycle of endless refinement and continuous improvement." Systems will keep us on the right path, especially when results are not immediately attainable or observable.

SYSTEMS VS. FLOW

The Flow State theory, also known as being "in the zone", is a state where you're fully immersed, focused, and thoroughly enjoying what you're doing. "Writer's block" is the term creatives use to describe this lack of flow. I believe many people hold a misconception that flow and systems cannot coexist: structure, routine, or a schedule limits creativity and productivity. You may believe that getting into flow is difficult, and once you're in it, interruptions should be avoided, as who knows when you'll be able to regain it again! However, that's not true. If used correctly, systems can help you more readily enter flow.

Work with, not against your schedule
Your schedule doesn't have to look like a typical 9am-5pm morning schedule. If you're a night owl, tailor your schedule to suit yourself and maximize productivity during the late hours.

Scheduling Tip: It may sound obvious, but tackle tasks that require the most energy (such as making important decisions, drafting proposals, or contacting key prospects) when you have the most energy. For most people, this is at the beginning of the day or their working routine, but for others, it could also be later in the day if they feel more refreshed after a nap or exercise.

Systems can help build focus
A requirement for entering the flow is focus. Don't burn the midnight oil because you're in the flow; the crash that follows isn't worth it. When you're mentally fatigued, it becomes a lot harder to re-enter the flow.

Following a schedule might mean you'll have to cut your productivity short to get the rest you need, but the long-term benefits outweigh the short-term interruption. When you consistently follow a schedule, your biological and mental clock will start to recognize when it's the scheduled time to do work, and you'll more readily enter the flow. To take it a step further, you can build a routine like taking a cold shower or drinking a cup of coffee to prime yourself. These actions will act as cues to trigger the flow state.

AUTOMATE, DELEGATE, VS. DO IT YOURSELF

Even if you're already convinced of the importance of systems, Rory Vaden argues that many of us are applying them incorrectly. This entire section paraphrases his TEDx Talk "How to Multiply Your Time":

Technology has made more possible than ever before, yet we still never seem to have enough time. The reality is that we can't manage time; it is the one thing we all have an equal amount of. We can only manage *self*. Therefore, time management is *emotional*, not logical. It's about giving ourselves emotional permission to work on the things we want to.

Let's look at existing time management theories:

1-dimensional thinking = Do things more efficiently (faster)
2-dimensional thinking = Prioritizing (Eisenhower Matrix)

	Urgent	**Non-urgent**
Important	Quadrant of necessity DO	Quadrant of quality PLAN
	Crises • Project meetings • Last minute demands • Deadline driven projects	*Goals & Planning* • Strategic planning • Working towards goals • Personal care • Relationship building • True recreation
Not Important	Quadrant of deception DELEGATE	Quadrant of waste ELIMINATE
	Interruptions • Phone calls, emails • Reports • Some meetings • Other people's minor demands • Busywork	*Distractions* • Web browsing • Social media • Binge-watching Netflix • Analysis paralysis • Any procrastination activity

(Eisenhower Matrix)

While both the 1st and 2nd dimension are important, there's still something missing: *the 3rd dimension = significance.*

"Spend time on things today
that will help you create more time tomorrow."
– Rory Vaden, Brand Builders Group

Most people don't get around to automating or delegating certain tasks because it takes them too long to do it. But that's the wrong approach, they aren't accounting for *significance* in their mental evaluation of a task. For example, setting up an automated bill payment might take 30 minutes; it's something neither important nor urgent. But if you do it, you'll save 5 minutes each month in manually paying your bills. After 6 months, you would have effectively broken even on your time investment; every month thereafter is bonus time!

Rory introduces the Focus Funnel, a life-changing concept I rigorously apply to all my tasks. It is a 5-step process for evaluating and prioritizing tasks:

1. Eliminate
The first step involves identifying whether a task or activity is of low value or unnecessary. We often say yes too easily. By eliminating these non-essential tasks, we free up time and mental energy for more important activities.

2. Automate
The second step is, if it is repetitive or routine, to determine if it can be automated. Automation reduces the need for manual effort, saving time in the long run.

3. Delegate
If it can't be automated, can it be delegated? If you don't have to be the one doing it, you shouldn't. We often resist delegating a task because it requires the upfront commitment of training someone on it and an accompanying decline in productivity as they are often subpar when they start. But this train of thought lacks the significance factor. Once delegated, the new person should eventually be able to do it as well, if not better, than us.

Once delegated, it is no longer something you need to dedicate your attention to, allowing you to focus on higher-priority activities. Delegating tasks not only saves time but also empowers others and encourages collaboration.

4. Procrastinate
Failing all the above, the task falls to you. The remaining question at this point is: does it need to be done now, or can it wait? If it's not urgent or important, you should intentionally delay acting on it.

This is not the same as avoiding responsibilities or neglecting what you know you should be doing because you don't feel like doing it. This form of procrastinating on purpose allows us to focus on more immediate priorities without feeling overwhelmed, revisiting those tasks at a more opportune time in the future.

Procrastinated tasks then enter a holding pattern where they eventually become urgent and you need to act on them now, you realize they weren't important and should have been eliminated in the first place, you find a way to automate them, or someone else takes them up and they get delegated.

5. Concentrate

If the task is urgent, important, requires your immediate attention, or has the greatest impact on your goals and objectives, we focus and concentrate on getting it done.

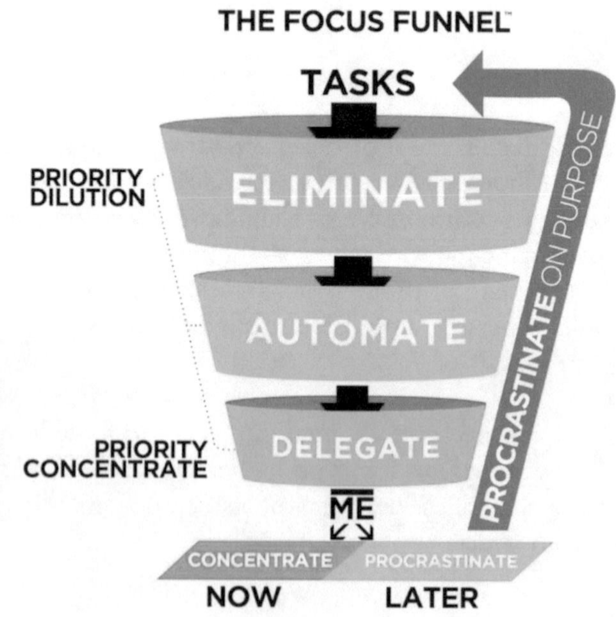

(Rory Vaden's Focus Funnel process for evaluating tasks)

ASSIGNMENT

Review your current to-do list using Rory Vaden's Focus Funnel:

1. What should you eliminate?
2. What could be automated?
3. What could be delegated and who could you delegate it to (employees/contractors/freelancers)?
4. Now vs. Later?

Notes:

HUMANE AUTOMATION

It's unavoidable; automation or any technological improvement is bound to displace some degree of human talent. Any process improvement that enhances the efficiency of a task creates the opportunity for more work to be done by fewer people. But is that a bad thing? No. We should view improvements as an opportunity to do more, not less; to do different things that add more value.

When considering automation, my main advice is to automate to be more, not less, human.

Less Human

For instance, if you follow up with customers who have recently purchases with a personalized phone call, automating that process with a scheduled email triggered after a certain date makes the interaction less human and provides a worse experience for your customer.

More Human

Instead, if you set up an automated reminder that triggers so that your SDRs don't need to track and remember to reach out to all their recent customers with the follow-up call, it alleviates their administrative and data entry work, thus freeing them up to spend more time with more customers.

Tech is a Loudspeaker

It's also equally important to realize that technology, automation, or any form of process optimization works like a loudspeaker. It amplifies everything, both the good and the bad.

If you have a prospecting process where you call 10 people and 3 of them will buy, and you decide to optimize for that, you may now be able to do a lot more and close 30 out of 100.

But if you jump to this without first testing and determining if this is the right approach or the right profile of prospects to be reaching out to, you could inadvertently create a lot of unnecessary noise. Perhaps there is another process or group of prospects where if you call 10, 7 of them will buy.

DELEGATION: LEGOS

In this article: https://review.firstround.com/give-away-your-legos-and-other-commandments-for-scaling-startups/, Molly Graham addresses many of the emotional turmoils that come with delegation in a rapidly scaling organization, drawing similarities between the experience and how a child feels when they have to share their Legos.

> *"One of the secrets of people who are really successful at fast-growing companies is how rapidly they're able to adapt to the chaos and uncertainty of adding new people. They become adept at redefining their jobs on a regular basis, and they become comfortable with the largely uncomfortable emotions that naturally happen when a team doubles or triples in a short period of time."*

Building on her analogy, here are some key points:

Don't lend them

If it's your favorite piece and you enjoy it, you might not want to give it away. If you delegate, make sure you're ready to commit to letting it go. Don't try to take something back if it's already been given away.

Don't give them away fully assembled

Where's the fun in that? It's boring when you give full and exact instructions and demand they be followed to the letter. If that's the case, you should be automating instead. Give people the opportunity to experiment, learn, and improve. You can share best practices and what you've found to be effective, but ensure you're open to having the person who takes over explore and find ways to improve. After all, what works best for you might not work best for them.

Nor with no instructions

The reverse is true. It's not a great experience for the person picking it up, and you can't expect them to perform well if you don't participate in the knowledge transfer to give them a good foundation to begin.

Don't leave it lying around

Don't be ambiguous, hoping someone will come around and pick up your mess for you. You need to explicitly designate responsibility.

PARETO PRINCIPLE

The 80-20 rule, also known as the Pareto Principle, is a widely recognized concept:

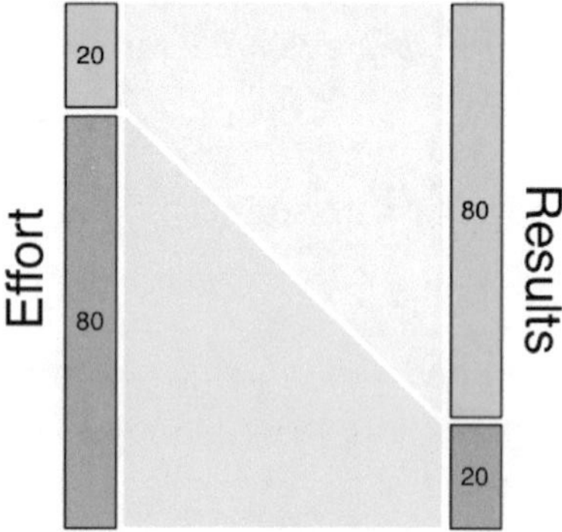
The 80-20 Rule
"For many events, roughly 80% of the effects come from 20% of the causes." - Pareto
Effort
20
80
Results
80
20
Therefore 20% of the effort produces 80% of the results but the last 20% of the results consumes 80% of the effort.
www.EndlesslyCurious.com

BUT! It's not universally true. In some instances, the mix might be closer to 95% / 5%, or in others, we might not even see this effect. However, I do want to raise it here because it encourages you to be more mindful of your activities and ensure you're working on the things that really matter.

Especially so in sales. Because selling is naturally uncomfortable for most, it's easy to avoid doing uncomfortable tasks and instead focus on the less confrontational activities to fool yourself into thinking you're being productive when instead you're merely preoccupying yourself with busywork.

This applies not only to your activities but also to your prospects and customers. Some prospects will require a disproportionate amount of time and effort to convert; ultimately, it's up to you to decide if it's worth it or if you might want to redefine your target customers. You might even want to fire certain high-maintenance customers, depending on your personal situation.

What and who are most important will differ depending on your business, solution, customers, and process. The point here is to take an occasional pause to reflect and ensure the proportion of resources and attention you give them is related to the return on investment.

ASSIGNMENT

Review your routines, SOPs, or regular sales activities.

1. How much time or effort are they consuming?
2. Are the results (both short-term, long-term, and possibly indirect) worth the investment?

Notes:

♦♦♦

PROCESS MAPPING

ASSIGNMENT

Try this exercise to identify the appropriate tools to acquire and determine the most effective ways to integrate and automate them.

Step 1: Identify the series of actions a prospect needs to take to complete a process.

Step 2: Do the same, but for your business. These are the opposing actions and assets you need to create to meet your prospects on the other end.

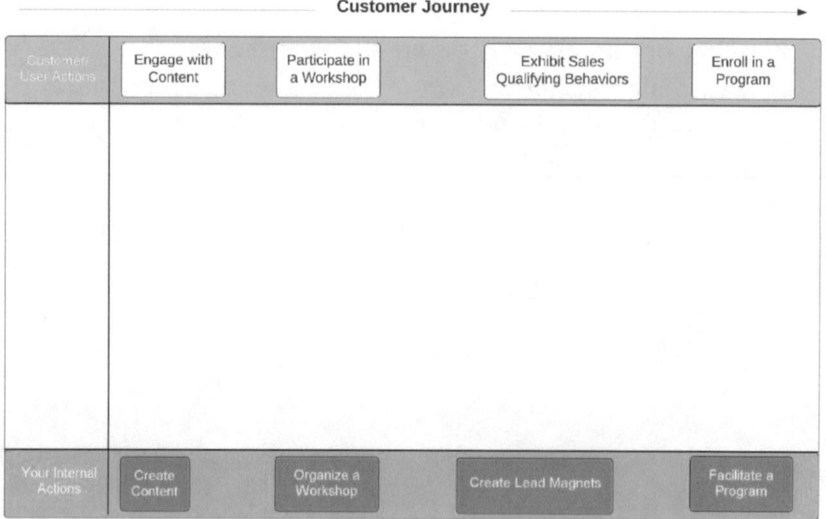

Step 3: Identify key decision points and qualifying markers.

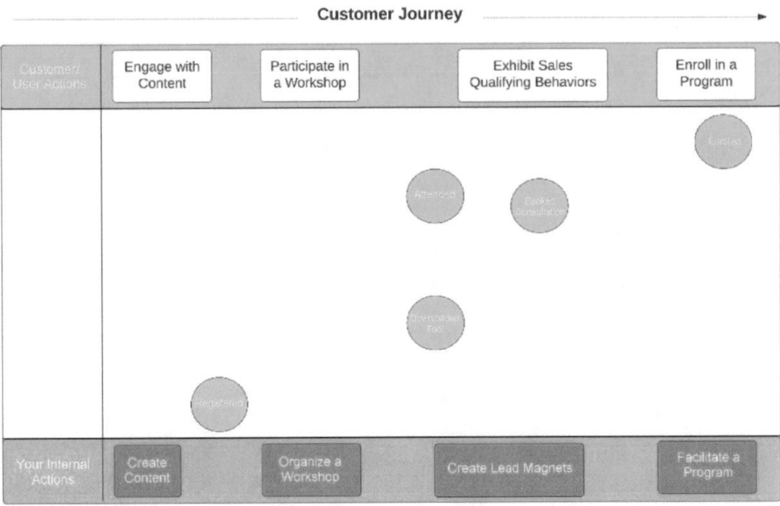

Step 4: Map out the actions and resources needed to get you to each decision point. Include IF…THEN…logic if there are multiple workflows.

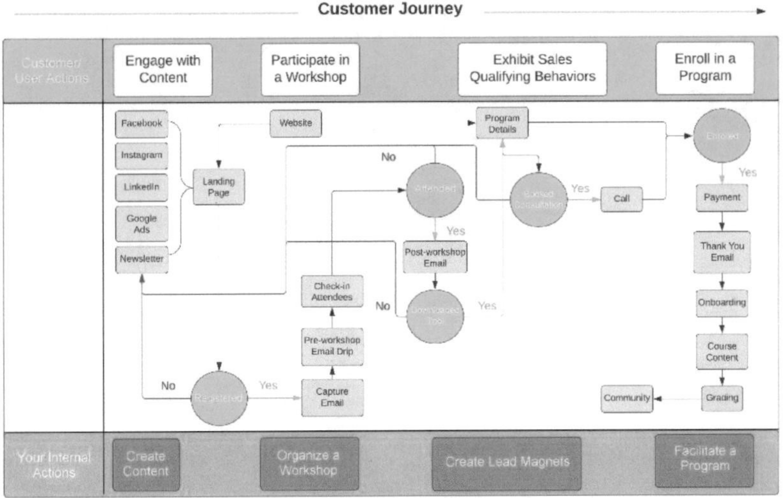

Step 5: Research tools that can satisfy your required functions and workflows.

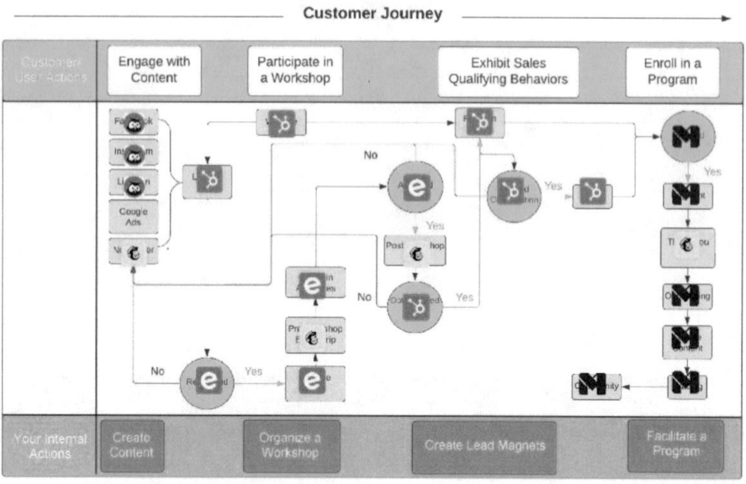

Ideally, it's better to have fewer tools that can do more, instead of having multiple individual tools for each function.

SALES TOOLS

Quick word of caution: Beware 凌遲 (Língchí) or death by a thousand cuts! Automation is often much more affordable than delegation; however, it still comes with a cost. Subscriptions for various tools can quickly add up, so it's especially important to track all of them and cancel those you no longer use.

CUSTOMER RELATIONSHIP MANAGEMENT (CRM)

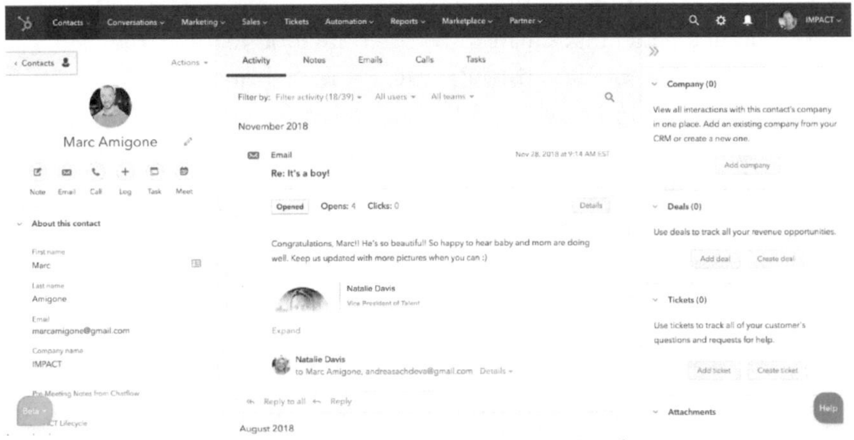

(Example HubSpot Contact Card)

A CRM is essential for every sales team as it serves as a system for managing interactions with both current and prospective customers. While different CRMs offer varying features, here are some important ones:

Data Collection
CRM tools start by collecting basic contact details, including names, email addresses, phone numbers, and other relevant information. Usually through a form that someone might fill out when they order a product, download something through your website, or register for an event. Once you have their contact, you can begin to track behavior or actions and associate them with their account.

Activity Tracking

Most of which is made possible through the use of local cookies (not the snack) stored on an individual's device when they browse your websites.

- Website Interactions: Many CRM systems integrate with websites to track visitor behavior. This can include the pages visited, time spent on each page, and actions taken (downloads, form submissions, etc.).
- Social Media Engagement: Some CRM tools integrate with social media platforms, allowing businesses to track interactions, mentions, and messages on social channels.
- Email Tracking: CRM tools often include features that track email opens, click-through rates, and responses.
- Transaction History: CRM systems often store details about purchases and transactions, enabling businesses to understand a customer's buying patterns and preferences.
- Logging Conversations with different prospects:
    - Documentation aids in resolving disputes or misunderstandings resulting from communication disagreements.
    - Helps maintain continuity in relationships, avoiding the need to start from scratch and rebuild trust. For instance, it enables another team member to seamlessly respond to Suzy's (a customer) inquiry while her assigned account manager, Amy, is on vacation, or in the event of an SDR's departure or termination from the organization.

Customization and Tags

You can use a CRM to customize fields and add tags or labels to contacts based on specific behaviors or characteristics. For example, a tag might be added for "Highly Engaged" or "Interested in Product X." This allows you to not only categorize, filter, prioritize, and search your contacts efficiently but also note important prospect preferences that will aid your interaction with them. For example:

- Noting key concerns preventing ABC company from

committing so you can address it in your next interaction with them.
- Knowing Sooyong's favorite food so you can order it at your next meeting to impress and show her that you're attentive.

Automation and Workflows
Most CRMs provide automation features, allowing businesses to set up workflows triggered by specific actions. For example:

- Sending a follow-up email after a prospect downloads a whitepaper
- An automated reminder to follow up with a prospect after a certain number of days have elapsed.
- Providing meeting booking links to reduce the back-and-forth needed to find a suitable time.
- Identify Marketing Qualified Leads (page 240) and Sales Qualified Leads (page 241), and initiate automation sequences for when a prospect is identified as such.

Analytics and Reporting
CRM tools also usually offer analytics and reporting features. Businesses can generate reports to analyze trends, customer preferences, and the effectiveness of various campaigns.

Funnel Optimization: Sales-oriented CRMs provide a funnel view to manage and track your prospects. This allows you to view the number of prospects at each stage of your sales funnel, along with specific details about each prospect. For example:

- Gain insight into Mohammed's position in the decision-making journey and the steps he has taken.
- Understand the duration spent at each stage and the conversion rate of each stage.

Machine Learning and Predictive Analytics: Some advanced CRM tools leverage machine learning algorithms to analyze historical data and predict future behaviors. This can help businesses proactively address customer needs and anticipate trends.

Integration with Other Tools
Many CRM systems integrate with other tools, such as marketing automation platforms, e-commerce platforms, and customer support systems. This enables a more comprehensive view of customer interactions across various touchpoints.

By combining these features, a CRM provides your organization with a holistic view of your customers and their behaviors, enabling you to make informed decisions, personalize interactions, and improve overall customer satisfaction.

Some of the most popular CRM tools are:

- Salesforce
- HubSpot
- Pipedrive
- Streak
- ZOHO
- Google Sheets
- Airtable
- Keela (for non-profits)
- ActiveCampaign (more marketing-centric)

Advice on Selecting The Right CRM to Start
1. Start with a spreadsheet: CRM tools are not cheap. Starting with a spreadsheet also helps you identify what you want to track and understand how you want to organize your data. Personally, if you're not familiar with CRMs or unclear on how you want to use your data, I don't recommend transferring to a formal CRM tool till you have over 10,000 contacts.

2. Ensure clean data capture practices: Messy data is challenging to accurately analyze and draw meaningful inferences from. It needs to be consistent. For example, if you pull a location report, the following would give you three different locations despite them being the same (and that's not even accounting for other variations or typos):

Vancouver vs. Van vs. Greater Vancouver
US vs. United States vs. America

Train all users on data entry standards, or better yet, automate data entry or cleaning if possible. Implementing automation for data entry not only saves time but also reduces errors and data inconsistency. It could even render it unnecessary to set standards or train people on them to begin with.

3. Don't let the daunting task of achieving perfection hold you back: It's better to take action than to do nothing at all. It's nearly impossible to have perfectly clean data, especially for a rapidly growing organization. Focus on adopting new best practices for incoming data, and consider tidying up old data as a secondary concern. Data policies are an iterative process; you should never set them and forget about them.

Beyond the CRM here are a few of my favorite sales tools:

ZAPIER (https://zapier.com/)

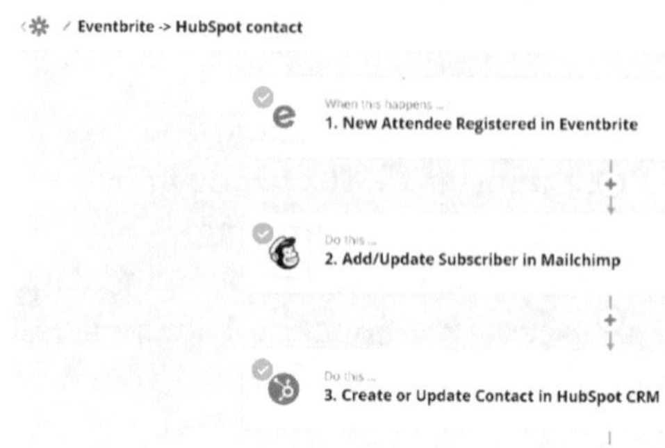

A great workflow automation tool that integrates with many others. It's awesome not only for automating sales but for pretty much every process in your organization. If you haven't already implemented something similar in your organization, this is game-changing! It allows you to automate workflows like:

Attendee fills out a form to register for an event → Creates them as a contact in your CRM → Adds them to your newsletter → Send an email notification to your SDR.

Or

New sales order → Automatically added as a line item in your spreadsheet → Send an email at the start of every day to your fulfillment center → If the order status is updated in the spreadsheet → Emails the customer to inform them of their expected shipment

You can even set up IF…THEN… logic, filters, and more. The possibilities are endless.

Alternatives: IFTTT, stands for If This Then That (https://ifttt.com/), Make (https://www.make.com/en) , HubSpot (https://www.hubspot.com/)

MAGICAL TEXT EXPANDER (Chrome browser extension: https://www.getmagical.com/)

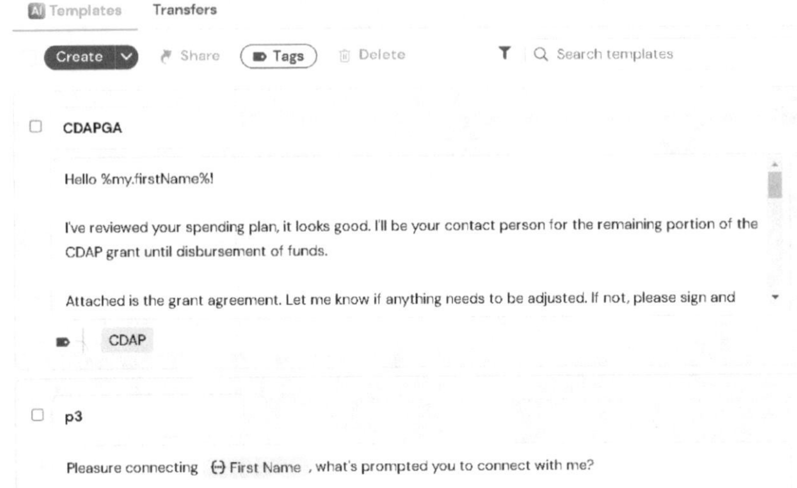

Allows you to use shortcuts to trigger the pasting of a longer text.

For instance, I can type the first 4 digits of my address, and it populates my full address.

It's much more efficient than navigating to different documents to copy-paste. I've saved an immense amount of time typing out messages for scheduling meetings, prospecting emails, sending my bio, responding to LinkedIn connection requests, filling out forms, and more. If you ever notice you're typing the same thing over and over, this is a great time saver.

DUX-SOUP (Chrome browser extension: https://www.dux-soup.com/)

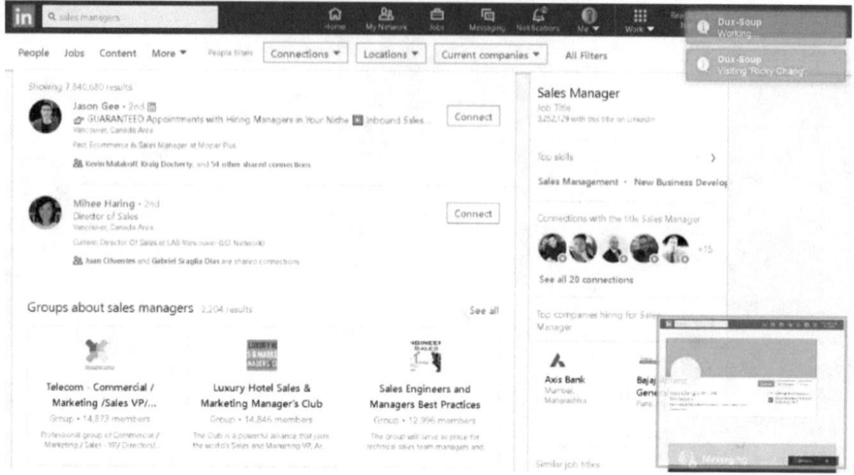

For automating LinkedIn prospecting & outreach.

Alternatives: PhantomBuster (https://phantombuster.com/), Dripify (https://dripify.io/) , Copilot AI (https://www.copilotai.com/)

HUNTER (https://hunter.io/)

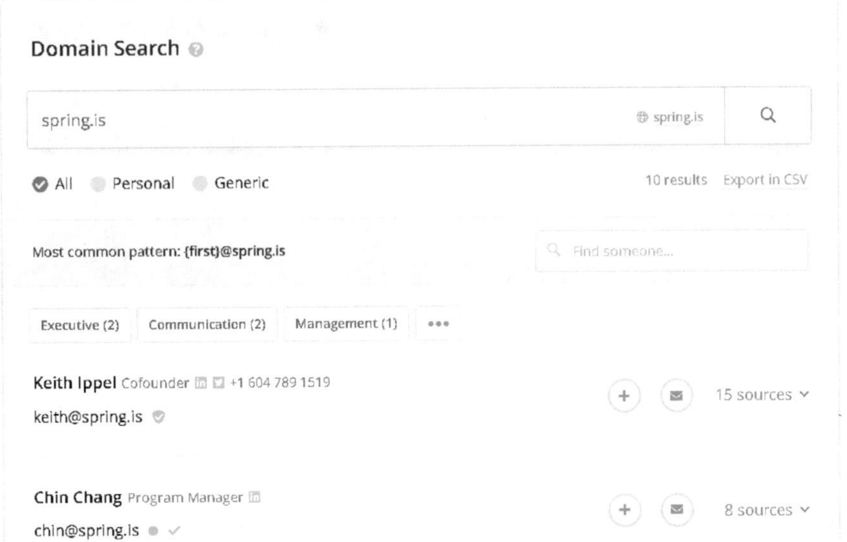

Scrapes the web to find publicly displayed emails for a domain. Great for uncovering common email address formats within an organization, enabling you to guess the email of the person you might be trying to reach.

Alternatives: VoilaNorbert (https://www.voilanorbert.com/)

BULK EMAIL CHECKER (https://www.bulkemailchecker.com/)

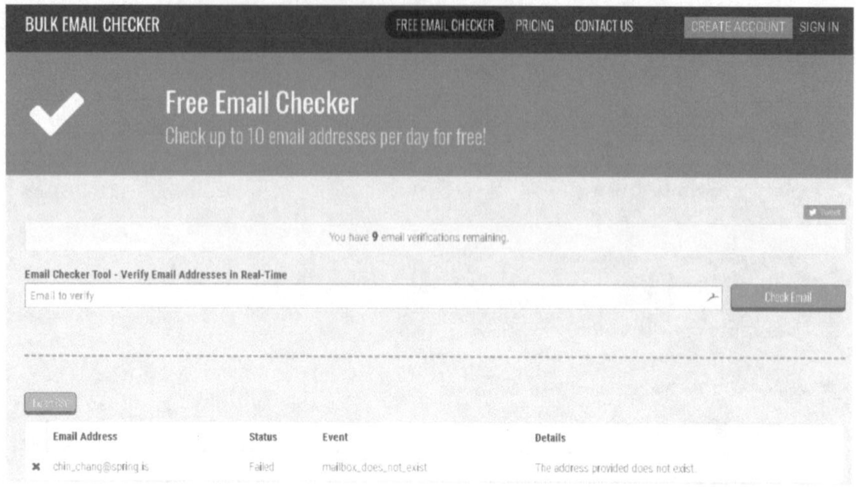

A necessary companion tool for prospecting, to verify if the email address you're guessing is correct or still in use.

Alternatives: Email Checker (https://email-checker.net/), EmailHippo (https://tools.emailhippo.com/)

MAIL TESTER (https://www.mail-tester.com/)

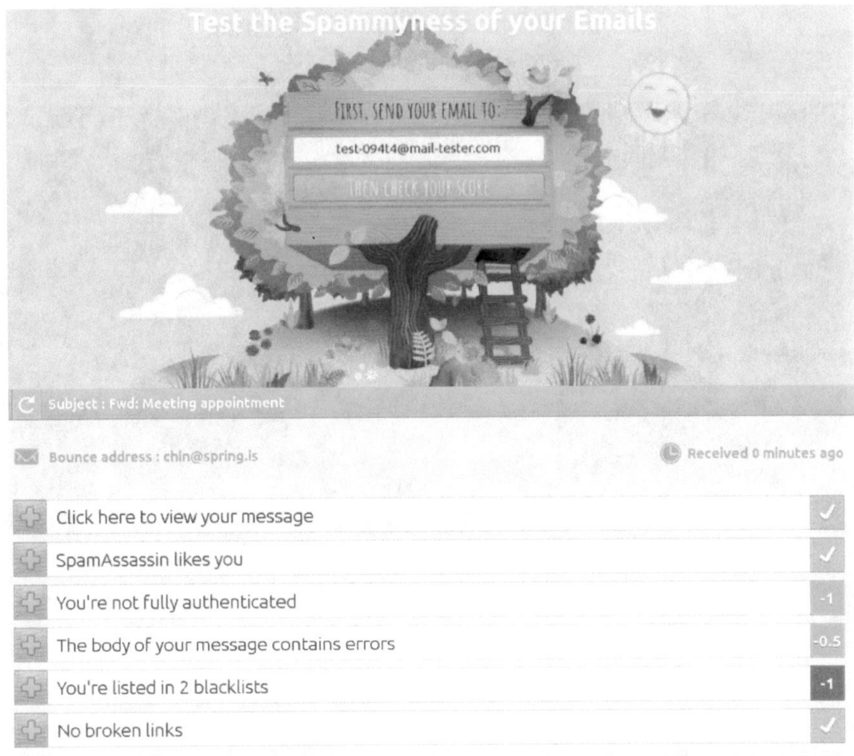

Audit your email for elements that may trigger spam filters.

Alternative: MailGenius (https://www.mailgenius.com/)

YET ANOTHER MAIL MERGE (Google Sheet Add-on: https://yamm.com/)

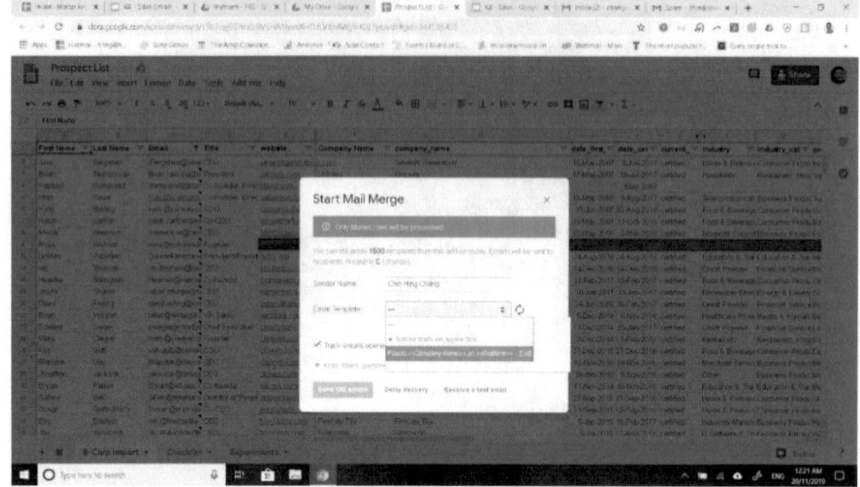

Allows you to send a mail merge directly through your Gmail account via Google Sheets.

A mail merge is when you send a mass personalized email. For example:

> *"Hello <<First Name>>,*
>
> *I found <<Company Name>> through <<Source>> and I see you're currently fundraising…"*

Mail merge tools enable you to replace and populate those merge tags with fields in your spreadsheet, facilitating the ability to send multiple highly personalized emails quickly.

Why is it important to do it via your personal inbox? When you send emails through a mailing client like Mailchimp, HubSpot, or Active Campaign, deliverability rates are often lower (industry average for email open rate is ~40%). This happens because these service providers are not only sending emails on your behalf but also behalf of many other organizations. As much as they try to put measures in place to maximize deliverability, there's still a high likelihood of your email from

them landing in your prospect's spam or promotions folder.
I won't go into the technical details of why, but emails sent from your domain server directly are much less likely to trigger these spam filters. Those email clients aren't bad; they're still good for mass marketing emails, but I don't generally recommend using them for targeted personalized mail merges to highly qualified prospects. To learn more about this and how to set up your email servers, check out Cold Email Academy (https://mailshake.com/academy/) & Cold Email Masterclass (https://mailshake.com/masterclass/).

The only caveat to sending a mail merge through your personal inbox or directly from your domain is if you haven't taken the time to properly optimize your deliverability:

- Verify the emails in the list you plan on sending to weed out emails that are no longer in use or have typos.
- Set up your DKIM/SPF settings.
- Conducted email warmup (Google it for more details).
- Test your email copy for spamminess.
- Run smaller batch manual tests to ensure good open and low unsubscribe or flag-as-spam rates.

There's a risk that your mail merge campaign could permanently harm the email deliverability of your primary domain or inbox.

As with my advice on automation, it shouldn't be done at the cost of being less human. Here are some tips on designing a good mail merge campaign:

- Don't compromise on research and personalization. For example:

  "I came across your profile in <<Source>>, <<Custom>>"

  Take the time to properly personalize that <<Custom>> field:
    - *"I really liked your recent article on how to increase innovation in the workplace, specifically your points on designing culture to PULL instead of PUSH those values."*

- Or "*I saw that you recently got promoted, congratulations!*"
- Or "*Yoseph said that you were an expert in the field and I should reach out.*"

- Don't draft your mail merge with merge tags. Doing so often results in writing in a less personal tone of voice. Instead, write the email as if you were writing to an actual recipient, then go back and replace the necessary fields with the merge tags.

CALENDLY (https://calendly.com/)

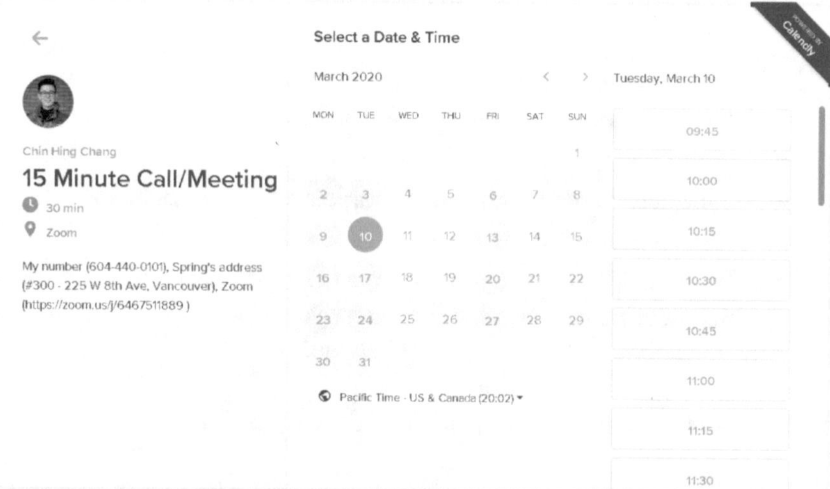

Appointment scheduler: save time by reducing back-and-forth via email when setting up a time.

Alternatives: Doodle (for groups to find a time, https://doodle.com/en/), YouCanBookMe (https://youcanbook.me/)

ZOOM (https://zoom.us/)

The tool that's now ubiquitous with virtual meetings.

Alternative: Whereby (https://whereby.com/), Microsoft Teams (https://www.microsoft.com/en-us/microsoft-teams/), Google Meet (https://meet.google.com/landing)

ACTIVE CAMPAIGN (https://www.activecampaign.com/)

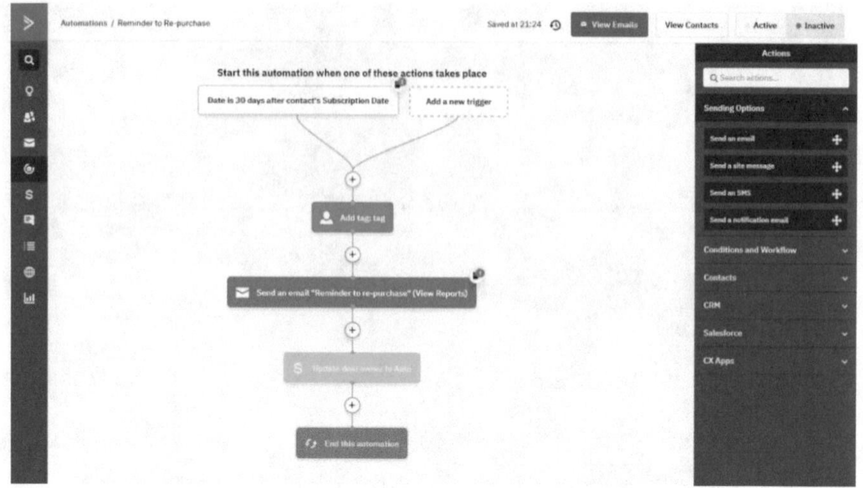

I like their built-in workflows allowing for IF…THEN…logic for email drip campaigns. They also have CRM functionality. For instance,

> *If a prospect visits the checkout page but doesn't purchase, send "Email 1";*
>
> *If they purchase, stop emailing them;*
>
> *If they still don't, start another email drip sequence or add them to a list.*

INBOX MANAGEMENT

As you've noticed, since emailing is one of the main sales activities, many of the aforementioned sales tools pertain to it. Given that inbox management presents challenges for many individuals, especially salespeople who handle high volumes of emails, let's explore this topic a little. Before we dive in, what works for me might not work for you.

Inbox Zero-ish

I prefer an uncluttered living and working space, so I strive to keep my inbox as uncluttered as possible. I've tested leaving emails in the inbox versus filing them away, and I find the latter works better for me. When I opt for the former, my inbox becomes overwhelming, and I'm more inclined to skip over some emails entirely if I'm overloaded.

You don't have to set up an elaborate labeling system for this to be effective. Most inboxes have pretty good search functionality, and the mere act of filing emails away if they don't require any action or if they've been acted upon is good enough. Out of sight, out of mind.

Snooze

If something requires my action, but there's a good reason to delay responding, I'll snooze the email so it's removed from my inbox and only reappears when action is needed:

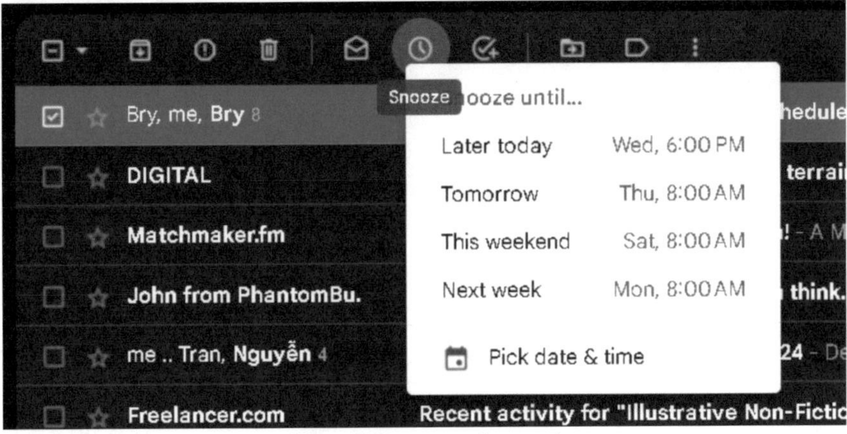

(Gmail Snooze feature)

This can also be done with an external tool such as Boomerang.

2-minute rule

If something takes less than 2 minutes to resolve (not only for emails), I generally try to get it out of the way as soon as possible instead of deferring and letting these pile up. Putting off a reply because you're lazy only wastes more time. You'll end up needing to reread the email again in the future.

Batch instead of Compulsively Check

Compulsive checking is a huge time-suck. I try to limit inbox checking to no more than 2-3 times a day to ensure I can carve out time for focused work.

Research has consistently shown that multitasking is not as efficient as we often believe it to be. Batching or time blocking is also a great practice for any other task, as it reduces the time needed to shift gears and refocus when we switch between tasks.

Unsubscribe

I'm pretty unforgiving when it comes to unsubscribing from any email I don't personally enjoy reading or don't find much value in. If I don't unsubscribe, I generally find myself wasting more time skimming over them, only to delete them right after.

SALES WORKFLOWS

Now that we're acquainted with certain sales tools, let's explore a few specific workflows that use them. Given the continuous advancements in technology, particularly with recent progress in AI, some of these tools or processes may become obsolete. Therefore, it's essential to prioritize understanding the process over solely relying on the tools themselves.

(Then vs. Now: Source Unknown)

LIST BUILDING/PROSPECTING

Here's an overview of the process, which we'll go into more detail:

Step 1: Create a list of companies
Step 2: Identify potential decision-maker(s)
Step 3: Guess their email
Step 4: Clean your list
Step 5: Craft and review your copy for spamminess
Step 6: Mail merge
Step 7: Automate the above

Step 1: Create a List of Companies
Your first step is to start a spreadsheet you can begin to populate. Begin by identifying potential sources for leads. Ask yourself the following questions:

- Where do my prospects hang out?
  - Are they active in certain groups or forums?
  - Do they attend industry or topic-specific conferences or trade shows?
  - Commonly have memberships in certain associations?
  - Are there specific certifications or awards they covert?
  - Listed in particular government directories?
- How do they currently seek solutions or address their problems?
  - What keywords do they use when searching?
  - What are some notable blogs on the topic?
  - Is a workshop or webinar a preferred method of learning?
  - Do they subscribe to specific newsletters?
  - Specific channels or content creators they might follow?
  - Popular videos they would have likely watched or engaged with?
- What are my competitors doing? If it works for them, it will probably work for you too.
- Who are potential referral partners? Who are non-competitors that also serve your prospects in different ways that you don't?
  - You can also leverage case studies or testimonials, not

only for credibility but also to drive referrals. This can be done by asking the company that was willing to provide it to share it with their network. They are often happy to do so as it features them as well. Similar companies will likely exist in their network.

- Are they self-identifying with specific keywords on platforms like LinkedIn?
    - In their job title, bios, experiences, or skills.
    - For instance, if you sell sales software, you may target a sales operations person who recently changed jobs (they may be more motivated to implement new changes).

As you build your list, differ judgment. Qualify as much as possible, but don't discard a prospect by assuming they won't buy. Your goal at this point is to compile a list of potential customers. As you work through the process, you'll qualify them in more detail. The process should also continue to evolve and improve; don't rush to populate your list yet. Aim for about 50 entries to start and test your lead source for effectiveness before proceeding. Discontinue a lead source if you find too many of the leads tend to be unqualified or uninterested.

Example Tools: Canada's Business Registries (https://beta.canadasbusinessregistries.ca/), Owler (https://www.owler.com/search) , LinkedIn Search

If you know a specific list, you can even try searching "list name.csv" to see if an unprotected spreadsheet exists on the web. For instance, when looking for social ventures, I decided it might be a good idea to build a list of companies that were B Corp certified. By searching "BCorp.csv", I was able to pull a list with over 14,000 entries from https://data.world/.

Step 2: Identify Potential Decision-makers(s)
Now that you have some potential companies in your spreadsheet, the next step is to identify potential decision-makers. The plural form is used because it's often difficult, especially with larger organizations, to identify the right decision-maker. Remember, as long as you do it correctly and don't spam everyone with the same message, it's also acceptable to reach out to multiple people in the same organization.

There are two main ways to do this:

1. LinkedIn: Search for people who work at the organization by viewing their employees on their company page

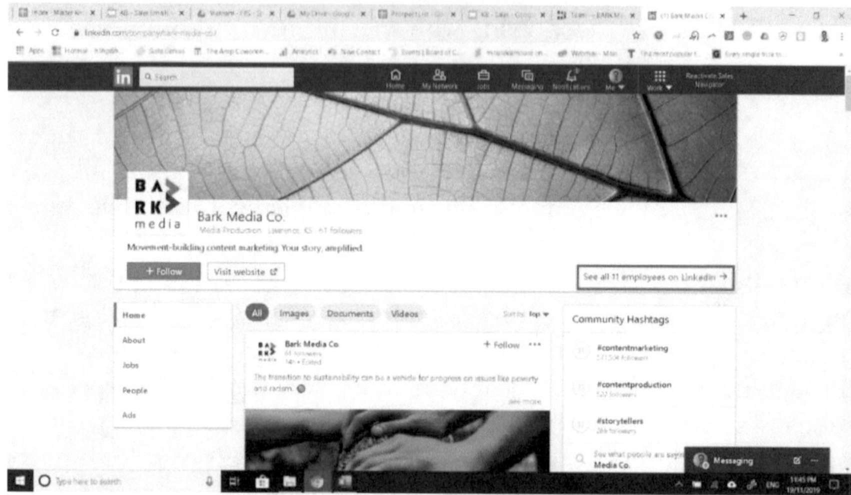

(LinkedIn company page)

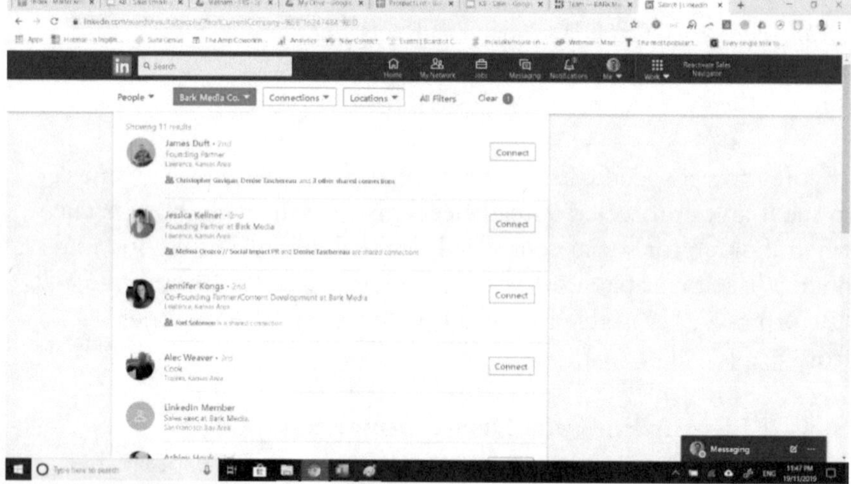

(LinkedIn "People associated with the company")

2. Navigate to their "About Us" or "Team" page on their website: This is often available with smaller or medium-sized organizations but rarely possible with larger ones.

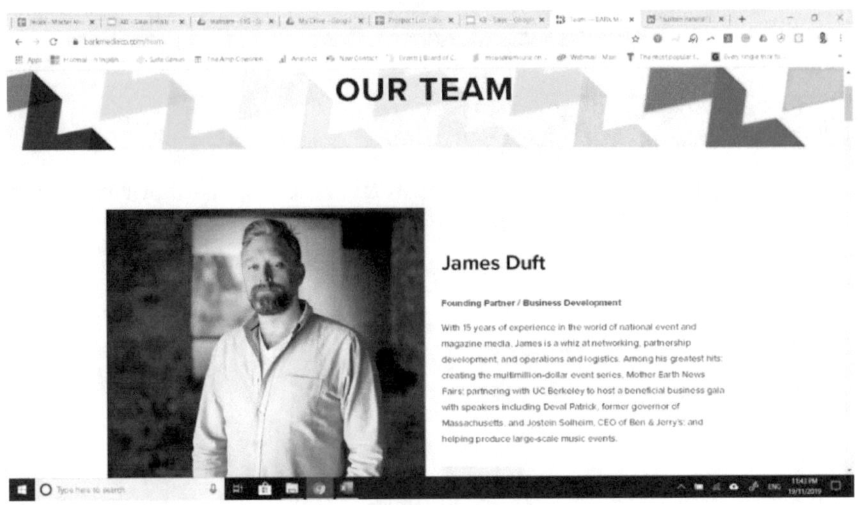

Step 3: Guess Their Email

Knowing their physical address might be the most effective if you're targeting a retail or restaurant establishment. But assuming you aren't, a person's phone number might be your best option. People are much less likely to change their phone numbers, and you can directly control the delivery of your messaging through it compared to a social media platform, where visibility is entirely dependent on what the most current algorithm favors. However, cold calling isn't always the best option. Not because I'm a millennial or an introvert, but because my generation and younger actually prefer text-based communication. Calling is sometimes too personal, and many others will have a similar policy as I do: to ignore all calls from unrecognized numbers. I have, however, found cold calling to be the best option in certain scenarios, like if you're going after baby boomers or targeting businesses in remote locations where internet access isn't their first choice.

The next best option is email. Like a phone number, it is relatively static and unchanging once assigned, and because the ROI on it is high considering the time invested in crafting an email and the ability to send multiple similar yet highly personalized emails at once via mail merge.

Tools: Hunter.io, VoilaNorbert

If nothing comes back, which can be the case for a newer company or one with strict email masking and public disclosure policies, here are some common formats you can try:

- Jordan@Company.com
- Chang@Company.com
- Jordan.Chang@Company.com (replace . with -, _, or remove it for alternative formats)
- Chang.Jordan@Company.com
- J.Chang@Company.com
- Jordan.C@Company.com
- Chang.J@Company.com
- C.Jordan@Company.com

If it's a high-priority prospect, you may even be willing to invest more time and resources to take a more direct and personal approach to connect with them and build a relationship, besides email:

Find a warm introduction
Do you have a direct contact who might know them and be willing to facilitate an introduction or refer you? If you don't already have a direct contact, it may also be easier to establish a relationship with someone else who is close to them (friends, colleagues, mentees, family, or peers in their industry). Do this sincerely, not solely for the sake of obtaining a referral.

A true story, not from a sales situation, but it applies. I have a friend who wanted to make a particular business leader his mentor. He got to know all the mentees of this leader and even his wife! When he was finally introduced, what the leader said affirmed his approach "I've heard so much about you, even my wife has mentioned you…". He did go on to work under this leader as a mentee for a few years.

Where do they hang out and engage, both in-person and online?
Are they vocal about specific topics or causes? Do they post in certain forums, are vocal about specific discussions, or engage with certain

hashtags? Are there specific events they attend? These could be either professional or personal. Try to find ways to get on their radar and be noticed where they're active.

For instance, we worked with an entrepreneur who was raising capital at Spring Activator. He was targeting a specific investor whom he really wanted for his investment round. He discovered that this investor was politically vocal on Twitter and deliberately engaged with him in a discussion thread. The entrepreneur didn't simply agree with everything or flatter the investor. In fact, he was well-informed and had a different opinion on some of the points the investor raised. He engaged in intelligent debate. This eventually led to him meeting the investor for a discussion over beer, and long story short, the investor invested in his company.

Step 4: Clean Your List

By now, you should have the following columns in your spreadsheet:

- Company Name
- Website
- First Name
- Last Name
- Email Address
- Job Title/Role

Exclude extra columns like these, even if they seem important unless you're deliberately testing their effectiveness:

- Company Size
- Industry
- Age of business

Here's a basic cleaning routine to follow:

1. Dedupe: Duplicate entries often occur during data entry.
2. Check First Names: Use personalized short handles if appropriate.
    a. E.g. Christopher → Chris
3. Tidy Company Name: Remove prefixes like "The…" and suffixes like LTD, LLP, Group, or Company.
4. Remove all leading and trailing spaces in any entry.

Tool: PowerTools by AbleBits (Google Sheet plugin: https://www.ablebits.com/google-sheets-add-ons/power-tools/index.php)

Put all the emails through an email verification tool because:

- There may have been a typo in their email.
- They may have already left the organization.
- Or perhaps the email format you guessed was incorrect.

Tools: Bulk Email Checker, Email Checker, EmailHippo

Step 5: Craft and Review Your Copy for Spamminess
Now's the time to draft your email outreach messages. I'll discuss a detailed outreach messaging workflow in the next section, but some high-level advice here is to avoid including too many links or salesy keywords like "free" or "buy".

Example Tools: Mail Tester, MailGenius

Step 6: Mail Merge
Most tools enable you to track email open rates, clickthrough rates (if links were included), and response rates. Additionally, you can add extra columns to your spreadsheet, such as status, objections, decline reasons, send date, and reply date. This allows for quick comparison and filtering when analyzing the effectiveness of your campaign.

Step 7: Automate The Above
Do a few of the above yourself so you have a rough expectation of:

How many entries you can capture in an hour
So you know what to expect when you outsource this work and have a benchmark to compare average performance vs. poor or excellent.

Quality of the list source
As mentioned before, tech is a loudspeaker (page 320); automating prematurely can result in a lot of unnecessary noise. It might be the case that there are other more suitable companies to reach out to or other directories with better quality or more updated information.

The right process
For instance, if there are multiple potential decision-makers, manual testing will give you the chance to better determine who is the right person to initiate the conversation with. Doing so will also allow you to test different email subject lines, copy, and CTAs to ensure you get the messaging right before you send en masse.

Once you're ready, you can "automate" this repetitive work by outsourcing it. I anticipate AI will eventually develop the capability to perform this type of simple research and data entry. However, currently, some degree of human judgment is still necessary for identifying the potential decision-maker(s).

Freelancing platforms: Upwork (https://www.upwork.com/), Fiverr (https://www.fiverr.com/), Freelancer (https://www.freelancer.com/)

When it comes to outsourcing list building, here are some helpful pointers:

Avoid buying lists
Some companies may offer to sell you lists of prospects. I generally don't recommend this approach, as these lists are often recycled and sold to multiple buyers. The contacts on these lists often receive a high volume of cold emails, meaning your email will likely get lost in the noise or, worse, end up in their spam or promotions folder.

When hiring freelancers, ensure you provide clear and specific instructions
Without them, some may not be the best decision-makers or problem solvers, leading to slower execution or even getting stuck on the project. For instance, you might specify:

- Identify decision makers in this priority order: Owner, VP of Sales, Sales Manager.
- Only enter a maximum of 2 contacts for a company (i.e., if you already have the Owner & VP of Sales, you do not need to find a contact for the Sales Manager).
- If no obvious potential decision-makers can be found, skip to

the next entry; do not spend more than 5 minutes per company.

- If their email format isn't discoverable through hunter.io, verify with these 3 formats and skip to the next entry if none of them are valid:
    - Jordan@Company.com
    - Chang@Company.com
    - Jordan.Chang@Company.com

Test multiple freelancers with the same list
This allows you to identify the best one to continue working with. Don't only look for the one that provides the most entries per hour; ensure they also maintain a low rate of duplicates and errors. Assign different segments of the list to each freelancer to minimize overlap and ensure data from each freelancer you're testing remains useful to you.

Automate gradually and in batches
Before going full throttle, restrict the number of hours your freelancer may work each week so you can test the list and refine your copy. If you're seeing positive results, feel free to proceed at full speed. However, if the outcomes aren't satisfactory, consider pausing or stopping your experiment to try a different list, subject lines, email copy, or CTA.

EMAIL OUTREACH

Everything in this following section comes from Ramit Sethi's "50 Proven Email Scripts". If you find my paraphrase summary valuable, definitely check out the original, as it goes into a lot more detail and even includes analysis and critique of many sample emails. This applies not only to email or sales but also to any other form of persuasive communication. This framework can effectively be applied to approach mentors, find investors, or even secure meetings with notable journalists.

START WITH THE SUBJECT LINE

You can write the best email or message, but if it doesn't get opened and read, it's pointless.

A good subject line should be:

- Short
- Personalized
- Invokes curiosity or asks a question

Some examples include:

"Still raising capital?"
"Read your LinkedIn post on Generative AI"
"Found COMPANY on AngelList"

MESSAGE BODY

The best practice for any message at any point in the conversation is to keep it simple. Complex discussions should be conducted over the phone or in a meeting. Deviation from this practice is acceptable as you become more familiar with someone, but it is still not recommended.

1. Scannable

If it's optimized for mobile, it'll probably be great for desktop too. Keep your paragraphs short, with no more than 2-3 lines, and space between paragraphs.

2. Formatting should be kept as plaintext instead of HTML

HTML emails may look prettier, but the formatting can trigger spam/promotion filters. Don't rely on graphics and formatting to keep your email readable; instead, put in the work to communicate concisely and effectively.

3. Avoid Jargon
Even when communicating with an industry expert.

Write as if you're writing to someone you know: When crafting cold outreach messages, we often default to a more distanced tone. As mentioned, when I discussed Yet Another Mail Merge (page 338), craft your email without merge tags and only replace them afterward.

4. Keep it simple
The more someone needs to think before responding, the less likely you are to receive a response. Sometimes it's not even because they aren't interested. They may leave your message in their inbox intending to reply when they feel more ready but forget to circle back. Use closed-ended instead of open-ended questions and avoid asking multiple questions. Make it as easy as possible for the recipient to reply.

Open-ended questions are valuable when you're trying to (A)SSESS your prospect; however, in outreach, it's still too early for them. Besides, those questions are best reserved for calls or meetings.

THE OUTREACH WORKFLOW

Message 1: Introduction/Ask
Message 2: Reminder
Message 3: Via a Different Channel
Message 4: Break Up

Applying the minimum of the 4-step follow-up process above almost guarantees improvement in response rates. I extensively use it myself and have seen it work with the companies I support when they adopt it as well.

Message 1: Introduction/Ask
Recall gradualization (page 230); rarely is it be appropriate to ask for a sale in the first interaction. The same applies if you're finding an investor, mentor, or anything else. Your goal at this point is merely to gain permission to continue the interaction.

1. Start by identifying and explaining how you found or know of them, using language and values with which they associate. For instance:

- *"I was researching restaurants with eco-conscious practices"*
- Or, take a look at this LinkedIn cold outreach message I received. The rest of the messaging could use some improvement, but it did catch my attention because as someone who advocates for profit through purpose, I felt like he was calling out to me directly:

to sell you anything. But I will reach out if I see or have an opportunity that may help support your business and I hope that you will do the same!

Feel free to take a look at my profile to see what I do or chat with me if you have any questions.

I will tell you that I typically work with businesses who:

1) Believe in profit through purpose
2) Are committed to engaging their people
3) Are ready to disrupt their industry or be ready if disruption does happen (Don't be Blockbuster!!)

If that's you, then I'm happy to chat or send you more info.

2. Follow closely with relevant and sincere praise about who they are and/or what they've done. Avoid superficial flattery.

3. Introduce yourself and why you're reaching out.

4. Close with an Ask:

- If asking a question, make it easy for them to engage and reply.
- If trying to find a time for a call or meeting, use the Wide-Narrow Technique. For example:

"I'd love to jump on a quick 10-minute call (make the commitment clear) to... (be clear about the purpose of the call). Is Monday or Tuesday at 11am good (Narrow)? If not, I can also work around your schedule (Wide)."

Narrow: Makes it easy to say YES and pick a time or decline. They don't have to figure out time zones or decide on options.

Wide: Acknowledges they are in the position of power and you're willing to work around them, given that you're often in the position of requesting in these messages. Power isn't a reference to authority here. There's usually someone who's asking for something, and someone in the position to give it (time, attention, etc.). The one giving holds a higher power dynamic.

Message 2: Reminder

Sent 2-3 days after Message 1. Your goal is to be persistent without coming across as pushy. Don't send them an unrelated email like *"thought you should check this out..."* or be apologetic about following up: *"I'm sorry for being persistent or annoying..."*. It should be short and simple, within two sentences.

1. Follow up. For example:

   "My email may have gotten lost in your mailbox"
   "Just wanted to follow up"
   "Sending this to bump it up in your inbox"

2. Repeat/reiterate the ASK and remind them of why you're reaching out so they won't need to refer to the previous email.

Message 3: Via A Different Channel

Sent another 2-3 days after Message 2 and only if they have not responded to either. Reach out to them via a channel different from what you used for the original message. It could be email, LinkedIn, a call, X (Twitter), or even Facebook. Use your discretion, depending on the objective, it may be too personal to reach out to someone via Facebook.

1. Phrase with something along the lines of:

   "Not sure if email is the best way to reach you, thought I'd try…"
   "Not sure if my emails are landing in your spam"

2. Repeat the ASK with new options for times (as the original timeslots have likely passed by now). But also, be prepared to engage in active discussion should they pick up the phone or are live on this social channel you're reaching out on.

Message 4: Break Up
You may not need to get this far, but if you still don't hear back, it doesn't necessarily mean they aren't interested. If they aren't, they could still reply and decline. I've seen many instances where someone is interested but delays replying because they were waiting for a more opportune time or got too busy to get around to it.

Sent another 2-3 days after Message 3.

1. In Ramit Sethi's framework, he introduces a concept called the Guilty Parachute:

   Guilt: To make them feel a little bad for not replying sooner.
   Parachute: An easy out so they won't feel like the bad guy when they finally reply. For example:

   "You might have been away over the weekend/ spring/ winter break"
   "Totally understand if you've been busy"

I'm not exactly a fan of the guilt part as it is manipulative. Keep the "Parachute", and instead of sending people on a guilt trip, emphasize why you sincerely want to hear back from them or believe your outreach will benefit them (not you, because we all already know there's something you stand to gain from this interaction). What could this look like?

> *"I see from your website that you're not currently selling your products online, and I truly believe our solution will help you unlock a lot of revenue by enabling you to do so."*

> *"I genuinely respect the advocacy work you do, and it would really mean a lot to me if you could give me some advice on…"*

2. Break up, make it clear that it's your last attempt. Something along the lines of:

> *"Thought I'd give this one last try. I won't bother anymore if you don't reply"*

3. Repeat the ASK

Additional Resource: https://bit.ly/cold-email-copywriting

That's a wrap!

AFTERWORD

Phew~! That was a lot more than just the C.A.R.E. Methodology. However, I believe it was necessary to cover all of it to establish the foundation of a successful sales organization.

TROUBLESHOOTING REVENUE PROBLEMS

As a final summary, here's the revenue troubleshooting process I go through with new companies I work with. Considered from the perspective of common challenges and potential ways to address them:

#1 TOP OF FUNNEL (TOFU): I NEED MORE CUSTOMERS!

Even if you're great at closing sales, it's going to be a problem if you lack enough prospects to work with.

Marketing Challenges?

Are you capturing data and tracking the right metrics that will help you improve your processes?

Refer to Top of Funnel (page 257) for some ideas.

Tips on addressing: Listen to your customers; focus on *their* problems and the tasks *they* want to accomplish, NOT your solution. Conduct some customer discovery (page 144); it will help you better articulate your messages to resonate with your audience.

#2 MIDDLE-BOTTOM OF FUNNEL (MOFU/BOFU): I'M HAVING TROUBLE CLOSING LEADS!

Refer to the Conversion Rate Between Stages (page 258) for ideas.

#3 LENGTH OF FUNNEL: IT'S TAKING ME TOO LONG TO CLOSE PROSPECTS!

Review and explore ideas for shortening your sales cycle (page 182).

#4 POOR RETENTION

You might be good at acquiring and converting prospects, but they're leaking out the other side as quickly as you can put them in the bucket. This is reflected in high churn, and low customer LTV, which results in poor profit margins.

What could be causing it?

- Bad User Interface (UI): It looks terrible?
- Poor User Experience (UX): They get frustrated? Too many steps or hoops for the customer to go through before they experience that Aha! moment?
- Or perhaps you're not delivering on your promise?

To address it: Pay special attention to your offering and explore how you can improve the experience. Quality testing, customer discovery, user journey mapping (page 235), and proactive experience design (page 96) are some ways to do so.

Refer to Improve Retention/Competitive Defensibility (page 165) for more ideas.

#5 POOR UNIT ECONOMICS

Typically the result of a suboptimal business model or pricing (page 222). This is why it's crucial to plan for revenue on day one instead of focusing solely on growth with the assumption that the revenue problem will resolve itself when you're large enough. Snapchat serves as a martyr, teaching us the importance of this.

Distinguish between customers & users and focus on the customer. Test business models early. Examples include subscription, freemium, refills, pay-per-use, and licensing. Explore how you can build recurrency (page 204) into your model.

COPY CHECKLIST

To finish it off, here's a checklist I use when reviewing websites, sales scripts, or outreach messages:

□ You test: Is your copy about *you* or *them* (the prospect)? □ Gradualization	
CONNECT	□ Be likable: Communicating like a human? □ Build trust: Credible? Social Proof? □ Avoiding jargon. □ Using their language. □ Relating to their pains? □ So what test: Why should they care?
ASSESS	□ Qualifying them? □ Open-ended questions? □ Quantifying value?
RECOMMEND	□ Clear and specific offering. □ Addressing their WANTS. □ Relating Features to Benefits and Values (FBV). □ Addressing alternatives.
ENGAGE	□ Are you giving something to say YES to? □ Addressing objections. □ Reducing risks. □ Authentic urgency. □ Setting **E**XPECTATIONS?

Here's an example of how a basic application of the above can make an invitation to join you for a hike much more persuasive:

Communication	Analysis
Let's go on an ADVENTURE! We've been sitting in the office all week.	**C**ONNECT • Communicating like a human. • Relating to their pain: In the office all week. • Their WANT: Adventure
What are your plans next Friday?	**A**SSESS • Qualifying
Instead of staying at home like any other regular weekend, let's go out and breathe some fresh air, see some great sights. Show them a breathtaking picture of the place you're going to visit.	**R**ECOMMEND • Addressing the alternative. • Hone in on all emotions and senses.
Deepthi and Shi Chang are coming too. I've got everything planned out already, don't worry about food, equipment, and the agenda. Just bring yourself. I'll drive too, let me know by this Friday if you're in as I only have 2 more seats left in my car.	**E**NGAGE • Social proof • Addressing objections • Authentic urgency

As you can see, even without checking off every single box on the checklist, this is already a much more persuasive invitation compared to a simple *"Hey, want to go hike Mount Garibaldi next Friday?"*

ABOUT THE AUTHOR

Chin Hing Chang is the founder of ClassyNarwhal, a sales consultancy firm that helps purpose-driven companies scale and amplify their impact by developing their sales processes and providing ethical sales training.

He began his career in sales in 2011 and transitioned to working with startups, incubators, and accelerators in 2014. Since then, he has collaborated with over 500 social ventures from various industries globally.

Chin is an active Entrepreneur-in-Residence for SwissEP, a highly sought-after advisor, and continues to mentor startups through the British Columbia Institute of Technology's Student Association, The Forum, and Futurpreneur. Additionally, he served as a visiting professor at IE University. He is also the author of a Kindle International Best-seller "UnReasonable Transformation: The actionable roadmap for Leaders and Entrepreneurs to create meaningful personal and professional change".

His personal motto is to *Learn, Grow, and Change the world* and he invites you to do the same.

Manufactured by Amazon.ca
Bolton, ON

40068426R00212